PHYSICAL EDUCATION-
INTRODUCTORY ANALYSIS

. . . for Courtney

PHYSICAL EDUCATION
INTRODUCTORY ANALYSIS

Daryl Siedentop
The Ohio State University

Drawings by Delbert Michel

WM. C. BROWN COMPANY PUBLISHERS
Dubuque, Iowa

PHYSICAL EDUCATION

Consulting Editor
Aileene Lockhart
University of Southern California

HEALTH

Consulting Editor
Robert Kaplan
The Ohio State University

PARKS AND RECREATION

Consulting Editor
David Gray
California State College, Long Beach

CONTENTS

FOREWORD

Physical education and sport—a title which is ascribed to our profession at this time for lack of a better term—has found a place in the educational system of America that seems reasonably secure. And yet greatly improved professional performance will be needed in the decades immediately ahead in order to maintain and perhaps to improve upon its present status. The aims and objectives of American education are being scrutinized most carefully, and physical education and sport leaders may be called upon to alter some of their most cherished goals and traditions to meet the pressures of sharply changing times. As one who has considered the prevailing "philosophical posture" of American physical education quite carefully, this writer believes that there is serious doubt whether those in the field now will be able to exhibit the needed "flexibility" that may well be required for survival in the 21st century. Perhaps the best hope for survival—based on a somewhat dubious distinction—is that "physical education has usually been ready to bend whichever way the shaky educational reed was inclining."

Another reason to look forward with reasonable optimism is the steadily improving quality of scholarly work being exhibited by men and women entering the field. Fortunately, this statement appears to be true whether one is considering: (1) teachers and coaches (practitioners); (2) professional educators (teachers of teachers); or (3) scholars and researchers (teachers and scholars who are adding to the "body of knowledge" upon which the profession rests).

Daryl Siedentop, the author of *Physical Education: Introductory Analysis,* is undoubtedly one of the third group mentioned above— those scholars and researchers who will help give the field its theoretical base. This endorsement of Dr. Siedentop and his work is not a case of "a friend helping a friend;" in fact, we have never met. My opinion is based on a careful examination of his material. There is absolutely no doubt that we have been provided with a superior analysis of physical education in America in the twentieth century, as well as a solid prescription for a direction to take in the years immediately ahead.

This is not to imply that I am in full agreement with his analysis and "philosophical stance." To expect complete consensus on the part of two philosophically-oriented individuals would be folly to the highest degree. In fact, those employing philosophy for their own purposes often take almost fiendish delight in the "dissection of their colleagues' work." Thus, it may well follow that some will decry what Dr. Siedentop has designated as "a new approach to physical education." But even allowing for this possible criticism, this writer believes that this book could be read with profit by every reasonably intelligent man or woman physical educator on the continent. Even if one does not agree with Siedentop's statement in Chapter 10 that "the aim of physical education is to increase human abilities to play competitive and expressive motor activities," the background and the development of other contemporary concepts of physical education in Part Two deserve most careful consideration through analysis and assessment.

This book is, therefore, one of those which can be used in many ways in the professional curriculum. It could be used in an introduction to a physical education course, in a so-called principles course, in a fifth-year course for master's students, or as excellent background reading for master's or doctoral students preparing for comprehensive examinations of one type or another. Still further, I would like to stress again that it "could be read with profit by any reasonably intelligent man or woman physical educator on the continent." Keeping up with recent scholarly and research developments in the humanities and science aspects of the field's body of knowledge is, of course, not a problem that is unique to the field of physical education.

This is an interesting and exciting book for many reasons. The approach is different, and the student is not offered "pablum." Dr. Siedentop wants our professional students to develop inquiring minds —a quality that is rare and which should be encouraged whenever it becomes evident to the slightest degree. Further, he readily admits taking a point of view, and he urges strongly that the reader develop his own specific beliefs and broader philosophical stance. Moreover, he realizes full well how difficult it is to do just this and then to communicate one's beliefs and attitudes to others. Ordinary language and professional terminology present language difficulties of their own, and we must study the effective use of words.

Someone has said most aptly on another occasion that "these are times that try men's souls." Who can doubt the wisdom of these words, even when they are applied to the 1970's and the 1980's? Prospective teachers, coaches, teachers of teachers, and scholars and researchers need knowledge as they face an uncertain, changing future. To have knowledge is to have power. Absolutely vital, also, will be care and concern for one's fellow man. Siedentop stresses precisely also the need to develop the ability to distinguish truth from fiction and fallacy. Physical education has an abundance of superstitions that may well be exploded by scholarly investigation.

Physical Education: Introductory Analysis is an important book for the profession. Eventually it may well be considered a significant contribution to the philosophy of physical education and sport. The organization is excellent, and it is readable. Dr. Siedentop has made every effort to separate editorializing from reporting. It is a real pleasure to be able to recommend a substantive publication of a professional colleague so heartily and without any major reservations whatsoever. This book will help the profession to untangle itself philosophically; the reader is urged to study and question.

Earle F. Zeigler
University of Illinois*
Urbana

*Professor Zeigler coordinates the humanities and social science aspect of graduate study in physical education at the University of Illinois, Urbana.

PREFACE

The purpose of this book is to introduce the reader to various concepts which undergird programs of physical education in the schools, and to do so in a manner that will sharpen the reader's critical skills thus enhancing his future study. Part One of the text is designed to place the study of physical education in proper perspective, and underscore the importance of what follows. Part Two describes and evaluates the most important of the contemporary approaches to physical education, enabling the reader to better clarify his own experiences with physical education, and provide the framework within which he might begin to develop a personal theoretical viewpoint. Part Three presents a basically new approach to physical education and suggests the major implications of the approach for various aspects of physical education.

Several strategies have been used in preparing the text and some of these need to be explained. An attempt has been made to address the reader as a young professional colleague. This results in more of a conversational style of writing than is normally utilized in textbooks. It is also hoped that this strategy will challenge the student to put forth his best scholarly effort in using the book. I have purposely avoided what might be described as a "primer approach" to writing (see John run, running is good, running makes you healthy).

A second strategy has been to quote from secondary as well as primary sources, even though this is not often considered to be good scholarship. The purpose is to introduce the reader to important secondary sources (reading books and anthologies, for example), with the assumption that such sources can provide natural leads to primary sources of research and criticism.

A third strategy has been to often use the full names of physical educators and to give direct reference to their important works. It is important that the future physical educator become acquainted as early as possible with the important contributors to physical education literature and to come to know them on more than a last name basis.

A fourth strategy has been to attempt to separate reporting from editorializing. Too often, physical education books present all viewpoints as if they are of equal value. The basic facts are reported here, but then some judgments are offered on the basis of those facts. It will become obvious that this text takes a point of view, but it is hoped that the point of view will be sufficiently divorced from the reporting of facts so that the reader will not be unknowingly coerced into accepting that point of view. Through it all, the reader is encouraged to form judgments of his own and to evaluate critically the point of view taken in the book.

I would like to acknowledge the aid of many people who directly or indirectly contributed to the development of the ideas presented in this book. My professional life has been greatly influenced by the combination of sensitivity, intelligence, and scholarship displayed by Anita Aldrich. John Cooper and Jack Daugherty greatly helped and encouraged my interest in writing. Bill Vanderbilt and George Kraft, my colleagues at Hope College, were always willing and intelligent reactors to my ideas. Bruce Bennett and Sy Kleinman offered me their expertise on the chapters which dealt with history and philosophy. I am grateful to Earle Ziegler for writing the introduction. Aileene Lockhart, who suggested that I write this book, and all the people at the William C. Brown Company were of real service.

Particular commendation should go to Delbert Michel who created the drawings found in this book. They display a consistent theme—the acquisition of skill—which is the central theme in the concept of physical education presented in Part Three. I am in debt to him for his excellent interpretation of this theme.

PART ONE

The Scope
of Physical Education

Introduction ⌐
On Studying Physical Education

The student learning a back flip on a trampoline is studying physical education. So, too, is the graduate student conducting an experiment on the effects of a particular teaching method on the acquisition of volleyball skills. The eight-year-old learning to dribble a soccer ball is also engaged in the study of physical education as is the undergraduate major in a physiology laboratory, in a seminar group, or listening to a lecture. In each of these situations, some "ways" of studying physical education might be better than others, and the differences among the "ways" of studying are seen in the goals stressed, the method used to reach the goals, and the learning environment within which the goals are pursued.

What we should be most concerned with now is how this book will be utilized in studying physical education, and the purpose of this introductory section is to clarify this matter.

Nothing characterizes the present more appropriately than the idea of change. Change has always been an important factor in society, but the rapidity with which it presently occurs is unparalleled in human history. We feel it in all facets of our lives; it affects and is affected by all of our societal institutions—family life, social mores, government, church, and school.

It is natural that education, normally one of our more conservative institutions, has also been affected. A most directly noticeable emphasis is the new view of "content" that is rapidly gaining adherents in all disciplines and at all levels of education. It was not too long ago that education was considered primarily to be the mastery of one type of "content"—"subject matter" per se—and all teachers, books, and educational methods reflected this point of view. Today, the idea that there

3

is subject matter that should be mastered by all students is beginning to be questioned, as much of it probably will be obsolete within a very few years, and the rapidly exploding and expanding amount prohibits its mastery by any one individual. Some educators who feel that this is the case have suggested that the entire educational program be refocused so that it concentrates primarily on the development of critical skills which should allow students not only to maintain an effectively intelligent position *vis-à-vis* an ever changing body of knowledge, but also to contribute creatively to it. Traditionally, educators have referred to such abilities as "critical thinking," and today a new emphasis is being placed on these process-skills (the language of youth vividly reflects this new emphasis on a process-oriented view of life in such terms as be-in, cooling it, making the scene, and happening). A greater educational emphasis on process-skills will, it is hoped, provide more of the kind of people that educator Fred Wilhelms has suggested are in great demand.

> ... one great essential ... is a certain daringness, a freedom of mind to break out of the rut, plus the nerve to go out on the edges of things. In the world of work we have Peter Drucker's expert word for it that the worst thing that we can do for a young man is to train him to do his first job with immediate competence—and industry cries for young men with the courage to take responsibility and leadership in ventures. In the civic world the cry is for young people who can shake off old preconceptions, analyze needs and problems as they are in the existential world, and venture creative, new solutions—and then do it all over again as the problems shift. In every case the cry is for a *kind* of person—a person equipped with knowledge and skill, yes, of course, but basically a person who can take it from where it is.[1]

Physical Education: Introductory Analysis has been written to help you to gain more than subject matter. One of these goals is to help you to think critically.

CRITICAL THINKING

Neil Postman and Charles Weingartner[2] have recently suggested that one possible way of viewing intellectual history is that it has been a constant struggle to overthrow half-truths and outright myths. Misconceptions, generalizations based on insufficient data, faulty assumptions, and superstitions need to be recognized and questioned. Much of that which we recognize as myth today was just a few years ago con-

---

1. Fred Wilhelms, "Curriculum Sources," *What are the Sources of the Curriculum? A Symposium.* Association for Curriculum Development, National Education Association, Washington, 1962, p. 20.
2. Neil Postman and Charles Weingartner, *Teaching as a Subversive Activity* (New York: Delacorte Press, 1969), p. 3.

sidered to be truth. The essence of critical thinking is to learn to recognize inconsistencies and inaccuracies when you meet them, instead of waiting for the time when everybody recognizes them for what they are. It wasn't too many years ago, for example, that most educated men believed that athletes were apt to develop an "athlete's heart," but it has now been demonstrated that participation in athletics per se does not damage the heart.

As you study physical education, whether as a beginning student, graduate student, or professional, you should not only be mastering a body of current knowledge, but you should also be sharpening the tools which allow you to think straight. This requires the identification and questioning of assumptions, evaluating the preciseness of definitions, examining the validity of generalizations, separating fact from opinion, and looking for evidence of the statistical and practical significance of experimental data. This book is designed not only to pass on some facts and opinions about physical education, but also to help you to acquire skills necessary for critical thinking.

A book is a learning environment, just as classrooms, gymnasia, and playing fields are learning environments. The *medium* of the book relays a *message* to the reader (you may be familiar with Marshall McLuhan's premise that "the medium is the message"). Postman and Weingartner have described the message that is too often transmitted through a traditional classroom environment.

> In order to understand what kinds of behaviours classrooms promote, one must become accustomed to observing what, in fact, students actually *do* in them. What students do in the classroom is what they learn (as Dewey would say), and what they learn to do is the classroom's message (as McLuhan would say). Now, what is it that students *do* in the classroom? Well, mostly they sit and listen to the teacher. Mostly, they are required to believe in authorities, or at least to pretend to such belief when they take tests. Mostly, they are required to *remember*. They are almost never required to perform any intellectual operations, formulate definitions, or perform any intellectual operations that go beyond repeating what someone else says is true. They are rarely encouraged to ask substantive questions, although they are permitted to ask about administrative and technical details. (How long should the paper be? Does spelling count? When is the assignment due?)[3]

It is hoped that this book will promote behaviours that are not in accord with those described above; behaviours that will instead continue to enhance your study of physical education long after most of the "content" of this book has been forgotten. The author hopes that studying

---

3. Ibid., p. 19.

this book will promote the development of the following types of behaviours.

1. You will ask more thoughtful questions of your teachers and your fellow students.
2. Your questions will become more relevant and more specific to the points of contention.
3. You will be more able to challenge statements made by "experts," other students, and teachers.
4. You will request evidence where you feel it should be available.
5. You will be encouraged to suspend final judgment on all issues where the data are insufficient to warrant such judgment.
6. You will become more willing to change your position when data and/or logic dictate such a change.

In order to accomplish these goals, each chapter of this book raises as many questions as it answers. Each chapter ends with topics about which you should be able to ask questions, instead of questions which you should be able to answer by simply referring to the "content" of the chapter. Many topics are left unanswered simply because there are no definite answers available at this time, but this makes them particularly interesting as subjects for discussion.

The book has a point of view, but an effort has been made to separate *editorializing* from *reporting.* It is hoped that by taking a point of view you will be encouraged to develop your own point of view. It is a basic law of nature that to move forward there must be effort, resistance, and friction. *I have supplied the initial effort, and it is up to you to supply the intellectual resistance which, although it will result in some friction between us, will also cause you to move forward.*

THE USE OF WORDS

Perhaps the most important part of developing the ability to think critically is to recognize the fundamental importance of words; how they are defined, how they are put together to express thoughts, and how they are used to influence readers or listeners to accept a particular point of view. To that end, it will be helpful to examine briefly some types of definitions and ambiguities.

Philosophers and logicians[4] seem to agree that there are four basic types of definitions: 1) stipulative, 2) bi-verbal, 3) conceptual or logical, and 4) ostensive or emotive.

---

4. See Francis Connolly, *A Rhetoric Case Book;* John Hosper, *An Introduction to Philosophic Analysis;* Francis Parker and Henry Veatch, *Logic as a Human Instrument;* and Israel Scheffler, *The Language of Education.*

A stipulative definition means that a given term is to be understood in a specific way for the space of particular discourse, even though it might have other meanings and usages. Stipulative definitions include all types of operational definitions, and these are important in understanding research. An operational definition merely means that the operations required to produce the word being defined are stipulated. For example, in an experiment designed to measure the effects of a specific teaching method on the learning of bowling skills, learning might be defined operationally as the total accumulative score of each subject over a period of twenty-five games.

A bi-verbal definition is descriptive in nature because it defines a term by describing its characteristics. If any one of the characteristics is sufficient for the term to be applicable, then the definition is a *disjunctive* bi-verbal definition. The definition of "strike" in baseball is an example. Its characteristics can be described as: 1) a pitched ball struck at by the batter which does not touch his bat, 2) a pitched ball which enters the strike zone in flight and is not struck at, 3) a pitched ball which becomes a foul not caught on the fly, 4) an attempt to bunt which results in a foul not legally caught, 5) a pitched ball at which the batter strikes, but misses and which touches any part of his person, or 6) a foul tip legally held by the catcher. The presence of any one of these characteristics is sufficient for the term "strike" to be applied; therefore, it is a disjunctive bi-verbal definition. If, however, *all* the characteristics must be present before a term applies, then the definition is a *conjunctive* bi-verbal definition. If you attempt to define the term "American flag" bi-verbally, you will have an example of a conjunctive bi-verbal definition; i.e., all the characteristics of the flag must be present before the term would apply.

A third type of definition is conceptual or logical. It places the subject to be defined in a general class (genus) and then differentiates it from all other members of that class. By doing this, the species of the class become logically designated into groups. Badminton, for example, is a member (species) of physical education (class), and it can be differentiated from other members (tennis, swimming, etc.) of the same class by references to rules, scoring, and court markings. It is much more difficult, however, to determine in which class physical education (as a species itself) should be placed, and the choice of class is a point of considerable dispute within the profession. Is it physical activity, sport, human movement, gross motor activity, or health? Chapter Nine of this book is devoted specifically to discussing a conceptual definition of physical education.

The fourth type of definition is ostensive or emotive. In this case, language is used emotively or sometimes not at all. You might ask "what is green," and I might reply by pointing to several green objects. Good behaviour might be defined by pointing to a specific example of behaviour. Pain might be defined by saying that "it is what you feel when you are hurt."

It is important for you to recognize that definitions are usually written to provide denotative meaning; i.e., to designate a particular meaning. This, however, does not prevent the addition of connotative meaning, which is usually supplied by the reader. The word fitness, for example, might be defined quite precisely; yet the term will nevertheless have differing connotations for individual readers depending upon their prior experiences. While it is often easy to arrive at some consensus in terms of denotation, it is much more difficult to assess or predict the various connotative meanings attached to terms. When you think critically, you will try to distinguish between the denotative and the connotative.

Words are often used ambiguously. The two types of ambiguity are equivocation (verbal or semantic ambiguity) and amphiboly (syntactical ambiguity). Verbal ambiguity exists when a word or phrase may be interpreted in many ways, yet no one single interpretation is stipulated. Your critical abilities will be at work if you notice the equivocation in a statement such as: "participation in physical education increases a student's level of fitness." "Fitness" is a term that has many interpretations, and the term "increases" needs qualification in order to be precise.

The second type of ambiguity refers to syntactical usage and is called amphiboly. While verbal ambiguity exists when a word may be interpreted in several ways, syntactical ambiguity exists when the position of the word in a sentence changes the meaning of the sentence. It is, therefore, the position of the word rather than the word itself which causes the ambiguity. A professor that I know always refers to a certain part of his physical education facility as "the old men's gym" (as opposed to the men's old gym). By shifting the placement of one key word, the entire meaning of the sentence can be altered.

Listed below are some statements which you might want to discuss and question. As you learn to think critically and to identify the illogical and imprecise use of words, then your questions will become more and more pertinent and penetrating, and the bases for your evaluations will be strengthened.

1. An important objective of elementary physical education is to make children physically fit.
2. Sports build character.

3. As representatives of your school, you should not wear your sideburns below mid-ear length.
4. Students should become acquainted with many activities.
5. Practice makes perfect.
6. Grades will be given on the basis of fitness, knowledge, skill, and attitude.
7. Experts suggest that a high level of fitness will increase a person's capacity to live well.
8. Our objective is to educate the whole man.
9. Long practices are not recommended because players can't learn as well when they are tired.
10. Physical education is an integral part of education.

Chapter 1 — The Significance of Physical Education

The scope and significance of physical education can be symbolically portrayed on a three dimensional grid. The vertical component on the grid represents the historical significance of physical education from prehistory to the modern era. It bears witness to the fact that man as a species has always been engaged in activity that can be called physical education. The horizontal axis represents the cross-cultural significance of physical education from primitive societies to the highly technological, industrialized societies of the present day Western world. The third dimension represents the individual meaning that has always been derivable from participation in sports, games, and dance both throughout time and across all cultures. An examination along any one or all of these three dimensions should enable the student of physical education to recognize more fully the significance of the field that he is studying.

HISTORICAL SIGNIFICANCE

It is highly probable that endeavors which might legitimately be called physical education were the first systematic attempts at instruction in the history of man. The concept of physical education, when used in this sense, embraces all the many and varied viewpoints which, although they have been known by different names and titles, can for this purpose be brought together under the one title of physical education. Archeological evidence has been amassed which shows that ar-

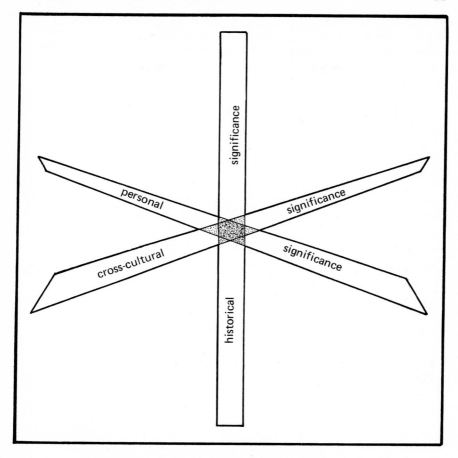

FIGURE 1. The significance of physical education

chaic types of man at the beginning of the lower Paleolithic[1] period, some 500,000 years before the birth of Christ, were utilizing missile stones and spears in their hunting operations. It is obvious that a high level of skill in these activities (hunting) was crucial to survival in prehistoric times. Because a high level of skill had survival value, it can be assumed that time was taken to instruct the young in the use of hunting

---

1. Paleolithic refers to classification of time in terms of cultural stages. The lower Paleolithic period is said to have begun *circa* 500,000 B.C., the middle Paleolithic period *circa* 200,000 B.C., and the upper Paleolithic period *circa* 40,000 B.C. This classification system is widely utilized in anthropology and its allied fields.

implements. The development of high degrees of skill in such gross motor activities is quite likely the first example of systematic instruction ("formal" education) and the first example of physical education.

During the middle Paleolithic period, *circa* 200,000 B.C., the use of missile stones and spears was further developed and the use of blade tools and scrapers became prevalent. There is evidence of hunting ritual and initiation during this period, which seems to validate the assumption that instruction of a systematic nature was probably prevalent among these primitive types.

This is not to suggest that prehistoric man "went to school." It means only that the adults of the community passed on to their young in some systematic method, the techniques necessary for skilled performance in these important survival activities. Margaret Mead has provided a remarkable description of what can be justifiably called a systematic program of physical education among the Manus, a primitive people in New Guinea. Much of the physical education of the Manu young had to do with aquatic skills and it is important that it be recognized that while the instruction was fairly informal, it was nevertheless of a systematic nature:

> As soon as the baby can toddle uncertainly, he is put down into the water at low tide when parts of the lagoon are high and others only a few inches under water. Here the baby sits and plays in the water or takes a few hesitating steps in the yielding spongy mud. . . . As he grows older, he is allowed to wade about at low tide. His elders keep a sharp lookout that he does not stray into deep water until he is old enough to swim. But the supervision is unobtrusive. . . . His whole play world is so arranged that he is permitted to make small mistakes from which he may learn better judgment and greater circumspection, but he is never allowed to make mistakes which are serious enough to permanently frighten him or inhibit his activity.[2]

The Manu child was swimming on his own by the age of three. This educational climate also allowed him to learn how to dive, to handle a small canoe, and finally to control the very large canoes that he would use as an adult member of the tribe. The entire process appeared to be very informal and unplanned, but the expert eye of the ethnologist was able to detect clearly the extent of planning and educational methodology present in the learning environment. It is, therefore, not stretching the point at all to call this type of endeavor physical education.

By the beginning of the upper Paleolithic period, *Homo sapiens,* man was living in artificial shelters, had means of crossing large bodies of water, had developed definite techniques in hunting and fishing, and

---

2. Margaret Mead, *Growing Up In New Guinea* (New York: Mentor Books, 1958), p. 25.

had begun to utilize dance as part of his ritual and ceremony. Much of the education of the young Homo sapien must have been devoted to activities which now would be called physical education.

The importance and scope of physical education, then, goes all the way back to prehistoric man. From those prehistoric days, when the first creature that one might correctly call man was fighting for his survival, down to the present day, physical education has remained an important part of the systematic instruction of the young. While its importance has fluctuated from time to time, it has always had some role to play in the educational scheme. Everywhere that scientists have been able to unearth and unravel the mysteries of ancient civilizations, the universal quality of play has been manifested. Throughout history, most societies have expressed play* in formal ways through organized games and sports, both for children and adults. The highly developed civilization of ancient Egypt was at its peak *circa* 1,500 B.C., and there is ample evidence that games, sports, and dance played a significant role in the cultural life of that society. There is evidence of widespread interest in wrestling, weight lifting, ballgames, racquet games, swimming, folk dancing, and formal dancing connected with religious rites.

The ancient civilizations of China also showed great interest in physical education activities. Archery, chariot racing, dance, football-type games, and wrestling were among the more widely practiced activities of the Chinese. A system of medical exercises called Cong Fu was established *circa* 2,500 B.C., and was in use for over 3,000 years.

The early civilizations of Greece are the clearest available examples of cultures in which great value was placed on physical education. One has only to browse through the 23rd Book of the *Iliad* to recognize the importance of games and sports in Homeric Greece. This book records the games and contests that were held in honor of the funeral of Patroclus, who was a close friend of the warrior Achilles. Boxing, wrestling, races on foot, chariot races, and many other contests were held during the funeral games. The seriousness of the contests can be noted by attention to the prizes awarded the winners. Fine trophies, oxen, horses, and women were the fruits of victory during the funeral games.

The education of the young Greek in the city-states of Athens and Sparta provides the historian with a glowing example of an educational program which held physical education in highest esteem and made it a truly integral part of the everyday education of the young. Many

---

*For the purposes of this chapter, the terms play, sport, and physical education are used almost interchangeably. The differences among these terms will become apparent as the book progresses.

physical educators have felt that the ultimate goal of physical education today is to recapture the spirit of Greek physical education; but while one might envy the important place granted physical education in the Greek scheme of education, it is doubtful that the philosophy that undergirded Greek education should be considered to be important for today's educational scene. As I have suggested elsewhere,[3] the dualistic philosophy of idealism considered physical education to be important for two reasons: 1) for the protection of the city-state, and 2) to build a strong body that would do no harm to the eternal soul which was enclosed within it. Nevertheless, the histories of the city-states of Athens and Sparta are fertile ground for the student of physical education who is interested in closely examining the central role that physical education can occupy within the educational program of a society.

The Roman Empire is also replete with evidence of widespread interest in sport and games. The Romans were very interested in vigorous physical exercise, boxing, running, jumping, ballgames, and dancing. The gradual decline and fall of the Roman Empire and its ultimate defeat by the Visigoths in 476 A.D. is particularly fertile ground for the sports historian and the sport sociologist. A link between the rise of professional sport in the United States and the rise of professional sport in the Roman Empire has often been suggested.

The fall of the Roman Empire ushered in a period of 1,000 years during which little emphasis was granted to systematic programs of physical education. It was no doubt the lowest ebb for sports and games in the history of man, especially as items of significant cultural importance. It was not until the Renaissance that physical education again was considered to be important as evidenced in the writings of philosophers and educational theorists, and it gradually worked its way back into formal programs of education. From the Renaissance on, through the Age of Enlightenment and into the Industrial Revolution, physical education became solidified as an important topic of educational theory and practice. In Europe, philosophers and practitioners such as Rousseau, Basedow, GutsMuth, Pestalozzi, Froebel, Jahn, and Ling provided the theoretical and practical basis for systems of physical education that were to last for well over one hundred years. Elements of their thinking are still in evidence in the concepts of physical education which form the subject matter of this text.

Throughout history, therefore, in both highly developed cultures and in primitive societies play, sport, games, and dance have occupied

---

3. Daryl Siedentop, "What Did Plato Really Think?" *The Physical Educator* 25:25-26, March, 1969.

significant roles. The historical scope of physical education is as old as man himself.

CROSS–CULTURAL SIGNIFICANCE

The significance of physical education can also be examined along another dimension. If time can be visualized as the vertical (historical) component on a grid, then it can also be viewed horizontally. There is no culture known to man in which at any one chronological stage in history, play was not prevalent and of significant cultural importance. Anthropologists Eliot Chapple and Carleton Coon have said: "Children among all peoples play, both imitatively and otherwise. So do adults."[4] One can be assured that wherever play forms have existed, there have also existed methods and techniques of "playing," and these methods and techniques have been passed down from generation to generation. As Celeste Ulrich has said in *The Social Matrix of Physical Education,*

> Play is a basic mode of behavior, an integrating thread in the design of life. It is an aspect of all societies, for the play group is the most fundamental of all peer groups."[5]

Thus, physical education seems to have been a part of all cultures, all societies, throughout time. It is important to recognize the significance of this evidence because it makes all that follows in this text more meaningful. There are very few cultural universals. Play is one such universal element in culture, and where play has been, physical education has also been. This fact lends seriousness and importance to the study of physical education, and it especially underscores the significance of examining different concepts of physical education, for it will provide a basis for understanding some of the many and varied approaches to this universal field of endeavor.

What should be most obvious, even after a short introduction to the scope and significance of physical education, is that there are many different reasons why skill in gross motor activities has been considered to be of such importance that it has been passed on to the young in some systematic way. The "whys" of the young prehistoric boy learning to throw his spear by practicing at a target and a modern young boy in the United States learning how to play baseball, while similar in certain respects, are vastly different in other respects.

---

4. Eliot Chapple and Carleton Coon, *Principles of Anthropology* (New York: Henry Holt and Co., 1942), p. 614.
5. Celeste Ulrich, *The Social Matrix of Physical Education* (New York: Prentice-Hall, Inc., 1968), p. 99.

The differences are usually best explained by an examination of the cultures within which the activities are pursued. While physical education may be a cultural universal, the reasons for organizing or participating in its activities will vary from culture to culture and from time to time. Spear throwing may be an activity that is pursued both by young men in twentieth century America and by young men in primitive tribal societies, but the activities are vastly different; because one culture utilizes spear throwing as a contest (javelin) in a festival situation (track meet), while in the other culture, the skill has dual survival value in hunting and war. Florence Stumpf Hendrickson has discussed the anthropological approach to physical education in her excellent article "Sport and the Cultures of Man":

> Research has shown that sports always play a complex role in cultures, from the simplest to the most highly developed. Underlying their obvious identification as amusements and pleasurable tests of physical supremacy are often unstated but implicit functions in the culture. As old as the history of sport itself is the story of the use of sport as an instrumentality for accomplishing something else. . . . Whether at any given time in history man plays for fun and self-expression, for prestige, power, and glory, for financial gain or political advantage, his motivations are to a large degree culturally determined. Whether or not sports hold a place of esteem as an expression of national pride and strength, as a respected instrumentality for propitiating the deities or upholding the honor of the tribe or the nation, or as an accepted means of educating the youth. . . . these things are culturally determined.[6]

A brief examination of the varying cultural roles that the activity of wrestling has played will serve well to illustrate both the scope of physical education and the often important meanings attached to the activities of physical education.

In the Ifuga country of the Philippines, the boundaries of rice fields were often a matter of dispute among landowners.[7] Without the use of man-made boundary markers such as fences or walls, natural boundaries often shifted. The resulting disputes were settled by wrestling matches. The landowners, or champion wrestlers appointed by them, would meet, and the dispute would be decided through combat. The Ifuga believed that the ancestral spirits of the two offended parties would know which party was right and see to it that the wrestler representing the "right" party would win the match. Thus this wres-

---

6. Florence Stumpf Hendrickson, "Sport and the Cultures of Man," in *Sport, Culture, and Society,* edited by John Loy and Gerald Kenyon (London: The Macmillan Company, 1969), pp. 89, 92.
7. Ibid., p. 92.

tling match, infused with religious meaning, became the judicial mechanism for settling land boundary disputes.

Among the Pukapuka, who live on an atoll in the Northern Cook Island Group, wrestling played a significant role in puberty rites.[8] In primitive cultures, boys are usually granted the right to assume adult status within the society after they have participated successfully in contests, ceremonies, or festivals. Most often, a test of skill, strength, and courage is necessary to "pass the test." Among the Pukapuka, all young men who were born within a six months' period underwent initiation to adult status at the same time. The boys were, on each of two successive days following the first new moon of each six months' period, required to make a trip in canoes to gather nuts. Returning from their journey, the boys placed their best wrestler in front position of the lead canoe. Awaiting him on the beach would be the champion wrestler of the young adult men of the village. The two would wrestle and this match would be followed by several bouts between the older and younger groups. These wrestling matches were held on the second day of the initiation rites and signaled graduation to adult status within the tribal society.

Among the Ona of Tierra del Feugo, family feuds of all sorts were settled by wrestling matches.[9] The men of each family agreed (through the use of an emissary which was always an older woman of the offended family) to meet at an appointed place and time. Upon meeting, they formed a circle and each side heard speeches which justified the opposing claims. Two wrestlers then went to the center of the circle and began to wrestle. The match continued until either all of the challenging or all of the opposing side had been thrown. Thus, the dispute was settled and the families returned to their villages.

In Nigeria, the Dukawa utilized wrestling matches for purposes of selecting a mate.[10] The young girls of a village would attend a festival wrestling match so that they might choose a husband. Each girl carried a small bag of flour. When the girl decided upon a suitable mate, she sprinkled flour on his head. The father of the athlete then would begin marital negotiations with the parents of the girl. Quite naturally, the better wrestlers were considered to be the more desirable husbands.

The tribal power of ancient Hawaiian chiefs was often decided upon the basis of wrestling matches.[11] Each tribal chief would have a group of wrestlers to represent him. Whenever two chiefs would meet

---

8. Ibid., p. 93.
9. Chapple and Coon, *Principles of Anthropology*, p. 625.
10. Hendrickson, "Sport and the Cultures of Man," p. 93.
11. Ibid., p. 94.

or visit one another, a challenge was customarily sent to engage in wrestling matches. The outcomes of these matches reflected the relative power of the chiefs. The wrestlers were, therefore, among the chiefs' most prized possessions.

In eighth century Japan, the Emperor began to utilize wrestling as part of the ceremonies that accompanied the harvest time.[12] Evidently, the first year that the wrestling matches were utilized must have been accompanied by a fruitful harvest because the custom was continued and became a very intricate and proscribed aspect of harvest festivals in Japanese culture.

One can be reasonably sure that the sport of wrestling has always provided a great deal of fun, satisfaction, and prestige for the winners, but the examples that have been cited above show that wrestling has often played a significant cultural role above and beyond the immediate satisfactions derived by the participants. Wrestling has been: 1) a legal mechanism for settling land disputes, 2) a means of symbolically gaining adult status within a society, 3) a judicial mechanism for settling family feuds, 4) a means of allowing young women to select mates, 5) a measure of the relative power of tribal chiefs, and 6) a significant part of a religious festival designed to insure a good harvest. These examples have all been taken from societies that are considerably less complex than our own. The homogeneity of the tribal or village society allows it to be less complex than our own. The heterogeneous makeup of our present day society has made it much more difficult to analyze the cultural roles that sport occupies.

The important point here is to recognize the importance that sport activities have enjoyed in various cultures. When an activity assumes an important role in a culture, one can be sure that serious efforts are made to develop the techniques and strategies of the activity. It is very reasonable to assume that instruction in the skills and strategies of wrestling was an important consideration in each of the six societal situations mentioned above. When these techniques and strategies are passed on from the older to the younger in the society, the process can be called physical education.

One cultural role that sport does occupy among the "big power" nations today is a political-propaganda role. Both the Soviet Union and the United States find a significant place for sport in their Marxist and capitalistic ideologies so that both the ideology and the sport are enhanced.

The growth of organized sport in the Soviet Union in the last two decades has been truly amazing. There are today at least 200,000 *killek-*

---

12. Ibid.

tivy (sport groups) with a membership of at least 40,000,000. Soccer fields, basketball courts, and volleyball courts are everywhere. Organized sport clubs are not the only example of interest in physical education:

> In Moscow and Leningrad people troop about happily on skis, although much of the park area is flat, and impromptu hockey matches are staged by youngsters in the shadow of the Kremlin. In summer, group hiking is encouraged, and hundreds of touring centers and camps are now being built. . . . Throughout the year the broadcasting day begins with the announcer cheerily on the job calling out morning exercises. And a unique program, on the job calisthenics, is a device, typical of the Party's utilitarian attitude, to improve labor productivity. Ten million workers in 28,000 plants engage in periodic exercises during working hours to stimulate tired muscles.[13]

The Soviet citizen is encouraged by his government to view sport as an important reflection of the Marxist state. Victory for an individual or a team is considered to be a victory for Marxism. Loyalty to a team or even to a training schedule is merely a natural extension of loyalty to the state. The nature of the political function of sport was stated clearly in a 1925 Communist Party resolution:

> Physical culture must be considered not only from the point of view of physical training and health but should also be utilized as a means to rally the broad working masses around various Party, Government and trade union organizations through which the masses of workers and peasants are drawn into social and political life. . . . Physical culture must play an integral part in the general political and cultural training and education of the masses.[14]

Group solidarity and individual achievement in the name of the state are two highly held values in the Soviet Union, and they are nowhere proclaimed more loudly than through Soviet sport.

Likewise, the American system is said to be mirrored through sport. Individual gain through individual achievement is a basic principle of American life and is widely applied to the world of sport. The social mobility that has long been a theoretical aspect of American society has for several decades now been a reality in the world of sport. The black athlete, the disadvantaged, and the uneducated have been able, in certain areas of sport, to rise on their merits. The degree to which sport activities have captured the imagination of the American people is truly unbelievable. James Reston, in a New York Times

---

13. Henry Morton, "Soviet Sport in the 1960's," eds. Kenyon and Loy, *Sport, Culture, and Society*, p. 194.
14. Ibid., p. 196, quoted from a Resolution of the Central Committee of the Russian Communist Party, July 13, 1925, Reprinted in Kalendar Spravochnik Fizkulturnika na 1939 God (Moscow: Fizkultura i Sport, 1939), pp. 5-7.

editorial of a few years ago, captured well the extent of sports-mania in the United States:

> These are hard days to write about politics in the United States. The country is in another of those lovely hypnotic trances over sports, and everytime you try to write the word "Johnson," it comes out Yastrzemski. This is something more than the annual madness over the baseball World Series. When President Johnson made a major address on the war in Vietnam the other night, NBC estimated his television audience at between 9 and 10 million. The next day when Carl Yastrzemski and his implausible Red Sox gored Minnesota in the last game of the regular season, the TV audience was estimated at 20 to 25 million. The frenzy in the capital of the Commonwealth of Massachusetts of course, has even surpassed the excitement at the election of John F. Kennedy. And that old chestnut about Beantown has been rewritten: And this is good old Boston/The home of the bean and the cod/Where the Lowells talk only about baseball/And Yastrzemski gets signals from God.

One does not have to be much of an analyst to recognize that both the Soviet Union and the United States utilize sport for propaganda purposes, and they each do so because they feel that sport reflects the best in their respective ideologies. Alex Natan, in his book *Sport and Society,* has severely criticized the political role that sport too often occupies in world culture today. Natan takes particular aim at the Olympic Games, which he suggests have become little more than another political testing ground that reflects exactly the same tensions which exist throughout the world on the political plane.

It is difficult to argue with Natan's criticisms. International athletics have become almost in every sense a socio-political tool. This fact need not be taken as a condemnation of sport or of the use of sport as a political-propaganda tool. What is important, and probably necessary to the survival of sport, is that the cultural roles that sport now occupies become fully recognized. The danger is not that our State Department sends thousands of athletes abroad each year to compete internationally on "goodwill" tours. The danger is that while this type of activity goes on, promoters and advocators of sport still attempt to characterize it as an essentially nonpolitical activity. As Natan[15] has suggested, the nations of the world can be placed on a scale according to the degree of involvement that the government takes in the organization and guidance of sport activities. On one end of the scale would be the nations where sport has become an official aspect of the political system and a tool for the use of the state. On the other end would be the nations in which the government takes no active control in the governance and

---

15. A. Natan, *Sport and Society* (London: Bowes and Bowes, 1958).

regulation of sport activities. Where each nation today might fall on such a scale would indicate, according to this logic, the cultural role of sport in the society.

One should recognize that all nations view success in sport as a measure of national vitality and as a reflection of the success of the national political system. As such, all national governments have entered the international arena of competition in search of political victories through sport. An analysis of the participants at Helsinki in the 1952 Olympic Games revealed the fact that 160 athletes had come to compete as representatives of underdeveloped countries in which the per capita income was less than one hundred dollars per year.[16] Peter McIntosh in his excellent book, *Sport in Society,* has alluded to the political role of sport on an international level.

> The best performers anywhere want to test their skill against the best from elsewhere, but because at international level the best performer merges some of his identity in the nation itself, whether he wants to do so or not, success in sport has political importance. This is true for the emergent nation as well as for the more highly developed countries.[17]

Physical education has been a part of every culture, from the simplest primitive society to the most complex society. Its role has not always been the same, but, when interpreted in terms of its own culture, it has always played a significant role.

PERSONAL SIGNIFICANCE

Another dimension that reveals the scope of physical education is the dimension of meaning. If a vertical dimension reveals the importance of physical education throughout history, and a horizontal dimension reveals the importance of physical education across all cultures, then a third dimension reveals the depth of meaning that participation in physical education activities has always offered an individual, a group, or a society. American author John Steinbeck once said that baseball was more than just a game or a contest, that it was a state of mind. For millions of American citizens, this is no doubt true, because baseball has been one of our great national games. The game is said to be a "state of mind" because of the meaning that people attach to it. This meaning is not, however, an inherent property of baseball, but is instead a property of national games. What is said of baseball fans in the United States might also be said of soccer fans in Brazil, bullfighting fans

---

16. E. Jokl et al., *Sports, in the Cultural Pattern of the World,* Helsinki, 1956.
17. Peter McIntosh, *Sport in Society* (London: C. A. Watts, 1963), pp. 197-198.

in Spain, or people who are fans of gymnastics in the Soviet Union. The point is that individuals and groups derive great meaning from athletic participation and spectatorship.

The individual and group meaning available from participation in sport, games, and dance activities is self-evident; to a greater or lesser degree, we have all experienced it. It is very doubtful that the core of this meaning has changed much through the years. It may be interpreted differently from culture to culture and from time to time; yet there are no doubt constants in terms of individual meaning. Becoming a skilled performer in a ball-type game, for example, affords the participant a certain type of meaning, and this core of meaning does not probably change much across time or across cultures. The skier, the surfer, the wrestler, the gymnast, the dancer, and the golfer also derive personal meaning from their participation. This meaning tends to be highly personal and holistic and, therefore, is not easily dissected and analyzed. Recently, scholars have become very much aware of the meaning available in both participation and spectatorship and have begun to try to analyze this meaning from several points of view. Howard Slusher, in his book, *Man, Sport, and Existence,* analyzed and described the meaning in sport from the point of view of existential philosophy. Arnold Beisser attacked a similar problem from more of a Freudian psychoanalytic point of view in his book, *The Madness in Sport.* Eleanor Metheny took a more empirical point of view in her *Connotations of Movement in Sport and Dance.*

Participation in sport, game, and dance activities provides certain types of meaning for those who play and those who watch. This is true for the play of children and the play of adults. Roger Bannister, the great British miler, has said that, "running has given me a glimpse of the greatest freedom a man can ever know," and those who run know immediately what he means. The spectator also participates in a vicarious way and derives meaning from the activity. Premier Nikita Khrushchev, an ardent soccer fan in Russia, said that, "whenever a player kicks the ball, it is Khrushchev who kicks it, and whenever a player gets kicked in the shins, it is Khrushchev who gets kicked."[18] Those who are fervent fans of some American sport know what this means. It would be easy to translate the sport and person and to say: "When Arnold Palmer sinks a putt, it is me who sinks the putt, and when Palmer hooks his drive, it is me who hooks the drive with him." This dimension of meaning is no doubt the most self-evident of all the dimensions of

---

18. New York Times, October 28, 1957, quoted in Morton, "Soviet Sport in the 1960's," *Sport, Culture, and Society,* p. 192.

physical education because it is the dimension that the reader will have personally experienced.

The significance of physical education can be defended along all three of the dimensions cited in this chapter. The dimension of time, of course, is the realm of the anthropologist and the historian. The horizontal dimension takes one across cultures, and this is the province of the ethnologist and the sociologist. It is the psychologist and the philosopher, finally, who are most interested in the dimension of meaning—that third dimension that is most responsible for the extent of the historical and cross-cultural significance of physical education. For whatever might be said concerning the historical or cross-cultural significance of physical education, it is most apparent that man has always found meaning in running, jumping, dancing, gaming, and competing in activities which require skilled performance.

WHAT QUESTIONS CAN YOU ASK ABOUT THE FOLLOWING STATEMENTS
1. To be called "physical education," activity has to occur in a school program.
2. The play of children is merely a release of surplus energy and has no personal or cultural significance.
3. Sport should not be used to promote any political ends.
4. Sport is more an expression of democracy than of totalitarianism.
5. The largest part of the personal meaning in sport and dance is that it is fun.
6. The capitalistic ethic is basically incompatible with sport.
7. Religion and sport have been historically antithetical institutions.
8. In American life, sport is more ritualistic than religion.
9. Russians do not play football because, as a people, the game is too rough for them.
10. The difference between primitive man and modern man is that modern man is a spectator instead of a participant.

Chapter 2—

The Development of Physical Education in the United States: Where We Have Been*

If you had been one of the fortunate young men attending the Round Hill School in Northhampton, Massachusetts in the 1820's, you would have had ample opportunity to participate in active sports and games because the school leaders were attempting to develop a total educational program based on aims and ideals associated with classical Greek schools. You also would have had the honor to receive instruction three days a week from Charles Beck, the first officially recognized teacher of physical education in the United States. Beck's program of physical education was derived directly from the gymnastic system developed in Germany by his friend and teacher, Ludwig Jahn.

During the same period, Charles Follen, a close friend of Beck's and like him a German political refugee, was using a converted dining hall to start a physical education program for the students at Harvard University. Follen was also an advocate of the Jahn system of gymnastics, and each of these programs relied heavily on apparatus work, which was at the heart of the Jahn system.

Before this period, there was little in any of the educational institutions in the United States that could be described as physical education. The "academy movement," which started in the middle 1700's and reached its pinnacle in the early 1800's, adopted a progressive educa-

---

*In the appendix, a chronology of events important to the development of American physical education is provided. The purpose of this list is twofold: First, dates, people, and events are the raw data for any discussion of history; and secondly, it is hoped that the list might provide a beginning for a lifetime acquaintance with the people and events which have shaped the development of our profession.

tional philosophy which allowed for sports and games after the regular school hours; but aside from some instruction in hygiene, little effort was made in the area of instructional physical education. It would be more accurate to describe the academy programs as forerunners of intramurals. Other schools during this early period had programs of manual labor, which was considered by many educators to be of much greater educational benefit than gymnastics or sports. Military schools, of course, had rigorous programs of military training which included many physical activities. Prior to the innovations at the Round Hill School, there was little effort made to incorporate instruction in physical education into school programs, and afterschool sports, manual labor, and military training were the only programs open to students in American schools.

In September of 1826, an open air gymnasium, similar to the ones that had become quite popular in Germany, was opened in Boston with Follen as the director. A year later, Follen was succeeded by another Jahn disciple, Francis Lieber. Lieber's appointment also included the charge to open a swimming school, which he did in 1827; and while the popularity of the gymnasium was to wane considerably in the next few years, the swimming pool venture was quite popular.

If male students had only limited access to organized programs of physical education, then the problem was considerably more difficult for women students. An early pioneer in higher education for women was Catherine Beecher. At the Hartford Female Seminary and later at the Western Female Institute in Cincinnati, Miss Beecher promoted education for women and included in her programs regular instruction in physical education. Miss Beecher's approach was one of calisthenics performed mostly to music with the goal of developing carriage and grace. Girls attending the Institute also had twenty-six lessons in physiology along with their courses in calisthenics.

The middle period of the nineteenth century was one of growing interest in physical education, but, as Leonard and Afflek point out, of little interest in terms of major innovations.

> In the third and fourth decades of the nineteenth century, four different systems of physical training had been brought forward for trial in the United States—the drill and discipline of the military academy, the Jahn gymnastics, manual labor on the farm or in the shop, and "calisthenics" for girls and women. The claims of each were pressed by imitators of the educational institutions in which each had first become incorporated; but for various reasons not one of the four was generally adopted or won for itself more than temporary foothold. From 1835 until 1860, though educators were increasingly alive to the importance of physical training, no one appeared with anything

that seemed more likely to meet the conditions and needs of the time.[1]

It was Dio Lewis who provided the kind of innovative program necessary for widespread acceptance. Lewis was a lecturer, leader in the temperance movement, advocate of women's rights, and a very important physical educator. His dissatisfaction with the skill and strength necessary to utilize the heavy apparatus in the Jahn system led him to create a "new gymnastics" that utilized light implements that were readily available in most schools. His goals were more in the areas of flexibility, agility, carriage, and grace of movement. In the 1860's, many schools adopted this new system, and it was not uncommon to find school children using wands, rings, and dumbbells as they performed exercises to music. Lewis also opened a school to train teachers in his new system, and this too helped the program to spread and prosper.

During the same period that the Lewis system of physical education was gaining acceptance, Edward Hitchcock was directing the first college department of physical education at Amherst. Like Lewis, Hitchcock's program tended to move away from the heavy apparatus work of the Jahn system to more of a light gymnastics program executed to music with the dumbbell as the primary implement. If you had been a student at Amherst during this time, you would have been required to report to the gymnasium four days a week to take part in the light gymnastics routine, run, and march. Hitchcock also began to take regular anthropometric measurements of all of his students, and his contributions to the area of tests and measurements in physical education are considerable.

In the 1870's, Dudley Sargent developed a program of physical education at Harvard, and his contribution was to be the dominant one of the next several decades. Sargent not only continued the trend in gymnastics and made important contributions in the field of measurement, but also began to develop "exercise machines" which allowed students to develop their capabilities according to their individual needs. This "functional" approach to exercise is still a very important part of physical education today, and its origins can be traced directly to Sargent. During the last two decades of the nineteenth century, many American colleges built gymnasia and began to develop programs of physical education utilizing the fine examples set by Hitchcock and Sargent.

---

1. Fred E. Leonard and George Affleck, *A Guide to the History of Physical Education* (Philadelphia: Lea and Febiger, 1947), pp. 255-256.

If you had been a student in the public schools of Kansas City in 1887, you would have heard a bell at 10:00 a.m., and this bell signalled the beginning of the exercise period. Every student in the school system did the same exercise at the same time each day. Such was the physical education program in many Midwestern cities during the last decade and a half of the nineteenth century, and the group responsible for the programs were the Turners.

The Turner movement had come to the United States in the 1850's and had flourished as a private gymnastic society to the extent that in the 1890's there were over 300 societies with almost 40,000 members. It was inevitable that this program of physical education would find its way into school curricula in those cities that had a substantial German population.

THE BOSTON CONFERENCE

In a certain sense, it is inaccurate to discuss the history of "physical education." When the term physical education is used, it is generally understood to signify a broad program of activities which might include team sports, individual sports, aquatics, dance, gymnastics, intramurals, and interscholastic sports. However, to use the term this way is, in an historical sense, misleading, as we have seen by examining a few of the early programs in the United States. Bookwalter and Vander Zwaag have pointed out that the term, as we now understand it, has definite limitations in time and place.

> First, physical education, as we know it, largely had its origins in the United States. Second, although the name "physical education" appears in the literature before 1900, physical education is by and large a twentieth century phenomenon.[2]

Our discussion of the history of physical education in the United States refers to the different kinds of programs which have eventually developed into what has come to be called physical education in the twentieth century. The names under which these programs have been conducted have been many and varied: physical activity, body training, physical training, military training, gymnastics, calisthenics, hygiene, physical culture, physical fitness, sports and games, recreation, health education, athletics, sports education, movement education, and physical education. Some have focused on only one activity. Others employed only one method of instruction. Some were connected with schools, while others were supported by religious organizations or eth-

---

2. Karl Bookwalter and Harold Vander Zwaag, *Foundations and Principles of Physical Education* (Philadelphia: W. B. Saunders Company, 1969), p. 44.

nic societies. Each in its own way, however, is interwoven historically in the development of physical education. It is important then to recognize that when the term physical education is used here it is used in a special historical sense signifying a program which is related to the development of contemporary programs of physical education.

Toward the close of the nineteenth century, interest in education in the United States was considerable. The theories and practices of the great European educators, Rousseau, Pestalozzi, Basedow, Herbart, Froebel, were beginning to affect seriously the course of American education. It was appropriate then that physical educators of that day would be concerned with moving toward a more uniform program of physical education and also with the development of a physical education profession. There were, however, many programs to choose from, and it was the competition among them that Arthur Weston in his book, *The Making of American Physical Education,* has called quite appropriately the period of "the battle of the systems."

> The years between 1865 and 1900 were a period of change and ferment in the United States, and the activity in industry and society was matched by advances in the field of physical education. Just as before the Civil War there existed, however, a variety of programs, no one of which had achieved supremacy when the period closed. Thus there existed, side-by-side, the foreign born programs of German and Swedish gymnastics, the modified programs of Catherine Beecher and Dio Lewis, and the new American programs of physical education taught by such leaders of the new profession as Edward Hitchcock, Dudley A. Sargent, Edward M. Hartwell, and William G. Anderson.[3]

The "battle of the systems" was given official attention at a conference in Boston in 1889. This Boston Physical Training Conference has come to be known simply as the "Boston Conference," and it is a landmark of great significance in the history of American physical education. The purpose of the conference was to answer the question "which gymnastic system should be adopted by the United States?" Each of the systems was presented and then discussed by the participants. Most leaders who were not emotionally and pedagogically attached to one of the systems concluded that no one system met fully the needs of the American nation. It is interesting to note that the idea of a program of sports and games went completely unrepresented at this conference, even though sports and games had at that time already made their way into the schools but only as extra-curricular activities and only as a result of the insistence and efforts of students.

---

3. Arthur Weston, *The Making of American Physical Education* (New York: Meredith Publishing Company, 1962), p. 47.

Another event of note which occurred during this period was the creation of the American Association for the Advancement of Physical Education. This was the first truly national professional organization in physical education and was the forerunner of the American Association for Health, Physical Education, and Recreation (AAHPER).

THE TWENTIETH CENTURY 1900-PRESENT

This is a rather large span of history, not only in terms of years but also in terms of the occurrence of important events and movements; however, for this brief survey it is sufficient to consider this period of time as one historical period. Tremendous sociological changes have occurred during this period, most notably due to the technological and economic advances which have contributed to increased urbanization.

Educational philosophy has generally broadened during this time, and the objectives of education are now couched in terms of sociological and psychological needs. Psychology has made significant strides forward, providing a scientific basis for studying teaching methodology and child development. A general organizational pattern has evolved with an elementary school, junior high school or middle school, senior high school, and various types of colleges. The mere number of students now attending schools is in itself a significant educational change. Materials and equipment have been refined and are constantly being improved. The experimental attitude has come to be more nearly accepted by the American public. Teacher training has come to be an important part of educational planning. The first two decades of the twentieth century produced the progressive movement in politics and in society in general. In education, the progressive movement was championed by men such as G. Stanley Hall, Edward Thorndike, John Dewey, and William Heard Kilpatrick.

In physical education, also, the changes since 1900 have been many and varied. During the first two decades of the century, men such as Thomas Wood, Clark Hetherington, and Luther Halsey Gulick formed the conceptual framework upon which the "new physical education" would be built.

The early Twentieth-Century programs of physical education were still dominated by formal gymnastics, the German and the Swedish in particular. They were rivalled, however, by a new concept of physical education known variously as the "new physical education," "natural program," and "natural gymnastics," which was in the process of formation largely through the efforts of a trinity of outstanding leaders in physical education; Dr. Thomas D. Wood, Clark Hetherington, and Dr. Luther Halsey Gulick. It was they who broke with the tradition of formal gymnastics and gave shape and content to a distinctively Twentieth-Century program of physical education, which centers upon the physical as an avenue for promoting education.[4]

This marked the first truly American program of physical education, and it became the first viable competitor of gymnastics programs in school programs. From 1920-1940, Jay B. Nash and Jesse Feiring Williams carried the banner of the "new physical education" and also did yeoman's work in terms of getting physical education accepted as a justifiable aspect of total education.

Dance education, health education, athletics, and recreation were fused with physical education into the one profession known as physical education; and while there are signs today that these are beginning to evolve into separate disciplines, they are still generally thought of as one. The profession has grown not only in terms of numbers but also in terms of conception and quality. Sport sociology, sport psychology, exercise physiology, kinesiology and motor learning have come to be recognized as foundational scientific disciplines which support physical education. The research work carried on in these areas has constantly improved and today has become highly sophisticated, thus necessitating extensive academic preparation.

Since 1950, many important developments have occurred, but it is difficult to view them with any amount of historical perspective. Physical education programs have broadened considerably to include many new activities such as scuba, sailing, skiing, and judo. Because of a recent trend which questions the advisability of required courses, many schools have had to reevaluate their programs after losing the school requirement of instructional physical education. Sports clubs have begun to flourish in many places, and women's athletics have grown to include many interscholastic sports. Several schools have instituted the lecture-laboratory approach to teaching physical education, rather than the more traditional activities approach. Movement education flourished in England and was transported to the United States where it found a very ready audience for its new approach to physical education.

IMPORTANT CHARACTERISTICS
IN THE DEVELOPMENT OF AMERICAN PHYSICAL
EDUCATION

The purpose of this chapter has been to introduce you to some of the historical movements and events which have shaped the develop-

---

4. Ibid., p. 51.

ment of physical education in the United States. No claim is made for complete coverage. You may secure more information by consulting the many excellent references that are available in this field.

Perhaps we should close by attempting to identify some characteristics of American physical education which seem important to an understanding of the many current approaches to the field. Our purpose has been to look at "where we have been" in order to help us to understand better where we now stand. It will be seen that some characteristics persist into the present time; while others have reversed themselves or are moving in new directions.

1. *Physical education as an "umbrella" concept.* As late as 1889 (The Boston Physical Training Conference), physical education for all practical purposes was considered to be synonymous with gymnastics. Sports and games were not a major concern of that significant conference. This fact is doubly important when one realizes that it was during this period of history that popular interest in sports and games was growing by leaps and bounds. Football, volleyball, bowling, tennis, basketball, and other activities were being invented and rapidly diffused throughout the American culture. From this time on, "physical education" became an "umbrella" term under which games, athletics, dance, recreation, and health education came to be identified.

By 1937, when the AAHPER was established, the profession was firmly rooted in the "umbrella" concept, and there have been signs that several of these programs which have historically been lodged under the "umbrella" have decided that it is time to establish themselves as distinct and separate disciplines. Health education, recreation, safety education, and dance have all indicated interest in standing apart from physical education. It is likely that we have passed through the "umbrella" period and are now in the beginning stages of becoming distinct and separate disciplines.

2. *Downward movement of innovation from college to high school to elementary school.* Bookwalter and Vander Zwaag have suggested that a downward movement in physical education is a curricular trend.

> For one thing, physical education was first introduced in college curricula and then gradually extended to, first, secondary school curricula and, later, to elementary school curricula. It is an unfortunate fact that the latter change cannot be noted as even approaching complete progress, since many elementary schools in the United States still lack organized programs of physical education.[5]

---

5. Bookwalter and Vander Zwaag, *Foundations and Principles of Physical Education,* p. 53.

Historically, the major innovations in physical education have occurred at the college level and they have then filtered down to the high school and then into the programs of elementary school physical education. This is true, for example, of fitness testing. Largely created at the college level, most fitness tests have then been used in high schools and finally in elementary schools; the test-activities used in the elementary schools have primarily been watered down versions of those first used in colleges.

There are, of course, some notable exceptions to this characteristic. The early program at the Round Hill school, the influence of the Turners, and Clark Hetherington's "play school" experiment were all instituted well below the college level. In this century, however, when sports and games became so important in physical education curricula, most innovations started at the college level and gradually filtered down to elementary schools.

There is some evidence that this downward movement is not as true today as it has been in the past. The profession of physical education has done a good job in encouraging innovation at all levels of physical education. While most innovations have been created at the university level, they are not necessarily created *for* university students. The large graduate centers have been especially important in providing means by which graduate students in physical education can focus on the various school levels in their research and study. It can be assumed that teachers of physical education in elementary schools will more and more provide their own innovations. One should expect that the future will bring increased specialization and innovation at all levels. This is an important change for the good in the development of physical education.

3. *Sports and games developed through outside sources.* The term "outside sources" refers here to sources outside of professional programs of physical education in the schools. Athletic associations, gymnastics societies, sports clubs, and individuals have contributed to the development of organized sports and games in this country. This situation existed until the 1920's, when sports and games became established parts of total physical education programs. The Boston Conference of 1889, as has been previously mentioned, did not have a major spokesman to advocate the use of sports and games in physical education programs.

Of great importance have been the sport associations such as the American Lawn Tennis Association and the National Bowling League. Associations such as these have fostered interest in participation. When the time came to incorporate such activities into programs of physical education, the transition was smoothly accomplished and well received by students. This point leads to a very closely related characteristic which we shall consider next.

4. *Selection of activities dictated by adult leisure trends.* After physical education passed through the transition from a gymnastics orientation to the "new physical education," the activities which were selected for inclusion in the much expanded programs became a matter of interest. Historically, additions have seemed to follow increased popularity of certain activities among the adult population of the country. Three recent examples are golf, bowling, and skiing. Not too many years ago, these activities would not have been found in any but a few isolated programs of physical education. Each sport, however, underwent a significant "popularity boom" among the adults of the United States. Golf courses and driving ranges were built by the hundreds; bowling alleys sprang up everywhere; and ski resorts began to multiply. The profession has made an attempt to meet the demand for instruction in these activities by adding them to our curricula.

It might be difficult to defend the profession of physical education in terms of its leadership role in promoting activities. Activities are too often included in programs of physical education for other reasons than because they are considered to be of value by physical educators. This is not to suggest that the "other reason" should not also be considered when making such decisions. It merely means that physical educators have not taken an active enough role in promoting new activities which they feel are of value, and they have not been too successful in educating the public to the relative value of activities. One of the major reasons for this lack of "public education" is, of course, the fact that the profession of physical education has not as yet come to any clear-cut decisions about the relative value of various activities, and this stems from the fact that physical educators are not at all in accord regarding the objectives of physical education. It is now fairly well documented that, in terms of cardio-vascular fitness, certain activities are of greater value than others, but this is only one criterion by which value can be measured; the profession has not made decisions which firmly establish priorities among the many other criteria that could be used to make judgments concerning the relative value of activities. We have often tended to follow rather than to lead public opinion.

5. *Unclear relationship between athletics and physical education.* Organized athletics, even of the inter-school variety, existed long before athletic programs were brought under the umbrella of physical education. Athletic programs were mostly started by students at eastern colleges, and they came to be included in the total program

of physical education not because this was the desire of physical educators, but because school administrators forced the union. E. F. Voltmer and Arthur Esslinger made note of that point in their book, *The Organization and Administration of Physical Education.*

> When school administrators decided to accept interschool athletics and introduce it into the school curriculum, they logically located it in the physical education department. It proved to be an unwelcome guest. Physical educators viewed this foundling with suspicion and reluctantly accepted it as a necessary evil. A bitter struggle was waged for the leadership of the combined department. Little harmony and co-operation existed between athletics and physical education, and considerable jealousy and antagonism developed.[6]

While the antagonism between these two programs has lessened considerably through the years, the relationship still presents problems which have never been completely resolved.

The relationship has often been described symbolically as a triangle, with the instructional program at the base as the foundation, the intramural program at the middle, and the inter-school program at the apex. (See Figure 2). While this is theoretically and symbolically ideal, it does not present an accurate reflection of conditions as they have existed in the past or as they still exist in the present. The symbolism of the triangle clearly indicated that the foundation or strength of the total program lies in the instructional aspects which should reach all of

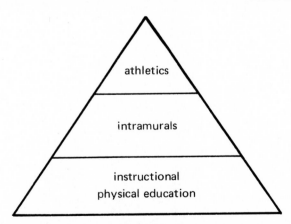

**FIGURE 2. Traditional symbolic relationship of
physical education, intramurals, and athletics.**

---

6. Edward Voltmer and Arthur Esslinger, *The Organization and Administration of Physical Education* (New York: Appleton-Century-Crofts, Inc., 1949), 3rd edition, p. 259.

the students, an ideal which seems consistent with the goals of American education. If put into practice, this would mean that teachers are hired first for their abilities to reach goals in the instructional program, that budgeting should clearly reflect the priorities suggested by the triangle, and that time allotment, equipment and space should also reflect these priorities. This certainly has not been the case. In many high schools, it is still the case that a coach is hired with his coaching abilities as the first prerequisite and his teaching abilities second. Budget, space and time allotments reflect similar discrepancies. The point is that physical education theory relegates athletics to a position that is inconsistent with that which it holds among at least the large vocal majority of the public. Inter-school sports are extremely important in American culture, particularly in the smaller towns and schools which dot the map of this country. Most universities operate with departments of athletics that are connected to physical education departments only in very minor ways, if at all.

One of the interesting relationships to follow in the future will be the one between physical education and athletics, and an interesting question to speculate about is to what extent the citizenry of this nation would support programs of physical education in high schools if they were completely divorced from programs of inter-school athletics. It will be interesting too, to follow the fast developing scene of girls' and women's inter-collegiate competition.

6. *Periodic returns to major emphasis on fitness.* Ever since the beginning of this century, many physical educators have felt that physical education could and should mean something more than physical fitness. These feelings were largely responsible for the abandonment of the term, "physical training" and the change to "physical education." Broadly based programs were advocated, and many educational goals were believed to be obtainable through the multi-activity approach. From time to time, however, the profession has returned to a major emphasis on fitness as the primary goal of the profession. Eleanor Metheny, an important current American physical educator, has made mention of these periodic returns to fitness as follows:

> At each stage in the development of educational thought, physical education has tried to move forward; but at each stage we have found it necessary to retreat and fire our old biological guns to ward off both real and imagined attacks made by other educators. We have made good use of our Nineteenth Century muskets. We have trained them on state legislatures to win many battles for laws and requirements; and recently we have triggered them with evidence that European children are more adept than American children in touching their toes and won for physical fitness a quasi-cabinet post in our national

government. At the moment it appears that the wheel set in motion by the physical trainers of the Nineteenth Century has come full circle. We are back where we started from a hundred years ago, and the tattered old biological banner of physical fitness is again waving triumphantly from our educational battlements.[7]

The profession of physical education returns to fitness whenever it is "called on the carpet" by public opinion. Such has been the case after the draft rejects in World War I, a severe polio epidemic in 1916, draft rejects in World War II, and the Kraus-Weber test reports to which Metheny referred in the above statement. In each of these cases, physical education programs became more fitness-oriented for several years before returning to the more broadly based approach. Fortunately, the recent Kraus-Weber crisis did not do as much injury to broadly based programs of physical education as did previous crises. Perhaps this is evidence that the American public has come to accept the value of a complete program of physical education. Only time will tell whether this trend will continue into the future. There are still strong "fitness first" voices in our profession.

7. *Increased specialization in professional training.* Physical educators originally were M.D.'s. Many of the great names in American physical education were medical doctors. In this century, this trend has very definitely changed. Professional courses in physical education beginning at Springfield College in 1887, the master's program at Columbia University in 1901, and a doctoral program in 1924, have been oriented in other directions.

Increasing specialization within the profession has also come about. Today it is commonplace for the undergraduate student to be required to elect a speciality in elementary physical education, secondary physical education, or in research oriented training. At the graduate level, the movement toward increased specialization is quite evident. The graduate student is likely to have to pick from among exercise physiology, sport psychology, sport sociology, administration, history, philosophy of physical education or from other such areas for his major specialization. It appears that the graduate student of the near future will not be trained as a "physical educator" but rather as a "sport psychologist" or as an "exercise physiologist." What this means for the profession and what this means especially for programs of physical education in the schools, has yet to be determined. The trend suggests both promising opportunities for the discipline of physical education

---

7. Eleanor Metheny, *Connotations of Movement in Sport and Dance* (Dubuque: Wm. C. Brown Co., Publishers, 1965), p. 101.

and perplexing possibilities for instructional programs of physical education.

Some characteristics of American physical education have been briefly discussed in this chapter. There are others. It is hoped that you will exercise your analytical capacities to pick them out and to attempt to make judgments about what they mean for the future of physical education.

It should be repeated that it has not been the purpose of this chapter to fully acquaint you with the history of American physical education. This, it is hoped, you will want to do later. The purpose has been merely to introduce you to the past of our developing profession so that you may better understand the remainder of this text which is largely designed to survey critically and analytically the question of "where we are." It is hoped that some ideas about where we have been will help you to understand better both where we now stand and where we will go from here.

What Questions Can You Ask About the Following Statements

1. The reason that German and Swedish gymnastics were so popular was that they produced recognizable results.
2. Sargent and Hitchcock were really health educators.
3. The United States is really more famous for the development of sports than for the development of physical education.
4. American physical education most basically reflects the progressivist philosophy of physical education.
5. The profession of physical education is now strong enough to withstand outside pressures for program change.
6. Physical education has played a large role in shaping the leisure activity patterns of the United States.
7. From the outset, physical education has been a profession where women have contributed just as much as men.
8. Physical education is meaningless as a term because it encompasses activities as diverse as driver's training and R.O.T.C.
9. Since the philosophy of idealism most favors the mind, it is incompatible with physical education.

Chapter 3—Physical Education as an Academic Discipline

I suggest that there is an increasing need for the organization and study of the academic discipline herein called physical education.

Franklin Henry, 1964

The above statement appeared in a 1964 *JOHPER*[1] article entitled, "Physical Education: An Academic Discipline." Henry's memorable article was an important contribution to physical education literature in the mid-1960's. In a serious and scholarly manner, he outlined the relevant issues concerning the viability of physical education as an academic discipline. The article was important not only because it stated well a position that needed to be stated, but also because it pointed to a change that most certainly will affect physical education for many years to come. The purpose of this chapter is to explain that change and to examine its possible effects on professional physical education.

Henry stated that his purpose was to define "the field of knowledge that constitutes the academic discipline of physical education in the college degree program."[2] It should be mentioned at the outset that no judgment was intended concerning the relative merits of an "academic" as opposed to a "professional" training. The merits of these different approaches is not necessarily the issue because, as Henry suggested, the two are not mutually exclusive. One of the questions that this chapter will attempt to answer, however, is how the academic

---

1. Franklin Henry, "Physical Education: An Academic Discipline," *JOHPER* 37:32-33, 69, September, 1964.
2. Ibid., p. 32.

discipline of physical education might affect programs of professional training. The question is one of potential influence rather than relative merit. It is likely that in the future there will be clear divisions between college physical education programs that are "academic" and those that are "professional." The purpose here is not to decide which of these is the better approach, but rather to explain the new academic approach and how this movement may affect the older, professional approach.

Henry defined academic discipline as "an organized body of knowledge collectively embraced in a formal course of learning."[3] A basic assumption underlying an academic discipline seems to be that the pursuit of the specific knowledge is self-justifying. What this means, of course, is that no practical application of the knowledge is necessary in order to justify the existence of the discipline. This is not to suggest that practical applications are not made or sought, but merely that the immediate practical use of the knowledge is not a necessary condition for the pursuit of that knowledge. It is of interest and worthwhile for its own sake. This is the basis of an important distinction, and no organized program can be called a "discipline" unless it meets this criterion. It is important that you recognize why this criterion must exist, because your immediate reaction might be to question the usefulness of disciplinary study.

Programs which are oriented toward the "applied arts and sciences," technical and professional programs, are necessarily concerned with short-run effects and examining questions whose answers have immediate practical significance. This, however, is not the only way that a body of knowledge is built-up and truth pursued. Disciplinary studies are "free" to pursue the answers to questions which may have no real or apparent immediate application. Disciplinary studies pursue truth with the faith that the pursuit is self-justified and that any answers they might come up with may some day be of practical "value."

MOVEMENT TOWARD AN ACADEMIC DISCIPLINE

During the early development of physical education in the United States, the young profession was tied quite closely to the general field of medicine. The primary benefits which were thought to accrue from participation in gymnastics and formal exercises were largely medical in nature. Most of the early leaders in American physical education were trained as M.D.'s; they did not hold pedagogical degrees. Such early leaders as Edward Hitchcock and Edward Hartwell were medical

---

3. Ibid.

doctors whose interest took them into the young field of physical education. John Warren, whose 1831 theoretical treatise on physical education was the first published in the United States, was a professor of anatomy and physiology at Harvard College. Catherine Beecher who created one of the very first "American" programs of physical education, built her system around twenty-six courses in physiology and two courses in calisthenics.

Henry[4] has pointed out in his article that the importance of this historical association with the field of medicine is that from the outset the profession of physical education has centered on what the activities of physical education can do for people, rather than being centered on the development of a specific body of knowledge. I should again like to point out that nothing is being suggested here that is critical of the historical tie with medicine or with the purpose of helping people, which is indeed a very altruistic service motive of which we should be rightly proud. The purpose here is merely to trace the development of the concept of the academic discipline of physical education.

Once physical education began to make inroads into programs in public schools, it was natural that it began to break its ties with medicine in favor of a closer tie with the field of education. As teacher training institutions grew after the turn of the century, departments of physical education began to develop. The first such department had been started in 1861 at Amherst College by Hitchcock. The rapid growth of similar departments did not, however, take place until toward the end of the nineteenth century. In 1898, the Society of College Gymnasium Directors was formed, and this is an obvious indication that some colleges had programs of physical education by that time.

It is interesting to note that the transition from a primary tie with medicine to a primary tie with education was not really accomplished until after the "new physical education" had been formulated and largely adopted by American physical education.

The three men who are most often cited as the founders of the "new physical education" were Thomas Wood, Luther Halsey Gulick, and Clark Hetherington. Wood and Gulick were both trained as physicians, whereas Hetherington developed his interest in physical education while studying under Wood at Stanford University. It was these men, however, who provided much of the impetus for attaching physical education to education rather than to medicine. They saw that physical education belonged in the schools. As early as 1890, Gulick foresaw the growth of the profession in the direction of general education.

---

4. Ibid.

If however, on the contrary, men of collegiate training, philosophic minds, of broad purposes, and earnest hearts, are induced to enter this field, the profession will show that it is intrinsically a broad, scientific, philosophic field, and *it will be recognized by thinking men as one of the departments in education,* fundamental in the upbuilding of the nation.[5] (italics added)

By 1920, physical education was firmly established as a part of education, and usually in universities as a department in the school of education. While Jesse Feiring Williams was trained as an M.D., most of his professional contemporaries received their degrees in physical education or in a foundation science. After Williams, there were few who held the M.D. degree, but more and more leaders earned the Ph.D. or Ed.D. degrees. Physical education has largely remained within schools of education from that time until the present. Even today, most graduate degrees are offered through departments of physical education which are administrative sub-units within schools of education. Some universities do offer a Ph.D. degree in physical education granted under the auspices of a school of physical education, but these are still the minority, and they are very often patterned after schools of education. In a few universities, however, the M.A. and Ph.D. degrees in physical education are offered through the graduate school and in this case tend to be liberally and academically oriented, the emphasis being on the discipline and not on teacher preparation.

Such is the history of physical education as a discipline. The movement toward an academic discipline has been given momentum in the past few years by a growing number of critics who view the technical-professional training programs as limiting. Henry pointed out in his article that physical education is perhaps the only subject matter that prepares students to teach exactly what they will teach in the schools.

In marked contrast, the student who obtains a bachelor's degree in physical education typically has a major that is evaluated and oriented with respect to what he is to teach in the secondary schools, and how he is to do the teaching or how he is to administer the program.[6]

Critics have also pointed out that the undergraduate major in English or Biology follows a sequence of courses and experiences which take him far beyond anything he might ever teach to high school students. The idea is not to train a chemistry teacher, but to train a chemist; not a psychology teacher, but a psychologist. Similar reasoning suggests that our emphasis should be on training a physical educator rather than a physical education teacher.

---

5. Luther H. Gulick, "A New Profession?" in *The Making of American Physical Education* by Arthur Weston (New York: Meredith Publishing Company, 1962), p. 149.
6. Henry, "Physical Education," *JOHPER,* p. 32.

With this background in mind, we should examine in more detail what it is that we have been referring to as the academic discipline of physical education. First, the discipline will be put in perspective as it relates to other disciplines, and second, sub-fields within the discipline will be examined.

THE ACADEMIC DISCIPLINE

For the most part, physical education has been viewed historically as a technically oriented profession to which several disciplines are foundational. These include physiology, psychology, anatomy, anthropology, sociology, history, philosophy, and physics. Physical educators have added to these bases specific courses such as exercise physiology, motor learning, and the history and philosophy of physical education. A question we are faced with now is where for example, does physiology, as a discipline stop and physical education as a discipline begin? Where does psychology stop and sport psychology begin? Let Henry explain the line or area of demarcation.

> One may well raise such a question as where is the borderline between a field such as physiology and the field of physical education? No simple definitive statement is possible, but it is not difficult to show examples that illustrate the region of demarcation. The existence of oxygen debt is physiology; the role of oxygen debt in various physical performances is physical education. We do not know why a muscle becomes stronger when it is exercised repeatedly. The ferreting out of the causal mechanism of this phenomenon can be considered a problem in physiology, although the explanation, when available, will be appropriate for inclusion in a physical education course. On the other hand, the derivation of laws governing the quantitative relation between an increase in strength and the amount, duration, and frequency of muscle forces exerted in training is surely more physical education than physiology. Determination of the intimate bio-chemical changes in a muscle during fatigue would seem to be a problem in physiology, although of direct interest to physical education. Here again, the quantification of relationships and the theoretical explanation of their pattern as observed in the intact human organism is more physical education than physiology. This is not mere application—it only becomes application when such laws are related to practical problems. The physiology of athletic training is not really application of physiology—rather it is physiology, of the sort that is part of the academic discipline of physical education, and only becomes applied when it is actually applied to practical problems.[7]

The same analysis could be undertaken for any of the sub-fields of physical education. The study of motor learning, for example, is not so

---

7. Ibid., p. 33.

much an application of psychology as much as it is a basic aspect of sport psychology and part of the academic discipline of physical education. The nature of aggression is a problem which psychologists must untangle, but the existence and extent of aggression in sports competition is a problem which physical educators must investigate because it is part of the academic discipline of physical education.

Disciplines such as physiology and psychology have long been considered to be directly foundational to professional physical education. What is now occurring is the development of the academic discipline of physical education itself. Physiology is a prerequisite to exercise physiology. Courses in exercise physiology should of course be preceded by a strong fundamental background in human or mammalian physiology. Psychology is foundational to the field of sport psychology, meaning that general courses in psychology should precede courses in motor learning, the psychology of motor activity, or personality factors in sports. Physical educators can now draw directly from the academic discipline of physical education. They can turn to sport psychologists or exercise physiologists for answers. Physical educators can now turn to physical education specialists and expect to receive expertise on the discipline of physical education. Distinctions as yet may not always be clear, but will in the future become clearer as the academic discipline of physical education is more fully established.

One of the primary reasons that the academic discipline of physical education has developed is that through the years a tremendous need has arisen for special kinds of investigation. As Henry said, "if the academic discipline of physical education did not already exist, it would need to be invented."[8] This is true because competence in any of the foundational disciplines provides no grasp of the knowledge necessary to understand physical education. One can study physiology and hardly touch at all on the function and effects of exercise. One can study psychology and not know much about how people learn sports skills or how and why people behave as they do in competitive sports situations. Basic texts in physiology treat exercise only as a peripheral topic. Texts in the psychology of learning treat motor learning briefly, if at all, and the material and research drawn on is largely of a fine motor skill nature that is carried on in a laboratory. The extent to which the conclusions of such research can be generalized to sports skills, which are gross motor skills, has never really been determined. The need arose for systematic investigation in these areas which were being treated only superficially by the foundational disciplines. The systematic investigation was forthcoming and marked the beginning of physical education.

---

8. Ibid., p. 69.

THE SUB-FIELDS OF THE ACADEMIC DISCIPLINE OF PHYSICAL EDUCATION

All academic disciplines have sub-fields, and physical education is no exception. The sub-fields of psychology include, for example, personality, behaviour disorder, and learning. While these obviously overlap, personality being an important factor in the study of behaviour disorders, they do form somewhat distinct aggregates within the larger disciplines. Sub-fields are not necessarily permanent groupings. From time to time, the emphasis within disciplines changes and produces a new sub-field. Stress physiology is an example of the recent development of a sub-field of physiology. The study of violence and human aggression is producing a new sub-field within the discipline of psychology.

Below are listed sub-fields of physical education as I see them at this stage of our disciplinary history. Other physical educators might prefer to alter the classification somewhat, and it certainly might change in the future; but at the present time, these sub-fields appear to represent a logical classification of the academic discipline of physical education.

1. Exercise Physiology
2. Kinesiology
3. Sport Psychology
4. Sport Sociology
5. History of Physical Education
6. Philosophy of Physical Education

The names given to these sub-fields may appear to be inconsistent (why sport psychology and not the history of sport). The reason that these names were chosen was that they are the labels that most often appear today in the ordinary language of the profession of physical education, and, therefore, it was felt that they would be the least confusing names to use for this classification. The names or labels for these sub-fields might change often without the basic content or focus of the sub-field changing at all. More will be said about names and labels at the end of this chapter when a look into the future is undertaken. It would be appropriate to pay particular attention to names and labels as you read the descriptions of the sub-fields.

EXERCISE PHYSIOLOGY

Exercise physiology is the study of human functions under the stress of muscular activity. It is concerned with the adjustment and regulatory activities of the bodily systems when placed under the stress of exercise. Some of the topics that are normally considered in exercise physiology courses are the physiology of muscle contraction, the effects of exercise on the heart, the effects of exercise on the circulatory system, respiration and lung ventilation, gas transport and internal respiration, exercise metabolism, and the effects of exercise on the endocrine system. Applied exercise physiology deals with such topics as fatigue, endurance, recovery, and strength development.

The field of exercise physiology has advanced considerably since the time when researchers were primarily utilizing instruments such as the stopwatch, the electrocardiograph, and the Douglas bag as means for gathering experimental data. Arthur Steinhaus, a pioneer exercise physiologist, has presented a graphic word picture of the type of activity that is now being carried on.

> In a Japanese laboratory a subject's arm is placed in a plethysmorgraph to show the changes in volume that reflect the changing blood flow in the exercising forearm muscles.
>
> In Germany catheters are passed up an arm vein into the opening of the coronary sinus in the right atrium to collect venous blood directly as it comes out of the heart wall. Then by analyzing this blood and representative arterial blood drawn simultaneously from the bronchial artery, researchers can tell that in strenuous exercise the heart gains more and more of its energy for the extra work by oxidizing lactic acid.
>
> On a Russian athletic field the heart rate of a trained runner is telemetered and found to accelerate more rapidly to its maximal rate than does that of an untrained one.
>
> In a Michigan laboratory large numbers of rats are forced to run, to swim, or to sit quietly or to run as they see fit. Some of each group are subjected to various anxiety-producing stresses. In histologic studies and chemical analyses of their hearts and other organs, researchers seek answers to some of man's most perplexing questions concerning the values of exercise in combatting the stresses of modern life, questions which today are answered usually by educated guesses.[9]

Recently, physical educator David Lamb[10] emphasized the importance of understanding the chemical nature of exercise and movement, thus underscoring the bio-chemical aspects of exercise physiology. Lamb points to methods such as Chromatography, Electrophoresis, and Spectrophotometry[11] as important approaches for exercise physiologists. This approach will broaden the scope of exercise physiology and

9. Arthur Steinhaus, "The Disciplines Underlying a Profession," *Quest* 9: 68-73.
10. David Lamb, "New Perspectives on Exercise Physiology," *New Perspectives on Man in Action,* eds. by Roscoe Brown and Bryant Cratty (Englewood Cliffs: Prentice-Hall, Inc., 1969), pp. 18-31.
11. *Chromatography* is a method used to separate chemical constituents of a solution from each other by differentially absorbing the solutes in various absorbing substances. *Electrophoresis* is a method of separating proteins in solution by determining their migration characteristics in an electrical field. *Spectrophotometry* is a method of determining the concentration of a chemical in solution by measuring the transmission of light through the solution.

basic research geared toward understanding metabolic pathways and energy production; an understanding of enzyme adaptation might someday contribute greatly to more efficient methods for training athletes. The sub-field of exercise physiology has in the past and no doubt will continue to contribute most significantly to the discipline of physical education.

KINESIOLOGY

Like so many words that we use in physical education, such as pedagogy and gymnasium for example, the term "kinesiology" is of Greek derivation. The suffix, *ology,* is familiar to you because of its common usage in terms such as psychology and biology. It can be translated as "the science of." *Kine* comes from the Greek word which means movement or motion, and, therefore, kinesiology means the science of motion or the science of movement. This term has been chosen to serve as a title for this sub-field, but you should be aware that several other terms are currently in use which, more or less, describe the same sub-field. Biomechanics is perhaps the term which is used most often as a substitute for kinesiology. *Bio* means life or living things, thus the term means the mechanics of living things. The two terms really focus on two separate aspects of this sub-field. One term, however, had to be chosen as a title for the sub-field and kinesiology is the more traditional and more widely accepted term. Other terms which have recently come into vogue are biokinetics and homokinetics. Both of these terms refer to the movement of living things or the motion of man.

At its present stage, kinesiology seems to have three major foci of attention. One concerns the understanding of the musculo-skeletal system. Such a study deals with the structure and function of joints, planes and axes of movement, and the muscular system which moves the bony structure of the human body. Too many students have had to memorize the attachments and actions of individual muscles. The current trend is a myological approach which emphasizes the group or aggregate action of muscles in producing movement. Thus, the term agonist (primary mover), synergist (helper), and antagonist (controller) are now essential in the study of muscular action. This focus of attention is the one that has traditionally been referred to as kinesiology.

A second focus of attention is that which has most often been referred to as principles of mechanics, principles of physics in motion, or just plain mechanics. The subject matter of mechanics is usually divided into sections dealing with gravity, buoyancy, equilibrium or balance, motion, leverage, force, work, and energy. Logan and McKinney[12] in the book, *Kinesiology,* have synthesized mechanical principles into three areas which they have termed "kinesiologic constructs": 1) summation of internal forces, 2) aerodynamics, and 3) hydrodynamics.

The third focus of attention in kinesiology is the analysis of activities, most often, of course, the activities common to physical education. This aspect of kinesiology is referred to as biomechanics or mechanical analysis. Often, the locus of the study is the specific activity. John Bunn's book, *The Scientific Principles of Coaching,* is divided into sections dealing with baseball techniques, gymnastic techniques, track techniques, and other sport activities. Others, such as John Cooper and Ruth Glassow in their book, *Kinesiology,* attempt a more generalized approach, preferring to focus on underarm patterns, pushing and pulling patterns, kicking patterns, arm-supported skills, and other general movement patterns.

Kinesiology is obviously a far-ranging field. The kinesiologist may do research on a human cadaver, or in a laboratory where he records the action potential of muscular patterns through the technique of electromyography, or on a sports field where he might record the movement pattern of an outstanding athlete through the use of high speed photography.

SPORT PSYCHOLOGY

If exercise physiology and kinesiology are relative "old-timers" in terms of their disciplinary strength, the sub-field of sport psychology is still in its infancy. The International Society of Sport Psychology is the oldest professional organization in this latter field and it is less than ten years old. This is not to say that there has been no interest in the psychological aspects of sports participation and performance. Certain topics such as motor learning and personality factors in sports have long held the interest of many investigators in physical education, but it was not until the last decade that sufficient interest in a wide variety of related topics resulted in the emergence of that which is now called sport psychology. It is still too early to predict the direction in which this field will move in the future, but it is possible to suggest several areas of investigation which seem to be developing within sport psychology.

One area which is considerably more developed than the others is motor learning. Some might argue, in fact, that motor learning is of sufficient scope to be a separate sub-field of the academic discipline of

---

12. Gene A. Logan and Wayne C. McKinney, *Kinesiology* (Dubuque: Wm. C. Brown Company, Publishers, 1970), p. xi.

physical education. Topics of concern to specialists in motor learning are the effects of practice, transfer, the role of stress in learning, knowledge of results, reinforcement, kinesthesis, retention of skill, mental practice, and the effects of different teaching methods on learning and performance.

Other areas of concern to the sport psychologist are the relation of personality factors to success in sports, motor activity in personality development, aggression in sport, social status and athletic performance, psychiatric factors related to sport, perceptual-motor development and therapy, and other such topics. It appears quite likely that the field of sport psychology will expand considerably in the future and that its research and scholarly contributions will be of great value to the profession of physical education.

Sport Sociology

Sport sociology, like sport psychology, is a recent addition to the discipline of physical education. When the *International Review of Sport Sociology* was first published in 1966, it became the first English language periodical dealing with this field. Several sport sociologists have given considerable thought to the emergence of their field. The first section of *Sport, Culture, and Society,* edited by John Loy and Gerald Kenyon, is devoted to "the sociology of sport as a discipline." Even more recently, Kenyon has ably discussed the topic in, "A Sociology of Sport: On Becoming a Sub-Discipline."[13]

Kenyon defines sport sociology as "the study of the underlying regularity of human social behavior within situations involving sport."[14] He suggests what he sees as necessary prerequisites for the development of this sub-discipline. The first is a conceptual framework within which research can be pursued. The second prerequisite is value free inquiry which is necessary for all disciplines, and which is comprised of descriptions, explanations, and predictions of behaviour in sport situations. The third prerequisite is a theoretical-empirical balance.

Sport sociology is concerned with all facets of social behaviour in sport situations. Among these are the roles of rules, ritual, and costumes, which are part of the form of sports. Also to be considered are the physical and social situations of sport. Involvement in sport is another basic area of concern and involves the athlete, the spectator, the sportswriter, and the television fan. Finally, sport sociology is con-

---

13. Gerald Kenyon, "A Sociology of Sport: On Becoming a Sub-Discipline," *New Perspectives of Man in Action,* eds. Bryant Cratty and Roscoe Brown.
14. Ibid., p. 165.

cerned with the coach, the instructor, the governing bodies, the refer-
ees, the promoters, the owners, and the manufacturers, all of whom
facilitate the on going existence of sport.

HISTORY OF PHYSICAL EDUCATION

Here, again, the terminology used is quite tentative. The term
"history of physical education" is a bit misleading since, as we have
seen, it is largely a twentieth century phenomenon. The future, no
doubt, will bring a developing study of the history of physical education
and, also, a developing study of the history of sport. It is quite likely that
the disciplinary study will be the history of sport, and that the history
of physical education will be a more professionally oriented sub-field in
teacher training programs rather than in programs dealing with the
academic discipline of physical education. At the present time, however, the two can still be considered under the umbrella term, the
history of physical education.

A great deal of research is needed in this field. Melvin Adelman[15] has pointed out that the sub-field is not likely to develop to its
fullest potential until sports historians shift their focus from the narrative-descriptive approach to history to the interpretative-comparative
approach to history. The narrative-descriptive approach merely
records past events. The interpretative-comparative approach attempts to explain past history, to formulate search for valid generalizations, and to search for patterns of change.

Marvin Eyler[16] suggested in 1965 that sports history would develop
through three periods: 1) the awakening period, 2) the fledgling period,
and 3) the approbatory period. Eyler felt that this field has already
moved through the awakening period and slightly into the fledgling
period. The final period, of course, should be characterized by a full and
rich body of knowledge covering the major periods of history, utilizing
the interpretative-comparative approach. Adelman,[17] on the other
hand, considers Eyler's views to be a bit optimistic. Adelman considers
the sub-field to be now solidly within the awakening period.

One of the changes that must occur is that more sport historians
must become active throughout their professional lives. Most of the
research that has been undertaken has been done by students pursuing
graduate degrees. Excellent work can be accomplished in this field as
is witnessed by the truly first-rate work done by H. A. Harris in *Greek*

---

15. Melvin Adelman, "The Role of the Sports Historian," *Quest* 12:61-65.
16. Marvin Eyler, "Sport Historians," *Proceedings of NCPEAM,* 1965, pp. 57-60.
17. Adelman, *Quest* 12:61-65, p. 63.

Athletes and Athletics and by David Quentin Voight in *American Base-ball: From Gentleman's Sport to the Commissioner System.*

We should look forward to an upsurge of activity within this sub-field and it should make for some interesting reading for us all.

PHILOSOPHY OF PHYSICAL EDUCATION

The same problems of terminology which were mentioned in con-nection with the history of physical education are also in evidence when philosophy of physical education is considered. You should recognize by now that philosophy of physical education and philosophy of sport are really two different areas of study, and they no doubt will separate in the foreseeable future. For the moment, however, I shall continue with the terminology that is most consistent with current practices.

Philosophers have traditionally neglected the general area of sport and physical education. Paul Weiss, Sterling Professor of Philosophy at Yale, in his book *Sport: A Philosophic Inquiry,* has spoken to this point:

> We will find in the Greeks some good historically grounded explana-tions for the neglect of sport by philosophic minds, then and later. Despite their evident enjoyment of athletics, and their delight in speculating on the meaning of a hundred different human concerns, the Greek thinkers never dealt extensively with the nature, import, and reason for sport. Since Plato and his fellows formulated most of the issues that have occupied philosophers over the centuries, the Greek failure to provide a philosophical study became a norm for the rest.[18]

Thus, the philosophy of sport and the philosophy of physical education do not share in the glorious history of philosophical inquiry that is available to most disciplines.

There has in recent years, however, been an increase in philosoph-ical speculation and analysis in sport and physical education. Such philo-sophical research is most likely to fall under three headings: 1) speculative philosophy, 2) normative philosophy, and 3) analytical philosophy. Speculative philosophy refers to extrapolations made beyond the limits of scientific knowledge. An example might be an attempt to explain the origins of play in human behaviour. The norma-tive method of philosophy refers to general statements that guide prac-tical activity. An example of such an effort might be a physical education curriculum for the elementary schools based on a progres-sivist philosophy. The analytical method deals with the clarification of words and concepts, especially the use of ordinary language. An exam-

---

18. Paul Weiss, *Sport: A Philosophic Inquiry* (Carbondale: Southern Illinois University Press, 1969), p. 5.

ple might be a conceptual definition of sport, or the use of the term "fitness" in the writings of Charles McCloy.

It should be expected that normative philosophy will, as it has in the past, provide an important link between the discipline and the profession of physical education.

A fourth force should be mentioned because it has already made substantial headway in the literature of physical education; the philosophical position most often called existentialism. One advocate of existential philosophy in physical education is Howard Slusher. His book, *Man, Sport, and Existence,* is an example of an existential approach. Existentialists tend to make widespread use of phenomenology as a philosophical method. Phenomenology refers to sensory perception and immediate insight as opposed to contemplative speculation or data gathering.

THE EFFECTS OF THE EMERGING DISCIPLINE ON PROFESSIONAL PROGRAMS

Even in its infancy, the academic discipline of physical education has already had important effects on professional programs of physical education. It should be expected that the discipline will continue to influence the profession, although the precise direction and quality of that influence is not completely clear at this time.

The first, most important, and longest range effect can be seen in the improved academic content of professional programs. In some cases, this means more emphasis on courses such as exercise physiology, motor learning, and philosophy of physical education. Academic content, however, is not necessarily synonymous with course divisions. Even if course divisions remain more traditional (introduction to physical education, organization and administration of physical education, teaching methods in physical education), their academic content will be improved because of work accomplished by exercise physiologists, sport psychologists, and other discipline-oriented physical educators. This will be true because of the second effect of the emerging discipline, which is a greatly increased research and scholarly effort which manifests itself in an improved professional literature.

Contrary to certain popular notions physical educators do read, both within and far afield from the professional literature of physical education. Many of the contributions to physical education are made by physical educators primarily involved with the academic discipline of physical education. Their research and ideas are diffusing gradually throughout the profession, and this will, in itself, improve the academic content of college courses in physical education. As the academic content of college courses in physical education improves, those students who are preparing to teach physical education will carry this expertise with them into their teaching situations.

A third effect will be an increased amount of rigor in approaching problems and ideas. Many of the "truths" of physical education have been built primarily on accumulated opinion, and may or may not have any real basis in fact. It should be expected that the academic discipline of physical education will attack certain ideas and concepts with the rigor that a research discipline necessarily exerts. This trend should produce a short-range and a long-range effect. In the short-range, the rigorous examination of certain "truths" (sports build good character) may create a great deal of uneasiness within the profession. It is never easy to put basic beliefs to the test, and many professionals will experience a bit of anxiety throughout this process. In the long-range, however, the rigorous examination of all assumptions and beliefs will bring a new respect for physical education in the eyes of the academic and scientific community. The "truths" that are indeed true can then be promoted vigorously on the basis of evidence, while the "truths" that are not true can be discarded.

A fourth possible effect is that the emerging discipline might produce conditions which bring about a division within physical education that is based on mistrust and jealousy. This would be most unfortunate, but it would be dishonest not to recognize that it might happen. If professional physical educators and disciplinary physical educators become divided so that hostility exists between them, then each will suffer a tremendous setback. We should certainly hope that this kind of division can be avoided. Perhaps recognition of the possibility of such division is the first step in avoiding the problem.

Overall, the emergence of the academic discipline of physical education is a very beneficial phenomenon both to the profession of physical education and to the academic community in general. The application of experimental and scholarly rigor to problems connected with sport and exercise will, in the long run, prove to be highly beneficial to all concerned.

THE FUTURE ROLE OF THE DISCIPLINE

It is difficult to judge what role the discipline will occupy in the future of physical education, and all that I now suggest is primarily speculative. There are signs and trends, however, which can be used to form some educated guesses.

One of the obvious problems that will have to be untangled in the future is the problem of nomenclature. Reading this chapter has probably thoroughly confused you about what names to use when describing the various aspects of the profession and the academic discipline. Gerald Kenyon has summarized well the basic quandary surrounding the use of labels.

> Thus, the expression "physical education" with its obvious professional connotations, is not a suitable label for both the professional and disciplinary aspects of human physical activity. However, because of its widespread currency, and despite the semantic difficulties long alluded to, the term might be retained, but in a restricted sense. Those who would use physical activity to change behaviour—whether it be cognitive, affective, or psychomotor—we may term *physical educators.* On the other hand, those whose objective is to understand the phenomenon, we may consider members of a discipline, the name of which is still a topic of much debate.[19]

Kenyon suggests that "the sport sciences" must be an appropriate label for the disciplinary studies. This certainly appears to be the direction in which the academic discipline will move. Some are suggesting "homokinetics," and other new labels are certain to appear in the literature.

Harold Vander Zwaag, a sport historian and philosopher, recently analyzed the problem in a speech entitled "Historical Relationships Between the Concepts of Sport and Physical Education." Vander Zwaag suggested that physical education should avoid searching for another label which is merely another "umbrella" such as "human movement."

> Physical education should not and will not be replaced by the concept of human movement. There has been a tendency to contrast the profession of physical education with the discipline of human movement. The net result is a comparison of one abstract entity with another. Both abstractions have risen from the search for appropriate umbrellas. In this search, concrete components have been overlooked. These components are sport and exercise.[20]

Vander Zwaag believes that adopting sport and exercise science as the focus would eliminate the need for organizational distinctions between the profession and the discipline. This organization would look like the chart on the following page.

---

19. Gerald Kenyon, *New Perspectives of Man in Action,* p. 165.
20. Harold J. Vander Zwaag, "Historical Relationships Between the Concepts of Sport and Physical Education," speech delivered at the 73rd Annual Meeting of the National College Physical Education Association for Men, December 29, 1969, Chicago, Illinois.

EXERCISE SCIENCE	THEORY OF SPORT
Understanding and Communication of Exercise Science	Understanding and Communication of Sport Theory
Conduct of Exercise Programs	Conduct of Sport Programs

This is one viable option that could be instituted. The departmental label would be the Department of Sport and Exercise Science. Working *across* the bottom tier would, of course, put you in the realm of professional training which is now known as physical education.

Another approach has been suggested by Wynn Updike and Perry Johnson. They suggest that "human physical activity" should be the label which describes the focus of the discipline.

> If an overall discipline can be defined as the study of human physical activity, physical education (the teaching of concepts, skills, and techniques), would logically become the educational arm of the discipline.[21]

Under this approach, a department might develop under the title, The Department of Human Physical Activity. The sub-divisions within the department would approximate what I have described here as the sub-fields of the academic discipline of physical education. In this approach, however, "physical education" as the educational arm of the discipline would simply exist as a sub-field within the department along with the other sub-fields.

Another option would be to separate the profession and the discipline into co-equal programs. They could exist as separate programs within a common department, and in time and with increased specialization, they might develop into separate departments. Thus, a Department of Physical Education and a Department of Sport and Exercise Science might co-exist within a university framework. In this type of organizational framework, the differences between the sport historian and the historian of physical education would be readily apparent.

The organizational framework which is adopted will be one of the interesting trends to watch unfold in the coming years. How it does

---

21. Wynn Updike and Perry Johnson, *Principles of Modern Physical Education, Health, and Recreation* (New York: Holt, Rinehart and Winston, Inc., 1970), pp. 19-39.

develop may well exert great influence on programs of physical education in the schools.

WHAT QUESTIONS CAN YOU ASK ABOUT THE FOLLOWING STATEMENTS

1. To develop a discipline, the subject must be a science, and physical education is not a science.
2. Physical education is becoming too academic.
3. The term "physical education" implies a philosophical dualism.
4. The discipline of physical education will affect teacher training programs by making the courses more academic and less practical.
5. The "truths" about physical education can be answered only through application of the scientific discipline.
6. The history of physical education is allied more closely to the history of education than it is to the history of sport.
7. The name of a discipline or a profession is not important.
8. The discipline of physical education should not make value judgments about the relative merits of different programs of physical education.

PART TWO

Contemporary Concepts of Physical Education

Introduction—
Examining Contemporary Concepts

In the second part of this text, an attempt is made to examine concepts of physical education that are of current importance in terms of their real or potential influence on programs of physical education in schools. A program of physical education in any school can be analyzed to determine what idea, concept, philosophy, or theory undergirds it. This is not to suggest that each program is developed from a philosophically oriented and consciously recognized point of view. It is true that many are developed by first stating a philosophy and then deriving goals from that philosophy. Many programs, however, just seem to happen. They are copied from other schools, or they just develop because of the contingencies which happen to be present at a given school at a given time. Even though no conscious attempt has been made to develop a program based on a particular point of view, nevertheless each program does *implicitly* reflect a certain set of beliefs and ideas about physical education.

We are now entering into a period of our professional history that may well be characterized by a diversity of physical education programs. There are many different types of programs in our schools. Some emphasize physical fitness, while others emphasize lifetime sports, and still others emphasize team sports. Some programs take the multi-activity approach, while others prefer specialization in fewer activities. Some new approaches are also being promoted and are making inroads into school programs. Movement exploration now dominates many elementary school physical education programs, and other schools now emphasize activities which purport to enhance cognitive development. Some physical education programs are organized around activities and techniques which aim primarily at emotional and psychological development. Such programs can be termed "motor therapy" or "play therapy" programs.

It is becoming increasingly important for physical educators to examine program aims and program content in order to determine the basic ideas and concepts which undergird the program. The physical educator should be able to make judgments about the relative merits of the various ideas and concepts which he encounters. It is important that you recognize that all ideas are not of equal value. The goal should be to be able to analyze ideas and the programs that reflect these ideas on the basis of the best current research evidence, the logic of the ideas, and the consistency with which the programs reflect the ideas. To help you to reach that goal is the purpose of this section.

Chapter 4—Physical Education for Physical Fitness

All forms of education may develop the mind and spirit of man but only physical education can develop his body.

Arthur Steinhaus, 1937

THE HISTORICAL BACKGROUND

It has been common practice among American physical educators to cite two "philosophies of physical education" as primary adversaries for dominance in twentieth century educational theory and practice. These two "schools of thought" have most often been referred to as education-*of*-the-physical and education-*through*-the-physical. Education-*of*-the-physical has applied mostly to programs of physical education in which the primary goal is physical fitness, defined most often as increased strength, speed, and endurance. Education-*through*-the-physical, on the other hand, has usually been associated with programs whose goals are similar to the goals of general education. It is the purpose of this chapter and the next to examine these two concepts, to chart their historical development, to evaluate their validity, and to judge their influence on programs of physical education in our schools.

The idea that the development of the body is an important educational goal is not new; indeed it is at least as old as Platonic Greece. Plato regarded the development of the body as a crucial educational goal but he valued the trained body not as an end in itself, but rather as a means toward an end. Plato considered the well-trained body a more suitable home for the immortal soul than the untrained body, and, thus, the trained body was used as a means for perfecting the moral and spiritual fiber of the individual. Also, as mentioned elsewhere,[1] the very practical fact should be recognized that physical education in ancient Greece was highly favored because it helped to prepare the Greek citizen to defend his city-state. Does Plato, then, reflect an education-*of*-the-physical point of view or an education-*through*-the-physical point of view? The answer is not easily drawn, but perhaps one criterion that we might utilize in deciding this and similar questions is whether the training of the body was sought as an end in itself, or whether it was pursued for other ends, such as for the development of moral stature or for purposes of military preparedness. If this is the criterion, then Plato obviously has to be placed in the education-*through*-the-physical category.

The early history of organized physical education in the United States has perhaps best been described as "the battle of the systems," for European systems of gymnastics vied for dominance in our school systems. As was pointed out in Chapter Two, an attempt was made at the Boston Conference of 1889, to resolve questions surrounding the value of the various systems of gymnastics, and this date marks a signal stage in the development of American physical education. It is correct, I believe, to classify the majority of physical educators of this era as adherents of the education-*of*-the-physical point of view, though there are statements that indicate that other goals which might be obtained through gymnastics were also recognized. Heinrich Metzner, for example, in a paper delivered at the Boston Conference of 1889 gave the following description of the goals of the German system of gymnastics.

> As gymnastic exercises, we denote all bodily exercises and movements produced by the controllable muscles with consciousness and intention, for the purpose of developing all bodily faculties in an agreeable manner, and at the same time of bringing out all those qualities which are the natural result of health and strength: namely, courage, self-reliance and joyfullness.[2]

Nevertheless, the main emphasis for physical education at that time was upon bodily development and health as ends in themselves.

That emphasis was particularly apparent in the Swedish system of gymnastics. Baron Nils Posse, at the same Boston Conference, suggested that the only exercises included in the Swedish system were those whose "local and general effects are fairly well known and proved to

1. Daryl Siedentop, "What Did Plato Really Think?" *The Physical Educator* 25:25-26, March, 1968.
2. Heinrich Metzner, "The German System of Gymnastics," *The Making of American Physical Education* by Arthur Weston (New York: Meredith Publishing Company, 1962), pp. 130-131.

be needed by the body."[3] Posse explained that movements were never chosen just for an aesthetic purpose, because exercises chosen by such a criterion had "but little effect toward physical development." Adherents of the Swedish system also disapproved of the use of musical accompaniment for gymnastic exercises.

One important point should be cleared up before proceeding further. The discussion in this chapter concerns the goals of the various European systems of gymnastics *as they were promoted and utilized in the United States.* If the history of physical education theory in Europe were the topic of discussion, then a most important consideration would be the *nationalistic* fervor of the important European physical educators. The nineteenth century in Europe is often characterized as the era of the rise of national states. The goals of German gymnastics, Swedish gymnastics, and Danish gymnastics, *as they were originally conceived in those countries,* were directly related to the development of nationalism. Strong and morally upright young men and women were considered to be the foundation of a strong national state, and the various gymnastics systems were considered to be important means of developing such a citizenry. When the European systems were imported to the United States, a change in the priority of goals was obviously necessary because German, Swedish, and Danish nationalisms per se were of little concern to American physical educators. The logical course to pursue was to emphasize the physical and health benefits of the gymnastics systems. Thus, the primary goals of the European systems of gymnastics as they were promoted and practiced in the United States were health and physical development. For this reason, they are characterized here as being within the education-*of*-the-physical viewpoint.

Several important American physical educators of this era clearly espoused the education-*of*-the-physical school of thought; the most prominent being Edward Hitchcock, Dudley Sargent, and Edward Hartwell. During the latter part of the nineteenth century, these three men were important figures in American physical education and were influential in promoting new programs in colleges and public schools. The following statement by Hitchcock summarizes well the bodily development and health goals of physical education during that period.

> Physical culture as expressed to Amherst College students by the experience of the past twenty years means something besides, something in addition to muscular exercise. It includes cleanliness of skin,

---

3. Baron Nils Posse, "The Chief Characteristics of the Swedish System of Gymnastics," *The Making of American Physical Education* by Arthur Weston, pp. 134-138.

> attention to stomach and bowels, relaxation from daily mental work, freedom from certain kinds of petty discipline, but with so much requirement and restraint as will give coherence, respect, and stability to the methods of maintaining health and the men enjoying them.[4]

Sargent,[5] in discussing the aim of physical education, also indicated that health, strength, and stamina were the long-range goals and the improvement of the physical condition of the student was the short-range goal. In contrasting the relative merits of gymnastics and athletic sports, Hartwell, while having good things to say about each, made it plain that he felt American physical education should concentrate on gymnastics training.

> Gymnastics, as compared with athletics are more comprehensive in their aims, more formal, elaborate, and systematic in their methods, and are productive of more solid and considerable results.[6]

The "solid and considerable results" to which Dr. Hartwell referred are improved strength, speed, endurance, and general health. Hartwell and his colleagues of that era promulgated the education-of-the-physical philosophy. American physical education in the latter part of the nineteenth century was dominated by leaders whose viewpoints and programs were oriented toward goals which had to do with the development of health, strength, carriage, endurance, and flexibility.

THE NEW PHYSICAL EDUCATION

The education-of-the-physical viewpoint, which was organized around various systems of European and American gymnastics and exercises, was to have a fairly short-lived dominance in American physical education. It is true (the Boston Conference of 1889 attests to it) that American physical education was originally organized with an education-of-the-physical viewpoint, but it is also true that even in its infancy that philosophical viewpoint was beginning to change. This is not surprising, because during this time, American education in general was beginning to undergo a vast change because of the influences of Froebel, Rousseau, Pestalozzi, Basedow, Herbart, G. Stanley Hall, and John Dewey.

---

4. Edward Hitchcock, "The First Academic Program of Physical Education in American Education," *The Making of American Physical Education* by Arthur Weston, pp. 107-112.
5. Dudley Allen Sargent, "The Sargent System of Physical Education," *The Making of American Physical Education* by Arthur Weston, pp. 113-117.
6. Edward Mussey Hartwell, "A Nineteenth-Century View of Physical Education," *The Making of American Physical Education* by Arthur Weston, pp. 124-129.

Reflections of this new movement can be seen in some early writings in American physical education. As early as 1893, Thomas Wood, who became one of the primary exponents of the "new physical education," described physical education in terms which became increasingly familiar and acceptable to professionals in the field.

> The term physical education is so misleading, and even misrepresented, that we look for a name which shall represent fairly the real idea of the science. What is physical education? This is one of the unsolved problems. Many people answer: "The training and development of the physical;" and they consider that the aim and end may be found in anthropometric apparatus, physical measurements and of averages. Now these things are very well in their places, but if our science is to be worthy of the best efforts of men and women, and of the respect and recognition of the educational world, physical education must have an aim as broad as education itself, and as noble and inspiring as human life. The great thought in physical education is not the education of the physical nature, but the relation of physical training to complete education, and then the effort to make the physical contribute its full share to the life of the individual, in environment, training, and culture.[7]

It should be pointed out that gaining for physical education "the respect and recognition of the educational world" was to become for the next half century one of the foremost goals of physical educators. While not always stated explicitly, this aim was implicit in the writings of most leaders in physical education during the first fifty years of this century. Physical educators of that time were literally fighting for their professional lives, attempting to gain inroads into school programs, to make physical education a required subject, and to insure the financial commitment necessary to make it all a reality. You should be aware of the reasons for this goal of "respectability" as you consider the criticisms of some who now feel that it forced physical educators to make claims and assurances about the outcomes of their programs that could not be substantiated.

The ideas suggested by Wood's statements are clearly within the philosophical framework of the education-*through*-the-physical viewpoint. This point of view was widely adopted during the early part of this century and by 1925 had become firmly entrenched as the major philosophical viewpoint of professional physical educators. In connection with this point of view, a greatly expanded program of physical education activities was utilized in efforts to pursue the general goals of education. This, in effect, tended to make physical education an equal

---

7. Thomas D. Wood, "The Scientific Approach in Physical Education," *The Making of American Physical Education* by Arthur Weston, pp. 150-158.

with other school programs that sought similar goals. The only difference was that the means used to reach the goals were of a different nature.

Thomas Wood, Luther Gulick, and Clark Hetherington were the most prominent of the early promoters of the new physical education (also called the natural movement in physical education). In a 1910 paper entitled, "Fundamental Education," Hetherington expressed ideas which dominated physical education for the next fifty years.

> This paper aims to describe the function and place of general neuromuscular activities, primarily general play activities, in the educational process. We use the term *general play* to include plays, games, athletics, dancing, the play side of gymnastics, and all play activities in which large muscles are used more or less vigorously. ... To present the thesis four phases of the educational process will be considered: organic education, psychomotor education, character education, and intellectual education.[8]

As you will see in the next chapter, Hetherington's four objectives left an indelible mark upon American physical education.

The work of Wood, Gulick and Hetherington was subsequently carried on primarily by Jesse Williams at Columbia University and Jay B. Nash at New York University. From 1925 to 1950, these two men were the most prominent spokesmen for the education-*through*-the-physical viewpoint and quite likely the most influential leaders in professional physical education. In his 1930 article, "Education Through the Physical," which may be the most famous single document in the history of American physical education, Williams drew the battle lines quite distinctly.

> No one can examine earnestly the implications of physical education without facing two questions. These are: Is physical education an education *of* the physical? Is physical education an education *through* the physical? ... Education of the physical is a familiar view. Its supporters are those who regard strong muscles and firm ligaments as the main outcomes. Curiously enough this restricted view is not heeded alone by physical educators but also by those who talk about educational values, objectives, and procedures. In effect, such a view is a physical culture and has the same validity that all narrow disciplines have had in the world. The cult of the muscle is merely another view of the narrowness that fostered the cult of mind or the cult of spirit.[9]

8. Clark Hetherington, "Fundamental Education," *The Making of American Physical Education* by Arthur Weston, pp. 159-165.
9. Jesse F. Williams, "Education Through the Physical," in *An Anthology of Contemporary Readings* eds. Howard Slusher and Aileene Lockhart (Dubuque: Wm. C. Brown Company Publishers, 2nd Edition, 1970), p. 1.

From that day to the present no prominent leader in American physical education has deviated far from the education-*through*-the-physical philosophy. To be sure, there have from time to time been physical educators who have criticized some parts of the viewpoint or have questioned the priorities or hierarchy of objectives within the total philosophy, but no major dissenting philosophy has been promoted until quite recently when the "movement education" philosophy began to become popular.

Two of the most important critics of the education-*through*-the-physical viewpoint were Arthur Steinhaus and Charles H. McCloy. It is often argued that McCloy represented the traditional education-*of*-the-physical point of view. This, however, is not borne out by an examination of his writings. To be sure, he was critical, particularly of what he considered to be the haphazard methods that were utilized in attempts to achieve the goals of the new physical education, but he nevertheless also believed that physical education was best characterized as a means of reaching educational goals through gross motor activity. Statements from two of his most important articles clearly show his dissatisfaction both with the traditional systems of physical education and with the priorities placed on physical education by the new physical education.

> The older systems of physical education in current use are, in most cases, educational anachronisms—hang-overs from the semi-military European systems of physical education; developed in nations constantly exposed on all sides to threats of war; invented by and for militarists, and impregnated throughout with angular never-to-be-used-in-life movements devised by the orthodox military mind.[10] (1927)

> For a profession that has glorified the physical side of man from before 500 B.C. until, shall we say, A.D. 1915, the physical education literature of today is strangely silent about the more purely body-building type of objectives. From the time of Homer to shortly after the time of Thorndike, the emphasis will be found to have been on the physical —education *through* the physical surely, but also education *of* the physical, for its own sake as well as in Education's sacred name. Then came the leavening influence of Thorndike's psychology and of Dewey's philosophy, enlarging our concepts of how to educate, and as a profession we made real progress. But this progress was made at the expense of the old model.[11] (1936)

---

10. Charles H. McCloy, "New Wine in New Bottles," in *Background Readings in Physical Education,* eds. Ann Paterson and Edmond Hallberg (New York: Holt, Rinehart and Winston, 1965), pp. 176-181.
11. Charles H. McCloy, "How About Some Muscle?" eds. Slusher and Lockhart, *An Anthology of Contemporary Readings,* pp. 5-9.

McCloy's primary goals were to encourage physical educators to scientifically attack, define, and refine the goals and methods of physical education while retaining the age-old emphasis on physical activity as the primary means for reaching the goals.

For thirty years, the ideas of Williams, Nash, and McCloy tended to dominate the physical education literature.[12] No suggestion is being made here that these leaders shared a unitary point of view. Indeed, their views were considerably different. Williams stressed social learnings through the medium of games. Nash stressed carry-over recreational skills. McCloy focused on strength and endurance training. What seemed to happen was that the physical education profession incorporated the work of the three so that it did become, for all practical purposes, a unitary point of view. The groundwork for this had been laid by Hetherington when he stated the four-fold objectives of the profession. Williams, Nash, and McCloy could be viewed as stressing different aspects of the total goal.

There have been attempts to define physical education more strictly in accord with an education-*of*-the-physical philosophy. Recently, Jerome Weber[13] has defined it as "the science of exercise." His argument is that the only demonstrable and obtainable outcomes available through physical education are physiological in nature. He further suggests that exercise is the only truly unique aspect of physical education. Weber proposes that we should consider a person to be physically educated if he: 1) possesses accurate knowledge about the effects of exercise, and 2) if he applies this knowledge to himself and exercises regularly. Weber's thoughts represent a very clear-cut, unequivocal statement of a contemporary interpretation of the education-*of*-the-physical viewpoint.

With this historical introduction in mind we can now turn to an examination of the facts and ideas surrounding the concept of physical fitness. Whether the development of physical fitness should be considered the sole objective of physical education or as one of several objectives can better be decided after the facts are examined.

PHYSICAL FITNESS: WHAT IS IT?

Virtually every book written about physical education discusses physical fitness; yet it is hard to find acceptable definitions of it. For the

12. Ellen Gerber, "The Ideas and Influence of McCloy, Williams, and Nash on Modern Physical Education," a paper presented at the Big Ten Symposium on the History of Physical Education and Sport," The Ohio State University, March, 1971.
13. Jerome C. Weber, "Physical Education, The Science of Exercise," *The Physical Educator* 25:5, March 1968.

most part, mention is usually made of the difficulty of interpreting the concept, and then a generalized definition is usually offered which relates physical fitness to some broader concept of total fitness. Total fitness is described as encompassing physical fitness, social fitness, moral fitness, spiritual fitness, and almost any other kind of fitness. Concepts of total fitness are usually meaningless because there is no way to measure the components, and no attempt is made to define them. Is, for example, a humanistic athiest "spiritually fit"? What criteria should be used to make judgments about social fitness? Often there is implicit in its definition an attempt to fit young people into preconceived modes of behaviour, so that the "totally fit" young man or woman is defined as the one whose behaviour reinforces the biases of older generations.

To circumvent the struggle, a concept of physical fitness such as the following may be given: "Physical fitness means an adequate amount of muscular strength and endurance to meet the needs of modern-day life." This type of definition is not very useful either. What are the needs of modern day life? Whose life are we talking about? What is adequate? Many businessmen and executives need virtually no significant amount of strength and very little endurance to meet the occupational and social needs of their sedentary urban lives. Does this mean they are physically fit? Is adequacy in meeting the *immediate* needs of one's occupational and social existence a sufficient criterion for making judgments about physical fitness? As you can see, such a definition raises more questions than it answers.

An alternative method to defining physical fitness is to list the components which comprise it. The listing of characteristics makes this a bi-verbal definition (types of definitions are discussed on pages 6-8). On the basis of a survey of research literature, Larson and Yocum have listed ten component aspects of physical fitness.

1. Resistance to disease: a broad component with degenerative and contagious diseases.
2. Muscular strength and muscular endurance: the ability to continue successive exertions under conditions where a load is placed on the muscle groups being used.
3. Cardio-vascular endurance: the ability to maintain effort when demands are placed on the functions of circulation and respiration.
4. Muscular power: the ability to release maximum force in the shortest period of time.
5. Flexibility: the degree of range of movement at specific joints and in total body movement.
6. Speed: the ability to make successive movements of the same kind in the shortest period of time.
7. Agility: the ability to change positions in space.

8. Coordination: the ability to integrate movements of different kinds into one single pattern.
9. Balance: the ability to control organic equipment neuromuscularly.
10. Accuracy: the ability to control voluntary movements toward an object.[14]

Even though this list of characteristics is two decades old, it still is quite representative of professional thought, and the only characteristic that might be open to question is the broadness of the resistance-to-disease component. The ability to resist disease is now thought to be largely hereditary and not particularly a function of the physical fitness of the person. There is no evidence to support the contention that fitness is a factor in preventing communicable disease, nor does it provide any automatic immunization against infectious illness.

As has been pointed out, attempts to define physical fitness by citing components, are examples of bi-verbal definitions (see page 7). As with all such definitions, one must determine whether the list of components should be regarded as a disjunctive or a conjunctive group. If such a definition is *disjunctive,* then the presence of any one of the components is sufficient to merit the use of the term physical fitness. Thus, if a person possesses a necessary amount of muscular power he is considered to be physically fit regardless of his status in terms of the other components. If, however, the definition is *conjunctive,* then it would be necessary for a person to possess a sufficient amount of each component in order to be considered physically fit. The advantages and disadvantages of conjunctive and disjunctive definitions are well exemplified in the Larson and Yocum list of physical fitness components. Obviously, the disjunctive approach does not have much merit in terms of this list of components. A person who is quite flexible, but can not be rated highly on any of the other components is certainly not considered to be a physically fit person.

The conjunctive approach appears to have more merit, but it also raises some questions. To be classified as physically fit, using a conjunctive approach to the Larson and Yocum list, one would have to exhibit a sufficient degree or amount of attainment on each of the components. This would be a great deal to ask unless the standard on each of the criterion measures was so low as to be meaningless. The term physical fitness as Larson and Yocum have defined it, then, must be a term that is restricted in its use to a very meager portion of the population. Even

14. Leonard Larson and Rachael Yocom, *Measurement and Evaluation in Physical, Health, and Recreation Education* (St. Louis: C. V. Mosby Co., 1951), pp. 158-162.

an Olympic marathon runner, for example, might not possess sufficient degrees of coordination to qualify as a physically fit person.

How then can physical fitness be defined so that it can become a meaningful term? How can physical fitness be defined so that it can provide useful directions as we build physical education curricula and implement physical education programs? *The first step toward answering these questions must be to recognize that physical fitness is not a unitary concept, i.e., there are different types of physical fitness.* Several physical educators have recently suggested approaches that may help us in understanding the concept and applying it meaningfully in physical education. Wynn Updike and Perry Johnson[15] have proposed that the components should be divided into two basic categories: physical fitness parameters that are essential for health, and motor performance parameters that are more directly related to motor skill performance.

HEALTH AND FITNESS PARAMETERS	MOTOR PERFORMANCE PARAMETERS
Circulo-respiratory capacity	Coordination
Flexibility	Agility
Muscular endurance	Power
Strength	Balance
	Reaction time
	Speed

The importance of recognizing the distinction between these sets of parameters is that two general categories of fitness are thus delineated. The first category has its foundation in health and seems to be the more general of the two. The second category has its foundation in motor performance and seems to be more functionally determined. Differing amounts of each of the motor performance parameters are necessary for different tasks. Thus, the *functional* and *specific* nature of motor performance is clearly recognized. A football tackle, a track sprinter, a soldier, a tennis player, and a bowler need different amounts of each of these motor performance parameters. This fact simply recognizes that there is a specific fitness necessary for performing as a football tackle, and that this fitness is quite likely to be different from the specific fitness needed to be a tennis player. This type of specific motor-performance-fitness should rightly be seen as fitness in the service of skilled motor performance. This type of fitness makes a person fit to play

15. Wynn Updike and Perry Johnson, *Principles of Modern Physical Education, Health, and Recreation* (New York: Holt, Rinehart and Winston, Inc. 1970), pp. 93-99.

football, fit to play tennis, or fit to dance. *This type of fitness is wholly performance oriented, and its purpose is to improve performance in the specific activity.*

The first category in the Updike and Johnson schema is related to general health and is, therefore, by its very nature less specific than motor-performance-fitness. Whenever you see definitions of physical fitness which include such terms as health, enjoying life, living longer, or maintaining adaptive effort, then you are in the realm of fitness as a health concept. Ultimately, this type of health-fitness is related to survival. Arthur Steinhaus recognized this when he said:

> The fundamental purpose of fitness is to assure survival—for animals, survival on an animal plane—for human beings, survival on a human plane.[16]

Fitness, then, can be tied to some concept of health, which in turn reflects judgments made about survival in contemporary society. It is easy to recognize that high levels of both health-fitness and motor-performance-fitness were needed by prehistoric man for survival purposes. It should be especially recognized that survival for early man was very much dependent upon motor-performance-fitness. Early man had to be fast, agile, and powerful. These characteristics had definite survival value. We no longer live, however, in an environment where survival depends on high levels of motor-performance-fitness. There are very few situations in modern societies where motor-performance parameters have actual survival value.

The question is, then, to what extent does survival in contemporary society depend upon health-fitness, and more specifically how do the components of health-fitness measure up in terms of the survival criterion? What levels of the various components—circulo-respiratory capacity, flexibility, muscular endurance, and strength—are necessary for fitness? When approached in this manner, a way out of the "fitness dilemma" begins to become apparent. Obviously, for health fitness only moderate levels of flexibility, muscular endurance and strength are necessary. In terms of strength Arthur Steinhaus has said:

> The ideal muscular development is that which has just enough margin of strength or power to maintain posture without effort, to do the day's work easily, and to handle one's body weight readily. Beyond this point it is wise to observe the maxims: "Truck-horse muscles are out of place on a buggy-horse job," and "Why bang around with a five-ton truck when a runabout will do?"[17]

16. Arthur Steinhaus, *Toward an Understanding of Health and Physical Education,* (Dubuque: Wm. C. Brown Co. Publishers, 1963), p. 63.
17. Arthur Steinhaus, in *The Making of American Physical Education* by Arthur Weston, p. 304.

Obviously, only a moderate amount of strength is necessary to be physically fit. Charles McCloy has also spoken to this point.

> In other words, strength would not necessarily be synonymous with physical fitness. An adequate amount should be desirable. An excess amount might be a handicap. The same may be true of some other developed qualities or characteristics.[18]

It should be obvious that the "adequate amount" criterion can be applied to strength, muscular endurance, and flexibility, but how well does it apply to circulo-respiratory capacity? Bowerman and Harris, in their popular book, *Jogging,* speak emphatically about the difference among the components of health-fitness.

> After all, when you're past 30, bulging biceps and pleasing pectorals may boost your ego, *but your life and health may depend upon how fit your heart and lungs are.*[19]

If the concept of fitness is discussed as health or survival, then what is being talked about is almost wholly circulo-respiratory capacity. The diseases that kill man today are primarily those that affect the circulo-respiratory system. Exercise physiologist Herbert deVries has spoken about the change in the nature of illnesses which plague man.

> The nature of illnesses that beset our American population has recently undergone a transition of sorts: from a predominance of infectious diseases to the present predominance of degenerative diseases. . . . The increase of such degenerative diseases as cardiovascular accidents (heart attacks and strokes), hypertension, neuroses, and malignancies offers a challenge not only to medicine but to physical education as well. It seems that as improvements in medical science allow us to escape the decimation of such infectious diseases as tuberculosis, diphtheria, poliomyelitis, etc., we live longer, but we fall prey to the degenerative diseases at a slightly later date.[20]

In terms of health, a man today might be strong, flexible, and possess muscular endurance, and yet not be fit unless he possess circulo-respiratory efficiency. If a person exercises to the extent that he develops circulo-respiratory efficiency, however, then his levels of strength, flexibility, and muscular endurance will be well above the moderate levels needed. Brent Rushall has summarized well this important point.

> One must accept circulo-respiratory endurance as the prime requirement for physical fitness, for associated with its improvement is improvement in all other areas of motor fitness. The attempt to develop

---

18. Charles McCloy, in *The Making of American Physical Education* by Arthur Weston, p. 309.
19. William Bowerman and W. E. Harris, *Jogging* (New York: Grosset and Dunlap, 1967), p. 7.
20. Herbert deVries, *Physiology of Exercise* (Dubuque: Wm. C. Brown Co. Publishers, 1966), p. 244.

all areas of motor fitness individually with specific exercise is inefficient, unsuccessful and not realistic in the teaching situation as it stands today. *Circulorespiratory endurance is a necessary and sufficient condition for physical health.*[21]

deVries has also recognized the importance of defining fitness in terms similar to those described here. He suggests that the concept of "physical working capacity" (PWC) should become an important part of the physical educator's attempts to define and measure physical fitness. deVries points out that "aerobic capacity" is measured when PWC is the goal.

> The best approach to the measurement of PWC is to have a subject perform successive work bouts of from three to six minutes duration, and of increasing intensity, with adequate rest periods between successive bouts. During each work bout the O_2 consumption is measured, and, when the O_2 consumption fails to rise with increased load, this "maximum O_2 consumption" value is a measure of the subject's aerobic capacity, or PWC.[22]

This type of measurement process obviously should be highly accurate, but also highly difficult to utilize in school situations. Fortunately, Kenneth Cooper, an Air Force physiologist, has recently provided the physical education profession with an easily applied test of circulorespiratory efficiency and a complete program for increasing circulorespiratory fitness. The "aerobics" phenomenon, although not representing any new fact, has now been received with enthusiasm by professionals and non-professionals alike. The important point to recognize is that it is becoming increasingly common to define fitness in terms of circulo-respiratory efficiency. This is definitely a step in the right direction, and this type of improved efficiency is by far the greatest benefit of the jogging phenomenon.

It now appears probable that certain therapeutic and prophylactic effects are obtainable through regular participation in exercise of certain types and quantities. Resistance to degenerative diseases as a result of increased circulo-respiratory efficiency is probably of greatest importance. Primarily through the work of Jean Mayer of Harvard University's Nutrition Laboratory, it has now been determined that the level of physical activity is the most important factor in weight control, outranking the more obvious factor of food intake. Mayer has said that "the massive difference between the fat and the lean is in the level of activity, particularly among young people."[23] Exercise is of value in the

21. Brent Rushall, *The Scientific Basis of Circulorespiratory Endurance Training,* unpubl'd master's thesis, Indiana U., p. 227.
22. Herbert deVries, *Physiology of Exercise,* pp. 205-206.
23. Jean Mayer, "Affluence: The Fifth Horseman of the Apocalypse," *Psychology Today,* January, 1970, p. 58.

treatment and prevention of certain organic diseases such as diabetes. There is some evidence that physical exercise can relieve neuro-muscular tension and, therefore, aid in relieving anxiety and tension.

It is important, however, for physical educators not to make claims for the benefits of exercise which they cannot verify scientifically. Physical exercise is not a panacea for all of man's ills. There are many happy, healthy people who live a full life to a ripe old age and seldom engage in any vigorous exercise. While research in exercise physiology has progressed rapidly in the past two decades, there are still many questions which need to be answered. The most important, of course, is what role does exercise (or the lack of exercise) play in the aging process?

When discussing physical fitness, the physical educator must choose his words carefully and examine his ideas thoroughly. It is not enough just to know that exercise develops circulo-respiratory efficiency, or to say that exercise builds fitness. It is easy to fall into traps. The ultimate result of thoughtlessness or carelessness is the physical educator who has his students do five minutes of calesthenics at the beginning of each class and thinks he has contributed to their physical fitness. We must be careful to say that certain exercises, done in certain quantities, at certain speeds, and with a certain regularity can produce a "training effect."

We must also be careful not to be premature in our claims. Many physical educators are now suggesting that physical exercise can relieve the accumulated tension and anxiety that plagues individuals who live in a society that does not provide many outlets for aggression. Sports psychologists are not at all sure that such a "cathartic" claim for exercise can be substantiated. Some who make this claim suggest that the degree of relief is proportional to the degree of involvement in the game or match. While this contention seems to clarify some questions about exercise as a cathartic for the relief of tension, it really makes the entire question exceedingly more complex. Is it the physical exercise that produces the cathartic effect or is it the absorption of the player in the game? If it is the exercise, then the desired relief might be achieved by a ten minute exercise bout on a treadmill. If it is the absorption in play that produces the desired relief, then painting or some other play activity might do just as well. As you can see, we still have a long way to go before we can pinpoint precisely the values of regular exercise.

FITNESS: HOW CAN IT BE ACHIEVED?

To answer the above question, the type of fitness desired must first be determined. Is the goal health-fitness or motor-performance-fitness?

Recognition of purpose is the biggest step in answering the question. If you answer—motor-performance-fitness, then it becomes obvious that you must go one step further and determine what kind of motor performance. With this in mind, it is necessary to take only a short step in order to determine a specific functional program of fitness activities. Sports coaches have recognized this for many years, and there are many excellent specific conditioning programs for various activities such as baseball, football, wrestling, tennis, and golf. Many books about activities include chapters which describe specific conditioning programs. There are even special books on the market which are directed toward specific aspects of conditioning, such as the application of weight lifting to various sports.

It now appears certain[24] that rhythmical exercises such as running, swimming, cycling, and walking when done without interruption are the best means for achieving the health-fitness training-effect. Next in value seem to be vigorous sports such as handball, squash, and basketball. Less vigorous sports such as golf, tennis, and volleyball are of intermediate value. Weight lifting and isometric training programs are usually of no value at all for this purpose, nor are most commercially promoted "exercise programs."

Obviously, it is the sustained nature of the exercise that produces the training effect. Such exercise require the body to use and process oxygen without producing an oxygen debt that makes further exercise impossible. The term "aerobic" means literally "with oxygen," and is therefore applied to such exercise. Kenneth Cooper, originator of the "Aerobic Program," has explained the basic principle behind such exercise.

> If the exercise is vigorous enough to produce a sustained heart rate of 150 beats per minute or more, the training-effect benefits begin about five minutes after the exercise starts and continue as long as the exercise is performed. If the exercise is not vigorous enough to produce or sustain a heart rate of 150 beats per minute, but is still demanding oxygen, the exercise must be continued considerably longer than five minutes, the total period of time depending on the oxygen consumed.[25]

How efficient does the circulo-respiratory system have to be before its owner is considered physically fit? This question has been answered with experimental precision. Cooper's research indicated that a maxi-

24. T. K. Cureton, "The Relative Value of Various Exercise Conditioning Programs to Improve Cardiovascular Status and to Prevent Heart Disease," *The Journal of Sports Medicine and Physical Fitness* 5:55, 1965.
25. Kenneth H. Cooper, *Aerobics* (New York: Bantam Books, 1968), p. 23.

mal oxygen consumption of forty-two milliliters of oxygen per minute for each kilogram of weight (42 ml/kg/min) results in an adequate level of cardio-vascular reserve and a satisfactory state of fitness for nineteen to thirty-five year-old-men. He has translated this goal into his now famous point system. For example, each of the following activities is worth five points in the Aerobic system, meaning that each is comparable in its aerobic training effect.

ACTIVITY	AMOUNT OF TIME
Running	1 mile in less than 8 minutes
Swimming	600 yards in less than 15 minutes
Stationary running	12-1/2 minutes
Cycling	5 miles in less than 20 minutes
Handball	35 minutes of actual play
Tennis	3 sets
Golf	27 holes

Cooper indicates that thirty points a week is sufficient to produce and to maintain a very high level of fitness. Plainly, the rhythmical activities (running, cycling, and swimming) produce the desired effect in the least amount of time. If you want to play golf to maintain your health-fitness, you had better be prepared to spend a great deal of time on the golf course because you would have to play twenty-seven holes a day, six days a week to score the required thirty points. Golf is a fine game but not for the purpose of developing health-fitness.

IMPLICATIONS FOR
PROGRAMS OF PHYSICAL EDUCATION

It should now be possible to make some judgments about fitness training in the schools. You should be at a point where you can begin to make intelligent, defensible judgments about the importance of physical fitness, and its present and potential role in school programs of physical education. The judgments which follow in this section are primarily those of the author. You should recognize them as editorial comments and not as the direct reporting of data. It is hoped that at this point you not only possess the tools but also the desire to question some or all of these judgments and observations.

More research is needed to determine when young children can begin to take part in endurance-training activities. We need a point system for junior high students that is comparable to the point system utilized in the Aerobics Program. The same is true for elementary school children.

It is now possible to assure an adequate level of health-fitness for each high school and college student. There is no need for special equipment, nor is there a need for special facilities. If each student could spend fifteen minutes a day in a jogging program, he could be assured of an adequate level of circulo-respiratory efficiency and all of the benefits which might accrue from this level of fitness. No special teacher would be necessary, only someone to administer the program and to see to the details of changing clothes, showering, and other administrative chores.

A third observation is that such a program is most accurately described as a health program and should, therefore, come under the administration of the health education department. In my opinion, a program such as the one described above, while of obvious benefit, is *not* a program of physical education.

A fourth observation is that the traditional "five or ten minutes of calisthenics" is largely worthless. It does not seem to contribute to either health-fitness or to any specific motor-performance-fitness. Calisthenics can be adapted to be functional to specific activities and, if so, are of value in improving performance capabilities. For many years, however, physical fitness has been functionally defined in physical education as the ability to do push-ups, sit-ups, and other such exercises. There is no evidence that practice for such activities causes a meaningful increase either in health-fitness or in the ability to perform in specific sports activities.

A fifth observation is that health-fitness needs to be maintained by regular exercise. Many of the effects of rhythmical exercise begin to reverse themselves after short periods of inactivity. This simply means that techniques for promoting regular aerobic exercise after the school experience are probably just as important goals as fitness during the school experience. In other words, we must find out what motivates the swimmer, cycler, or jogger. Under what conditions is it most probable that a person will pursue a regular program of aerobic exercise? Is the motivation of the jogger different from the motivation of the week-end golfer? Can a "need" for exercise be developed?[26] Obviously, there are many questions that remain to be answered.

---

26. At the University of Michigan, research studies have indicated that when young rats are forced to exercise for a period of thirty-five days (roughly comparable to three years in human life), they will spontaneously participate in exercise for the next 180 days (approximately fifteen years in human life). The period of forced exercise has created a "need" to exercise. This is not to suggest, of course, that we should force youngsters to exercise. The important implication is that exercise can become self-reinforcing.

What are your observations? What role do you feel that exercise should occupy in programs of physical education? What will your feelings be the next time you are required to participate in or to administer a so-called physical fitness test? Is aerobics training education-*through*-the-physical or education-*of*-the-physical? Can we motivate people to value health-fitness by telling them about the benefits of exercise or must they experience the feelings which accompany regular aerobic exercise? The answers that you formulate to these questions and to ones like them will form a large part of your total approach to physical education.

WHAT QUESTIONS CAN YOU ASK ABOUT THE FOLLOWING STATEMENTS

1. The nation needs young men and women who are physically fit.
2. If you can't pass the items on the Kraus-Weber test then you are not fit.
3. If you want to stay thin, you have either to exercise a lot or be willing to go hungry.
4. Fitness is no longer necessary for survival in modern society.
5. Handball is better exercise than tennis.
6. Football players do calisthenics to get in shape for the season.
7. Running cross country will help you to perform better in basketball.
8. Motor-performance-fitness is useful only in athletics.
9. Physical fitness is more a concern of health education than of physical education.
10. We should create a "need" for exercise by requiring exercise programs in the early elementary years.
11. The AAHPER Youth Fitness Test is a good measure of physical fitness.
12. The physically fit person is better able to meet the exigencies of life.

Chapter 5 ⌒
Physical Education as a Means for Achieving the Goals of General Education

If American education aims at normal adjustment of the individual to his world then so does modern physical education in American schools.

Delbert Oberteuffer, 1945

THE IDEA OF EDUCATION THROUGH THE PHYSICAL

The idea of utilizing motor activities as a means for reaching the general goals of education is primarily a twentieth century phenomenon. It is true that the seeds of this important concept were planted toward the end of the nineteenth century; but in terms of acceptance and implementation, education-through-the-physical belongs to this century. Thomas Wood in an 1893 speech played the role of prophet.

> The great thought in physical education is not the education of the physical nature, but the relation of physical training to complete education . . .[1]

In the first half of the twentieth century, this basic premise was generally accepted as the cornerstone of physical education theory, and a consensus of support for this idea grew and thrived within the physical education profession.

In 1910, Clark Hetherington presented his paper entitled "Fundamental Education"; the first thorough and succinct statement of the

---

1. Thomas Wood, "The Scientific Approach in Physical Education," *The Making of American Physical Education,* by Arthur Weston (New York: Meredith Publishing Company, 1962), p. 151.

education-through-the-physical viewpoint, which rightly earned for Hetherington the title of "father of modern physical education." With a clarity gained through a judicious use of words, Hetherington described both the scope and the categories of the new physical education.

> This paper aims to describe the function and place of general neuro-muscular activities, primarily general play activities, in the educational process. . . . To present the thesis four phases of the education process will be considered: organic education, psychomotor education, character education, and intellectual education.[2]

Authority	Organic development	Interpretive development	Neuromuscular development	Personal-social adjustment
AAHPER	X		X	X
Bookwalters	X	X		X
Brace	X	X	X	X
Barnnell—Hagman	X	X	X	X
Bucher	X	X	X	X
Clarke	X			X
Cowell-Hazelton	X	X	X	X
Daniels	X		X	X
Dow-Lawther		X	X	
Duncan-Johnson	X	X	X	X
Evans-Gans	X	X	X	X
Hughes-French	X	X	X	X
Irwin	X	X	X	X
Knapp-Hagman	X	X	X	X
Korman et al.	X	X	X	X
LaPorte		X	X	X
Lawson-Hill	X	X	X	X
LaSalle	X	X	X	X
Mathews	X			X
McClay	X	X	X	X
Miller-Whitcomb	X	X		X
Nash-Hetherington	X	X	X	X
Nelson-Van Hagen	X	X	X	X
Nixon-Covens	X		X	X
Oberhuffer	X	X	X	X
Okeefe-Aldrich	X	X	X	X
Salt et. al.	X	X	X	X
Seaton et. al.	X	X	X	X
Sharman	X	X	X	
Staley	X			X
Vannier-Fait	X	X	X	X
Volmer-Esslinger	X	X	X	X
Williams	X		X	X

Data from Miller K. Adams: Principles for determining high school grading procedures in physical education for boys, Doctoral thesis, New York University, 1959; from Charles A. Bucher: *Foundations of Physical Education,* 5th edition, (St. Louis: The C. V. Mosby Co., 1968), p. 147.

FIGURE 3. Frequency of physical education objectives as listed by leaders in the field

2. Clark Hetherington, *The Making of American Physical Education,* p. 160.

Hetherington's four phases were to become the four objectives of the new physical education, and wherever education-through-the-physical has been promoted and applied, the chances are excellent that it has been explained and interpreted by reference to the four-fold objectives originally proposed by Hetherington. The degree to which these objectives have received professional support can be seen by perusing the preceding figure which lists objectives of physical education as found in the professional literature.

Twenty-three of the thirty-three leaders cited in this figure agreed completely with the four-fold objectives, and all except three of the leaders mentioned at least three of these four objectives. The immediate question that arises is how did this unanimity of support occur within a profession that was developing rapidly in every part of the nation? There are several approaches that might be taken in attempting to answer this question. I shall attempt to suggest two reasons, expecting that you will be able to come up with several other plausible solutions.

When any group of people tend to hold similar thoughts and ideas on a particular topic or concept, the possibilities exist that they arrived at this consensus point of view either through independent judgement after an examination of the relevant data, or by a chain of influence in which each individual accepted in part or in total the views of another individual. In the case of the four-fold objectives of the new physical education, the latter explanation is almost certainly the correct one.

The chain of influence is, in fact, quite evident. Wood taught at Stanford University from 1891–1901. In his last year at Stanford, he greatly influenced a bright young student named Clark Hetherington. Before he left Stanford, Wood appointed Hetherington as Director of the Gymnasium, even though Hetherington was still studying for his degree. Wood left Stanford to take a position on the faculty of the Teachers College of Columbia University, a position which he held until 1932. Hetherington, in his later teaching years, was on the faculty at Teachers College and New York University. Jesse Feiring Williams took his M.D. degree at Columbia University in 1915 and joined the physical education faculty of the Teachers College in 1919. Williams became the primary disciple of Wood and most important interpreter of the education-through-the-physical viewpoint. In 1929, a bright, young student named Jay B. Nash took his Ph.D. degree in physical education from New York University where he was already a staff member and was to remain until his retirement in 1953. Nash became the primary disciple and interpreter of the ideas of Clark Hetherington.

Thus, the Wood-Hetherington-Williams-Nash influence was possibly accepted by the profession as a unitary point of view. As mentioned in the previous chapter, this is not to suggest that the views of these leaders were identical. Nash and Williams, for example, emphasized quite different goals and programs. Their views were, however, considered by many professionals to be emphasizing different aspects of a total education-through-the-physical philosophy. Since Teachers College and New York University were the early leaders in graduate training in physical education, it should come as no surprise that many leaders in physical education took their graduate training at these institutions and came under the influence of Williams and Nash, both of whom were dynamic and inspiring teachers.

A second possible explanation for the professional consensus on objectives is simply that conflicting points of view on objectives would breed controversy. The resulting critical analysis that would necessarily accompany such controversy would seemingly have done harm to a profession that was attempting to establish itself as a rightful aspect of public education. When a profession is fighting for such things as adequate funds and compulsory-requirement laws, a united front is the best way to gain widespread acceptance. Karl Bookwalter and Harold Vander Zwaag have discussed the opportunistic genius of the leaders of the new physical education.

> Regardless of any philosophical bias one might hold against Gulick, Wood, Hetherington, Williams, Nash, and others one would at least have to admit that they were opportunists. They were alert to the changing philosophy of their time, and they seized upon the opportunity to bring physical education under the broader umbrella of education. They also recognized that educational "experimentalism" offered great promise for physical education to achieve recognition as a legitimate part of the total educational curriculum. What other area was prepared to offer more experiences in learning by doing?[3]

Thus, we have two possible explanations for the fifty year consensus of opinion within the physical education profession regarding its objectives. First, there was a direct chain of influence, starting with Wood, which saw the four-fold objectives transfer from teacher to student through a series of personal, educational experiences. Students who studied under Williams at Teachers College and Nash at New York University took these objectives with them as they accepted positions all across the country during a time when teacher training programs in universities were rapidly developing, and trained physical educators were needed to staff the physical educator departments in these schools. Secondly, the focus of the profession was not on analyzing,

---

3. Karl Bookwalter and Harold Vander Zwaag, *Foundations and Principles of Physical Education* (Philadelphia: W. B. Saunders Company, 1969), p. 57.

defining, and refining its objectives, but rather on gaining acceptance as a legitimate aspect of public school education.

It was not until quite recently, when the concept of movement education or human movement began to gain broad acceptance as a theoretical concept, that education-through-the-physical had a serious opponent and the four-fold objectives came due for a bit of scrutiny by leaders attempting to formulate theories of physical education undergirded by the concept of human movement.

THE IMPLEMENTATION OF
EDUCATION-THROUGH-THE-PHYSICAL

As we have seen, the new physical education attempted to achieve the general goals of education through the medium of motor activity. In the broadest sense, general education developed in the first twenty-five years of this century with an "education for living" or an "education as living" philosophy. Greatly influenced by John Dewey and the "experimentalist" approach, American education aimed to develop within its young citizens the capacity for full living within a democracy. Thus, Jesse Williams reflected this general goal when he wrote what has become a famous sentence:

> Education through the physical will be judged, therefore, even as education for life will be judged—by the contribution it makes to fine living.[4]

To achieve this general goal, physical education adopted the four-fold objectives first proposed by Clark Hetherington in 1910: organic development, psychomotor development, character development, and intellectual development. In 1964, Charles Bucher defined these objectives in terms that were remarkably similar to the original concepts, demonstrating not only the broad acceptance of the goals but also their persistent longevity.

> Physical development objective: The objective of physical development deals with the program of activities that builds physical power in an individual through the development of the various organic systems of the body.
>
> Motor development objective: The motor development objective is concerned with making physical movement useful and with as little expenditure of energy as possible and being proficient, graceful, and aesthetic in this movement.

---

4. Jesse Williams, "Education Through the Physical," *An Anthology of Contemporary Readings,* Howard Slusher and Aileen Lockhart, eds. (Dubuque: Wm. C. Brown Company Publishers, 2nd Ed., 1970) p. 3.

Mental development objective: The mental development objective
deals with the accumulation of a body of knowledge and the ability
to think and to interpret this knowledge.

Social development objective: The social development objective is
concerned with helping an individual in making personal adjustments, group adjustments, and adjustments as a member of society.[5]

The goals first proposed by Hetherington in 1910 were given even
greater strength in 1918 when the National Education Association published what it considered to be the "7 Cardinal Principles" of American
education. These goals were: 1) health, 2) command of the fundamental
processes, 3) worthy home membership, 4) vocational competence,
5) effective citizenship, 6) worthy use of leisure, and 7) ethical character.[6] Three of these principles, health, worthy use of leisure, and ethical
character, were considered by leaders in physical education to be most
directly applicable to physical education. Thus, these three goals
became the "remote" or most general goals of physical education, and
the four-fold objectives became the intermediate objectives of the
profession. Karl Bookwalter, who studied under both Williams and
Nash, has provided the most fully developed example of the education-
through-the-physical viewpoint. The schematic presentation on page
89, developed by Bookwalter during his teaching years at Indiana University, is very useful for gaining an understanding of how the education-through-the-physical viewpoint was translated into school
programs of physical education.

As you can see from studying the schematic, the four-fold objectives were to be pursued in a variety of school programs, primarily the
basic instruction programs, the intramural program, and the interscholastic program. Education-through-the-physical had, as we have
seen, a diversity of goals. From the beginning, this acceptance of plural-
istic goals brought with it the concommitant acceptance of a variety of
activities. Perhaps the most obvious difference between the new physical education and the gymnastics oriented systems of the late nineteenth century was the scope of the program in terms of activities.

Recognition of the differing needs of children and the widespread
goals was thought to require a variety of activities for satisfactory implementation of the new physical education. These activities were usually classified into five categories: 1) aquatics, 2) rhythms, 3) gymnastics,
4) individual sports, and 5) team sports. It was felt that children needed
experiences in each of these areas in order to meet the goals of physical

---

5. Charles Bucher, *Foundations of Physical Education,* pp. 155, 157, 160, 161.
6. National Education Association, *Cardinal Principles of Secondary Education,* 1918,
pp. 27.

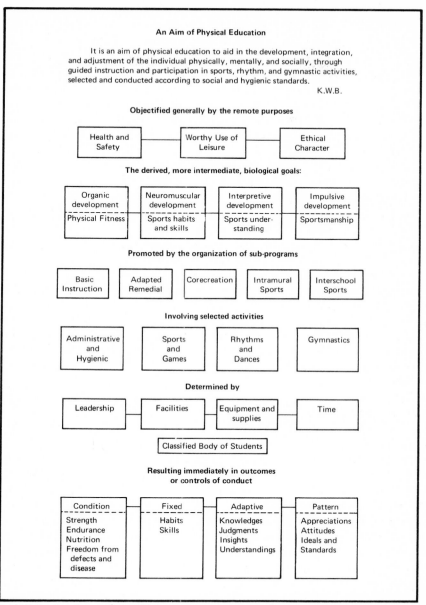

An Aim of Physical Education

It is an aim of physical education to aid in the development, integration, and adjustment of the individual physically, mentally, and socially, through guided instruction and participation in sports, rhythm, and gymnastic activities, selected and conducted according to social and hygienic standards.

K.W.B.

Objectified generally by the remote purposes

| Health and Safety | Worthy Use of Leisure | Ethical Character |

The derived, more intermediate, biological goals:

| Organic development | Neuromuscular development | Interpretive development | Impulsive development |
| Physical Fitness | Sports habits and skills | Sports understanding | Sportsmanship |

Promoted by the organization of sub-programs

| Basic Instruction | Adapted Remedial | Corecreation | Intramural Sports | Interschool Sports |

Involving selected activities

| Administrative and Hygienic | Sports and Games | Rhythms and Dances | Gymnastics |

Determined by

| Leadership | Facilities | Equipment and supplies | Time |

| Classified Body of Students |

Resulting immediately in outcomes or controls of conduct

| Condition | Fixed | Adaptive | Pattern |
| Strength Endurance Nutrition Freedom from defects and disease | Habits Skills | Knowledges Judgments Insights Understandings | Appreciations Attitudes Ideals and Standards |

Karl W. Bookwalter and Harold J. Vander Zwaag, *Foundations and Principles of Physical Education* (New York: W. B. Saunders Company, 1969), p. 224. Used by permission of the publisher.

FIGURE 4.   Education-through-the-physical

education. The result of this approach was a program which has come to be labeled as the "multi-activity" approach to physical education.

The multi-activity approach is quite evident in the prescription made by the La Porte committee for a national program of physical education. In 1927, William Ralph La Porte was appointed to chair a Committee on Curriculum Research of the College Physical Education Association. In 1938, this committee published its findings in a monograph entitled "The Physical Education Curriculum."[7] This popular monograph has been revised several times and is now in its seventh edition.

Part of the monograph was devoted to a scorecard on which programs of physical education could be judged. The scorecard was designed so that individual school programs could be compared with the "ideal" program. One criterion measure in the scorecard suggests the "block" or unit approach as the ideal.

> Program calls for systematic class instruction in activity fundamentals on the "block" or "unit of work" basis (continuous daily instruction for from three to six weeks).[8]

If the three week block is utilized, then students will experience from ten to twelve activities yearly. If the six week block is utilized, then students will experience from five to six activities yearly. This criterion was, of course, designed with daily instruction in mind. Daily instruction, however, was the exception rather than the rule in most school systems. Nevertheless, the block system approach became widely accepted and most physical education curricula attempted to cover from six to twelve activities yearly, regardless of whether classes met daily, twice weekly, or three times a week.

Thus, the four-fold objectives of education-through-the-physical were sought through a multi-activity program. Since the four objectives were generally considered to be of equal emphasis, physical educators attempted to plan programs and classes so that some attainment of each objective might be realized. Thus, the five or ten minutes devoted to conditioning exercises fulfilled the physical development objective. The variety of activities fulfilled the neuromuscular development objective and also worked toward the social development objective. An emphasis on rules, strategies, and history of the activities fulfilled the mental development objective.

In the evaluation process of such programs, the four-fold objectives again charted the course. A physical fitness test was given to measure

---

7. William Ralph La Porte, *The Physical Education Curriculum,* College Book Store, Los Angeles, 1937, 7th Edition.
8. Ibid, p. 74.

the degree of attainment of the physical development objective. A skills test was given for each activity. A knowledge test was usually given at the end of each unit, and sportsmanship attitudes were taken into consideration when grading was done. While school systems applied this pattern in slightly different ways, with the usual variations common to regional and personal differences, it is not unfair to suggest that this basic pattern has dominated American physical education for the past fifty years.

AN EVALUATION OF EDUCATION-THROUGH-THE-PHYSICAL

Bob Dylan, in one of his prophetic folk songs of a few years ago, wrote that "the times they are a'changin'." This is no less true for physical education than it is for any other area of American society. We appear to be in a period of theoretical transition within physical education, and it is still difficult to determine the exact direction in which we will move. It does appear that education-through-the-physical, as traditionally formulated, has reached its peak as the primary theoretical concept undergirding programs of physical education and is presently being challenged on several fronts. It might be that the concept has sufficient strength and merit to prevail as the major theory of American physical education, but it will probably have to undergo some modification if it is to retain its position.

How can a concept such as education-through-the-physical be evaluated? There are many approaches that might be suggested. You should know by now that this author does not believe that the idea of education-through-the-physical is a sufficient base for contemporary programs of physical education. If this bias is too evident in the following evaluation, you should take that into account in your evaluation.

There is always danger in change. We develop educational theories to meet special needs but then we tend to guard the theories like religious beliefs even though the needs of the day may have changed, and consequently, new formulations may be in order. If it is suggested that education-through-the-physical has outlived its usefulness as a major theoretical idea, this is not to suggest that it was not a most useful concept during its time.

In fact, education-through-the-physical was a very useful concept in many ways. The idea solidified a young profession that needed solidarity in order to grow both in breadth and in depth. The physical education profession has grown enormously during the past fifty years —in the number of school programs it affects, the number of people it directly concerns, and the quality of effort it elicits on the practical and scholarly levels.

A second benefit derived from the acceptance of this idea was the infusion into physical education curricula of a broad variety of physical education activities. The number of activities that physical educators feel have a rightful place in school programs has grown steadily over the past fifty years. Today, one encounters sports activities as diverse as fencing, scuba diving, synchronized swimming, sailing, badminton, and karate. The profession has come a long way from the time when the curriculum consisted only of touch football in the fall, basketball in the winter, and softball in the spring.

A third accomplishment of education-through-the-physical has been the broad acceptance of physical education as a legitimate part of school programs. The day has not yet come when it can be said that physical education is an *integral* part of school programs; at least not if that term is used with any strict adherence to meaning, but progress certainly has been made in that direction.

It is also possible to evaluate education-through-the-physical by examining the objectives generated from the concept and the programs used to implement the objectives. This can be done in a practical sense by noting the degree of attainment of the objectives, and in a logical sense by examining what can rightfully be expected to occur, given the standard interpretation of the objectives.

PHYSICAL DEVELOPMENT OBJECTIVES

If physical fitness is operationally defined in a standard sense (that is, the ability to reach certain levels on a test which includes pull-ups, push-ups, etc.), then education-through-the-physical has not done at all well in meeting this objective. In 1936, McCloy questioned the degree of attainment of this objective.

> I doubt if more than one-fifth of our physical education classes in the schools of today get enough exercise to contribute materially to any significant organic stimulation.[9]

Several studies in the past fifteen years have tended to confirm this criticism as equally relevant now. The Kraus-Weber testing program found American youth to compare most unfavorably with European youth on tests of "minimum muscular fitness." Because these tests were concerned primarily with flexibility of the lower back, they were rightfully criticized when attempts were made to pass them off as physical fitness tests. To remedy this situation the AAHPER developed a battery of tests which have come to be known as the AAHPER Youth Fitness

---

9. Charles H. McCloy, "How About Some Muscle?" *An Anthology of Contemporary Readings,* Howard Slusher and Aileen Lockhart, eds. (Dubuque: Wm. C. Brown Company Publishers, 2nd ed., 1970), p. 6.

Test.[10] Comparative studies[11] have been completed with this instrument, but the results are not encouraging because foreign children score consistently higher than do American youth.

What does all this tell us? Obviously, it tells us that American youth have scored consistently lower than European youth on certain test items. Whether or not these exercises constitute a valid measure of physical fitness is another question. If health-fitness is the matter of concern, then no item on the Kraus-Weber Test or the AAHPER Youth Fitness Test adequately measures circulo-respiratory endurance, which is the necessary and sufficient condition for health-fitness. Doolittle and Bigbee[12] investigated this question by measuring 153 ninth grade boys on the 600 yard run-walk, a twelve minute run-walk, and maximum oxygen intake. They found that the twelve minute run-walk item correlated highly with maximum oxygen intake ($r = .90$), but they found a much lower relationship ($r = .64$) between results on the 600 yard run-walk and maximum oxygen intake. These results substantiated an earlier study by Falls.[13] Since a correlation coefficient of .64 accounts for only 41 percent of the variance between the two variables, and since we know that maximum oxygen intake is a highly reliable and valid measure of circulo-respiratory efficiency, it can only be concluded that the 600 yard run-walk will not give adequate information regarding the health-fitness status of a subject.

With regard to motor-performance-fitness, the results are equally unclear. As has been pointed out previously, motor-performance-fitness is performance oriented for specific activities. To assess the degree of attainment for this type of fitness, one would have to measure performance in specific activities; that is, specific sports skills. Since cultural differences render sports skills comparisons among countries meaningless, it becomes impossible to make comparative judgments like those made with the AAHPER Youth Fitness Test. The important point here is to recognize that motor-performance-fitness is meaningless unless it improves the level of performance in specific activities. To measure it

---

10. The AAHPER Youth Fitness Test consists of sit-ups, pull-ups, broad jump, 50 yd. dash, softball throw, and 600 yd. run-walk.
11. H. G. Knuttgen, "Comparison of Fitness of Danish and American School Children," *Research Quarterly,* 32:190, 1961; N. Ikeda, "A Comparison of Physical Fitness of Children in Iowa, U.S.A. and Tokyo, Japan," *Research Quarterly,* 33:541, 1962; A. W. Sloan, "Physical Fitness of College Students in South Africa, United States of America, and England," *Research Quarterly* 34:244, 1963.
12. T. L. Doolittle and Rollin Bigbee, "The Twelve-Minute Run-Walk; A Test of Cardiorespiratory Fitness for Adolescent Boys," *Research Quarterly* 39:491, October, 1968.
13. Harold B. Falls *et al.,* "Estimation of Maximum Oxygen Uptake in Adults from AAHPER Youth Fitness Items," *Research Quarterly* 37:192, 1966.

directly makes no sense because it is of value only if it improves the level of performance in the skill.

MOTOR DEVELOPMENT OJECTIVES

This brings us to the second objective, that of neuromuscular or motor development. This objective refers primarily to the attainment of skill through participation in physical education programs. It is virtually impossible to assess the degree of attainment of this objective in any meaningful way. There are several reasons for this. First, many other agencies (YMCA, summer camps, boys clubs, etc.) contribute to the development of skill in the same activities which are pursued in physical education. This makes it difficult to determine the exact amount of skill gained through physical education. A second reason is that the construction of reliable and valid sports skills tests is still a most monumental task which faces our professional experts in measurement. It is obviously easy to assess skill in track, golf, and archery, but just as obviously difficult to assess skill in volleyball, basketball, and dance.

Some judgments can be made, however, concerning the degree to which we should expect skill acquisition to occur given the circumstances within which an education-through-the-physical program normally operates. First, we have already seen that education-through-the-physical has been traditionally devoted to a multi-activity program. Charles Cowell and Helen Hazelton,[14] in their book, *Curriculum Designs in Physical Education,* present many sample programs of physical education for various grade levels. In a two day a week sample program for seventh and eighth grade boys, they suggest ten activities for the year. In a five day a week sample program for ninth and tenth grade girls, they suggest thirteen activities. The two day a week example would allow seven class meetings for each activity, while the five day a week example would allow eleven class meetings for each activity (based on a thirty-two week school year). Such classes are usually forty-five minutes in length and consist of twenty-five to forty students.

A case can be made which suggests that a multi-activity program carried on within a learning environment such as the one described above has little chance, if any, of producing significant and meaningful degrees of skill acquisition. Moreover, it might even be suggested that for many students the short amount of time available to develop skills allows them to experience only the frustration connected with early

---

14. Charles Cowell and Helen Hazelton, *Curriculum Designs in Physical Education* (New York: Prentice-Hall, Inc., 1955), pp. 225 and 253.

attempts at skill development and the resulting possibility of developing avoidance behaviour(s) as a result of the frustration.

One problem connected with evaluation of the skill development objective is that curriculum developers tend to equate activities and skills. Volleyball is an activity that is made up of many different skills. While it might appear that allotting ten class periods for one activity provides enough time to develop skill, it would be far more realistic to focus on the number of skills rather than on activities. Learning to play volleyball well enough to have it be a meaningful experience—satisfaction from the attainment of skill, social reinforcement for acceptable participation, reinforcement from being able to compete with reasonable success, etc.—requires the development of ability in serving, fist or bounce passing, forearm passing, set-up passing, spiking, and blocking. Some of these skills are more difficult than others and, therefore, require more time to learn. The important point here is to recognize that volleyball is a sport activity that is made up of a series of complex skills. To acquire a reasonable proficiency in each requires time (more precisely it requires a certain number of trials under conditions conducive to learning).

The important question to consider when examining the amount of skill acquisition potentially available in a physical education class is how many trials each student gets and to what degree precise information-feedback and reinforcement are continually present during each trial. It would not be difficult for you to make a crude estimate of this in any physical education class. Start with the total amount of time in the class period. Subtract the time allotted for administrative matters —role taking, testing, showers, dressing, etc. Subtract the time taken in verbalization by the teacher. Determine the amount of equipment available in terms of the number of students in the class (five volleyballs for thirty students, for example), and from this estimate the number of trials each student might get per minute (one per minute, one every two minutes, etc.). You can now estimate the number of trials each student will get per class meeting. By examining the learning environment, you can make a judgment about the accuracy and the contiguity of the information-feedback (when a student serves does he have a definite target and how can he measure how close he comes to the target?), and you can also make a judgment about the reinforcement potential of the learning environment—teacher encouragement, self-competition, class competition, squad competition, competition against a standard, etc. After gathering this information, you can make a crude, but nevertheless, meaningful estimate about the number of trials each student will get for each skill being taught. Stated quite directly and simply, my contention is that the number of reinforced trials is never enough to get the average student beyond the novice level.

Novice learners can best be described as learners searching for strategies[15] to perform the skill successfully. This search for strategies takes time and involves many deadends in terms of strategies that do not prove to be successful. The early part of the learning curve, particularly for complex skills such as those encountered in sports, involves much of this trial and error strategy seeking behaviour. If students are not allowed to move beyond this part of the learning curve, they might react adversely to the frustration of non-success and develop avoidance behaviours when confronted with skill learning environments. In this case, none of the objectives of physical education would be reached, and we would have succeeded only in fostering bad attitudes toward physical activity in general and physical education in particular.

MENTAL DEVELOPMENT OJECTIVE

Two distinct meanings could be suggested in reference to this objective. To some physical educators it has meant the contribution that participation in physical education activities has made to cognitive development. To others, it has meant the acquisition of knowledge about the history, rules, equipment, and strategy of the activities, and knowledge about physical education in general. The two meanings differ radically and will be discussed separately.

Physical educators often claim that participation in physical education contributes to cognitive development. The following statement exemplifies an extreme position that physical educators too often take.

> To aid in the mental development of each child is most definitely a realistic goal of physical education. The fact that physical and mental development are very inter-related has been substantiated repeatedly. The quick, alert potential athlete is most often a child qualified for reaching a high academic standing. As one's physical abilities increase, he is better able to attain higher classroom standards.[16]

It is very doubtful that definitive statements—certainly none as positive as the above statement—can be made concerning the contribution of physical education to cognitive development. This is not to suggest that at some level of development physical activity does not contribute to mental development, either in a direct or indirect manner. It may well

---

15. The learning curve associated with strategy-cue learning theory is an S shaped curve in which the early trials involve no substantial increase in performance. Once successful strategies are developed the increase in performance is much more abrupt. See Frank Restle, "The selection of strategies in cue learning," *Psychological Review*, 69:329, 1962.
16. Layne C. Hackett and Robert Jenson, *A Guide to Movement Exploration*, Peek Publications, 1966, p. 74.

be that in early childhood such a causal relationship does exist (the work of Piaget, Kephart and others tends to confirm this). Does such development, however, normally take place beyond the age of school entrance and, if so, to what extent may the activities of physical education contribute to such development? Almost all of the evidence concerning this question is based on research using correlational techniques. John Lawther has commented on a summarization of this research evidence.

> The literature on the relationship of academic intelligence tests scores to motor learning scores is too extensive and so uniform in its findings that mere mention will be made of it. In general, correlations range from zero to .50, with the average being .20 or less. When motor learning is correlated with intelligence in groups of lower intelligence levels, a somewhat higher relationship tends to appear.[17]

A correlation of 0.20 accounts for less than five percent of the variance between the intelligence and the motor performance scores. This is hardly what one could call valid evidence of anything, let alone that improved physical abilities will improve work in the classroom.

The appearance of higher correlative relationships in the lower intelligence brackets is explainable. The same phenomenon occurs when pre-school children are measured for such abilities. Many of the motor tests utilized, the Lincoln-Oseretsky Tests for example, have fairly significant cognitive loadings. In other words, to complete the specific motor task requires a cognitive judgment and the person with higher cognitive ability will of course then have a better chance to complete the motor task. On the other hand, all of the non-verbal tests of intelligence, the Stanford Revision of the Binet-Simon for example, have very high motor loadings. These two factors, taken together, point to the strong possibility of spuriously high correlation coefficients.

Another important factor to consider is that all such coefficients between these variables may be spuriously high because such factors as good health, good nutrition, and personality traits may well contribute to favorable performances in both cognitive and motor tasks. It must be remembered that correlational techniques give evidence of association and relationship, but not of causation. Even a high correlation coefficient presents no evidence that one variable is the cause of the other.

Specific programs which may contribute in this area will be considered in chapter seven, among these being the Kephart and Doman-Delacato procedures. At this point it should suffice to say that it is difficult to defend an assumption of causal relationship between cognitive development and physical education activity, at least beyond infancy.

---

17. John Lawther, *The Learning of Physical Skills* (New York: Prentice-Hall, Inc., 1968), p. 138.

The second interpretation of this objective is by far the more common. It assumes that knowledge about the history of games, the equipment used, the dimensions of the court or field, the strategies involved in successful participation, knowledge about health, fitness, first aid, and other related topics are mental constructs. Knowledge testing has become an important aspect of physical education. We have probably made greater strides in perfecting good knowledge tests than we have in perfecting good skills tests. Many schools give grades in physical education, but whether this is true or not in individual situations, most physical education teachers try to stimulate their students mentally. Many new "sports skills series" books have appeared on the market, and, at least at the college level, most students are required to buy a textbook for their required courses in physical education. This "knowledge phenomenon" has developed partly because the mental development objective has traditionally been stated as one of the four-fold objectives of education-through-the-physical, but also this practice has been stimulated by the academic content emphasis of the current approach to physical education.

There is a trend in certain colleges and high schools to make the basic course in physical education "knowledge oriented." Such programs will be considered in chapter seven.

SOCIAL DEVELOPMENT OBJECTIVE

This objective has also been interpreted in two ways, one of them broader than the other. One assumes that through participation in physical activities, students gain in social skills, develop desirable attitudes, and develop worthy values. It is often believed that these skills, attitudes, and values carry over into the student's everyday world and, therefore, increase his effectiveness and worth in society. One of the most widely quoted statements in physical education is that "competitive sports provide the best training ground for 'the game of life'." A second interpretation is that through participation in physical activities students acquire good sportsmanship attitudes. This interpretation is, of course, much more specific than the first.

Evaluation of this objective takes us along lines of thought very similar to those followed in evaluating the mental development objective. Gerald Kenyon has reviewed the research in this area, and a summary of his comments will help to clarify the results of experimental efforts which have dealt with value, attitude, and character development in relation to physical activity in general and physical education programs in particular.

Although the majority of conclusions arising from the several studies reported were based upon statistically significant observations, closer examination renders the practical significance of the findings questionable. Correlations rarely exceed 0.50, hardly high enough for even crude prediction. Where t and F ratios were significant, the differences among means were often of limited import.[18]

Kenyon's interpretation of the research in this area is very similar to that which we considered earlier which dealt with possible contributions of physical activity to cognitive development. He reminds us again that causation is often erroneously implied from data that are relational in nature and suggests that successful participation in activities requires social characteristics that are already in the personality of the performer. There appears to be little research evidence which suggests that participation in programs of physical education will change habits, attitudes, and values. Robert Singer in his recent review of research concerning the personal-social development hypothesis suggests that "unfortunately, the absence of confirming studies is a thorn in the side of physical educators."[19] Kenyon suggests that it is time to modify traditional claims, and this appears to be an entirely reasonable suggestion.

Physical educators have tended to disregard psychological theory concerning these questions. Psychologists Robert Peck and Robert Havinghurst[20] suggest that character—value and attitudes—is remarkably well defined by the time the child is ten years old. They suggest that values and attitudes change little from this point on, and that teachers and educational programs are not as influential as commonly supposed in changing attitudes and values. Now, it is not that teachers and educational programs cannot do anything about these matters. The truth is, and it is well supported by psychological and psychoanalytic data and opinion, that to change attitudes and values requires a great deal of time and, most importantly, the right kind of person handling the entire affair. Even with these requirements, it is not the activity itself that causes any change that might take place. It results from the interaction among persons as they participate in the activity together. Sportsmanship, fair play, and playing by the rules are not learned by the physical act of playing the game. Like all attitudes and values, they are learned by the process of identification, by emulating persons that are admired and with whom there is an emotional attachment.

---

18. Gerald Kenyon, "The Contribution of Physical Activity to Social Development," *Symposium on Integrated Development*, Indiana, A.A.H.P.E.R. Lafayette, 1964, p. 49.
19. Robert Singer, *Motor Learning and Human Performance* (New York: The Macmillan Company, 1968), p. 307.
20. Robert F. Peck, with Robert J. Havinghurst, *The Psychology of Character Development*, Science Editions (New York: John Wiley and Sons, 1964), 267 pp.

Lambert and Lambert generally concur with the idea that attitudes and values that are learned early in life are highly resistant to change:

> At first glance, the changing of attitudes might seem to be a simple matter. Since attitudes are learned, it should be easy enough to modify their intensity or replace an undesirable one by learning another. The complicating fact, however, is that attitudes are not as easily modified or replaced as they are learned. ... Well-planned attempts to modify attitudes often succeed only in altering the thought-belief component without affecting feelings and reaction tendencies so that in time the attitude may revert to its former state.[21]

Psychologist, Donald Green,[22] has said that the facts permit the conclusion that basic patterns of values and attitudes are not usually established by school, nor are they readily changed by schools. Green says that schools can form and change attitudes when they have the attitude-area to themselves. When the attitude-area is such that students will encounter different opinions outside of the school, however, it becomes highly unlikely that the school will bring about any change.

From the standpoint of psychological theory, then, it seems unlikely that present physical education programs are doing much to change attitudes and values. It therefore seems that the development of attitudes and values does not deserve to be ranked as a primary objective of physical education.

This is not to suggest that character change cannot take place within environments in physical education. All of the ingredients needed for character development are *potentially* present in certain athletic environments. Coaches work with young men in small groups over long periods of time. The situation becomes a "dominant environment."[23] Champion swimmers, for example, may be within a dominant sports environment five hours a day for over three hundred days a year. If an athlete in such an environment identifies with the coach, then character change *may* take place. The student is in this environment for a much more limited amount of time and with a much larger group of students. The potential for identification with the teacher is less probable than in the dominant athletic environment. Generally speak-

21. William Lambert and Wallace Lambert, *Social Psychology* (Englewood Cliffs: Prentice-Hall, Inc., 1964), p. 64.
22. Donald Green, *Educational Psychology* (Englewood Cliffs: Prentice-Hall, Inc., 1964), p. 106.
23. I am indebted to Brent Rushall, a fine young Australian sport psychologist, for this concept of dominant and non-dominant environments as they relate to physical education and sport which he described to me in a conversation.

ing, character, value, and attitude will change very little, if at all, within this environment.

It is possible, however, for physical educators to achieve the much more limited goal of developing attitudes of good sportsmanship, particularly those that are specific to activities. If the teacher is consistent, and is the kind of person that young people might identify with, and if the students are unlikely to encounter serious differences of opinion outside of the physical education environment, then it is possible to develop attitudes of good sportsmanship. If, however, any of these basic ingredients is lacking, it is doubtful whether attitude development will occur.

IMPLICATIONS FOR PROGRAMS OF PHYSICAL EDUCATION

While reading the following, your goal should be first to evaluate the author's comments and observations critically, and then to see how they might differ from conclusions that you have reached.

It is the author's opinion that education-through-the-physical, while a useful concept at one time, is no longer acceptable. The physical education profession would have been far better off to reevaluate its objectives periodically, as general education has. Education-through-the-physical still refers to the "7 Cardinal Principles" developed in 1918. In 1938, the Educational Policies Commission (EPC) of the National Education Association (NEA) reexamined the goals of education and consolidated the objectives from seven to four: self-realization, human relationships, economic efficiency, and civic responsibility. In 1961, the EPC took another look at the goals of general education and decided that its central purpose was to develop the rational powers of students so they could think clearly. The change from seven to four to one was explained by suggesting that while the previous objectives were all desirable, that "neither the schools nor the pupils have the time or energy to engage in all the activities which will fully achieve these goals."[24] The same reasoning holds true for physical education. In attempting to reach a myriad of goals, we have too often come close to achieving none of them.

In the author's opinion, multi-activity programs are of very limited usefulness and do not promote the acquisition of skill. Much more concentrated experience over longer periods of time is necessary in order to develop any significant degree of skill in average students.

A possible explanation for many of the unfortunate attitudes toward physical education found in high school and college students is

---

24. NEA, *The Central Purpose of American Education,* NEA, 1961.

that they have developed avoidance behaviours as a result of the frustration of non-success which they have experienced in previous physical education situations.

The evidence leads me to believe that the widespread idea of character, attitude, and value development through participation in competitive sports is largely a myth. It appears to be wishful thinking. It sounds good in an after-dinner speech at athletic banquets. We would be far better off if we defined clearly and unequivocally what we consider to be good sportsmanship in specific sports situations and then taught these specific behaviours.

If any attitude, value, or character change is to come about in physical education or athletics, it will do so only to the extent that the physical educator or coach exemplifies the attitude, value, or character trait in his own personal and professional life. As psychiatrist, Joseph Jacobs, has pointed out, this means something more than talking about values.

> We can immediately grasp the obvious implications that what teachers are as people, their own real commitments, will have more to do with imparting values than anything they say. . . . The verbal discussion of values has a place, but only if you and the people with whom you are talking have some sense of mutual respect. It is in this area that the absorption and acceptance of values depends first on their acceptance of you as a person. This means that in the long run your own commitment, what you feel and what you believe, will show.[25]

I question whether the mental development objective, when this is interpreted to mean increased knowledge about activities and physical education, deserves to have equal status as a major objective. I have always felt that there was a distinct difference between "knowing an activity" and "knowing about an activity." The first is impossible without gaining some experience in the activity and developing some skill in it. The second is possible without ever experiencing the skill directly. I consider the former to be of much greater importance than the latter.

What do you think? Have I been too harsh? What do you feel about the multi-activity program? You had better decide, because you may be teaching in such a program now or in the near future.

WHAT QUESTIONS CAN YOU ASK ABOUT THE FOLLOWING STATEMENTS

1. Athletics are valuable because they motivate students to do good work in the classroom.
2. Academic eligibility requirements are discriminatory against below average students.

---

25. Joseph Jacobs, in *Value in Sports,* AAHPER, 1963, pp. 17 and 38.

3. Playing by the rules in football helps you to be a better citizen.

4. "Using" a rule for purposes of strategy is bad sportsmanship even though most fans believe it to be a smart move.

5. Learning to control your temper in a tense sports situation will help you to cope with stresses encountered in your vocational life.

6. Just because physical education has not always reached its goals, this does not mean that the goals need to be revised.

7. The only difference between the good sport and the bad sport is that the bad sport is more honest.

8. The alertness and quick thinking necessary for success in sports is also useful in learning academic skills.

9. The creative dancer is more likely to be a good student than the wrestler or tennis player.

10. In order to allow for individual differences, a multi-activity program should be utilized.

11. Physical education is the only school subject that deals with the "whole man."

Chapter 6—Physical Education as Human Movement

But we who love so dearly the sensory perception identified as kinesthesis, we who have found some of the most valued meanings of our lives in the perceptions identified with movement, have never spoken out about the unique meanings we know are implicit in our movement experiences.

Eleanor Metheny, 1959

THE HISTORICAL BACKGROUND

In the past fifteen years, the term "human movement" has emerged from a position of obscurity to become the most widely used theoretical term in American physical education. To some, it denotes the generic focus of a discipline; the "what" in "what physical education is all about." To others, it means only a program of activities that are used in the primary grades. To still others, it denotes a method of teaching, or more broadly a way of treating children. If the denotation of the term varies greatly within the profession, the connotation of the term raises even greater differences, with each position investing more than a little emotional currency in the particular feelings which the term arouses.

To some the term connotes a theory and a process that will lead physical education out of its present position, which they consider to be one of near total failure in terms of results. To others in the profession, particularly some of those connected more closely with interscholastic athletics, the term is almost meaningless; but because it might encroach upon their well defined programs, they consider it to be a threat. For the majority of physical educators, the term arouses feelings that fall somewhere between these extreme positions. What is important

105

to recognize at the outset is that "human movement," either as a theoretical concept, process, or content area, has become an important part of the language of physical education and has made itself felt in all parts of the profession.

The use of human movement as an important concept in physical education developed in England in the late 1930's. Throughout the war and post-war years, the importance of human movement as a potential theoretical focus for physical education grew until by 1952 it had become widely accepted in England as *the* theory and program of physical education which was most relevant to modern education.

There can be no doubt that the most important name associated with what Lawrence Locke has called "the movement movement" was Rudolph Laban. Laban came to England in 1937 after having been forced out of Nazi Germany, but he did not come as an unknown. Many British dancers and dance teachers had visited the continent and brought back some of his ideas and theories; so Laban had a small but established following before his arrival. Laban, along with his prize pupil and assistant, Lisa Ullman, began immediately to work with dancers and dance teachers and to spread his ideas about human movement.[1]

The physical education scene in England at that time was one of established success and apparent solidarity. Physical education programs had become established in almost all British schools, and the 1933 *Syllabus of Physical Training for Schools*[2] included a standardized curriculum and teaching method. Teacher training colleges provided programs of physical education based on Swedish, Danish, and Austrian gymnastics; Scandinavian and English folk dances; Greek dance; and various kinds of eurythmics. There was however, a small but determined group of physical education teachers (mostly women) who were not satisfied with the apparent success of British physical education. They were disturbed mostly because the new systems of physical education tended to retain the formality that had characterized the nineteenth century systems. They felt that even in dance and gymnastics, the formality prevented children from expressing themselves fully and naturally. In this group, the refugee Laban found a receptive audience and a number of eager pupils.

Slowly but surely the ideas of Laban began to spread, through lectures, workshops, and summer courses. Throughout the war years, the idea of human movement as the basis for a "new" approach to physical education in England grew and prospered. Perhaps one of the

---

1. Diana Jordan, *Childhood and Movement* (Oxford: Basil Backwell, 1966).
2. Board of Education, *Syllabus of Physical Training for Schools,* London, H.M.S.O., 1933.

factors contributing to the rapid acceptance of the idea was the predominance of women physical educators during the war years in England. Diana Jordan, an English physical educator and dance instructor, has given evidence not only of the history of the movement but, also, of the prevailing mood.

> The present approach to physical education stemmed from the war years 1939–1945 as women teachers began to understand the fundamental aspects of movement—how physical skill and agility as well as dance and drama could grow from a "common root" in all human movement. Since then, understanding and knowledge has grown with practice and to many children of all ages and widely differing endowment. So from 1940 all over the country, here and there, individual teachers, training college lecturers and Local Authority advisors were, through their experimental work with children, building confidence in a fresh approach to physical education based on the needs of children and a better understanding of human movement gained from the teaching of Laban.[3]

Concurrent to the Laban-influenced developments, another factor contributed to the growing importance of human movement as a major theoretical construct in English physical education. After the famous British evacuation from Dunkirk, army personnel in charge of military training decided that a new approach was necessary in order to instill courage and adventurousness into young military recruits. Here too, the older methods of physical training were found lacking because of their formalism. The method chosen to reach these goals can best be described as the "obstacle course" method. When inspectors of physical education were introduced to the new training methods, they immediately saw the potential application to elementary school physical education. Because no pedagogical method was available for teaching this new method in the schools, teachers allowed children to freely discover the many ways in which the apparatus could be used. Thus, another impetus for the use of the "discovery method" was brought about.[4]

In 1948, Laban published *Modern Educational Dance*. This important book provided both the name and the framework for a substantial part of the new human movement curriculum. The obstacle course program came to be known as "modern educational gymnastics" and along with the modern educational dance formed the basic curriculum of English physical education. In 1952, a new government syllabus, *Moving and Growing*, brought the two content areas together and gave

---

3. Diana Jordan, *Childhood and Movement*, pp. xxiii-xiv.
4. P. C. McIntosh, "The Recent History of Physical Education in England with Particular Reference to the Development of Movement Education" a paper delivered at the Big Ten Symposium on the History of Physical Education and Sport, The Ohio State University, March, 1971.

them official sanction. Human movement in physical education had come of age.

From its historical development in England, the movement movement has taken several somewhat different but still related directions. Rapid growth is largely responsible for the confusion in terminology that is encountered when investigating this concept. Today one is likely to encounter educational dance, educational gymnastics, women's gymnastics, movement exploration, movement education, developmental movement, and other such labels. Each is in some sense related to the developments in England during the 1940's.

Exactly how and when human movement became an important concept in American physical education is difficult to determine. This would, in fact, be a very interesting and important topic for a historian of physical education to investigate. How much of this movement in the United States is directly imported from England is an unanswered question. It was in the late 1950's that the concept of human movement began to appear in a significant way in professional physical education literature. To be sure, some leaders had, before 1955, been thinking and writing about the significance of human movement, and Eleanor Metheny was, perhaps, the most influential of these leaders. In 1954, she published an article entitled, "The Third Dimension in Physical Education." In that article, Metheny made the following statement which even today finds considerable acceptance as a basic definition.

> If we may define the *totally educated person* as one who has fully developed his ability to utilize constructively all of his potential capacities as a person in relation to the world in which he lives, then we may define the *physically educated person* as one who has fully developed the ability to utilize constructively all of his potential capacities for movement as a way of expressing, exploring, developing, and interpreting himself and his relationship to the world he lives in.[5]

Shortly after this time, Metheny and her colleague, Lois Ellfeldt, came under the influence of the philosophical thought of Susanne Langer and Ernst Cassirer. Starting from Cassirer's theory of symbolic forms, they began to devise a theory of human movement as a significant symbolic form, and they began to recognize that from this viewpoint the intellectual content of physical education could be organized into a body of knowledge.

In 1958, the physical education faculty of the University of California, Los Angeles, attempted to define and clarify the body of knowledge of human movement and to organize an undergraduate

---

5. Eleanor Metheny, "The Third Dimension in Physical Education," *JOHPER* 25:27, March, 1954.

curriculum based on that concept. Two members of this faculty, Camille Brown and Rosalind Cassidy, were at the same time beginning to work on a text which was later published in 1963 under the title, *Theory in Physical Education.* This text has become one of the primary theoretical statements about the movement movement.

By the early 1960's, the concepts of human movement and movement education had become part and parcel of the language and ideas of physical education. In 1964, the faculty of the Department of Physical Education for Women at Purdue University adopted the concept of human movement as the focus for guiding curriculum development at all levels, and began to conduct an extensive research program with human movement as the unifying focus. Their reliance on a Gestalt-psychology approach added a new dimension to the growing interest in human movement.

In 1965, Metheny published a compilation of speeches and articles under the title, *Connotations of Movement in Sport and Dance.* A majority of the elementary school physical education texts published since 1965 have human movement or movement education as a central focus. The movement movement has arrived.

THE CONCEPT OF HUMAN MOVEMENT

It was Rudolph Laban who was primarily responsible for the broadening of the concept of human movement to a point where it could be considered as an important factor in human existence and a primary method of human expression. This intellectual refinement of the concept of human movement paved the way for it to become an important idea in art, education, industry, and physical education. Laban's daughter, Juana de Laban, has explained the scope of his interest in human movement.

> The ideas propounded by Laban in *Die Welt Des Tanzers* (1920) were revolutionary. He declared that movement as the basis of existence is poorly understood and that the obligation of the dancer is to aid man in knowing himself through his movement. He wrote "There is no emotion (affective process) or intellectual action without bodily movement manifestation or vice versa." Further Laban defines: tone as gesture, thought as gesture, an analysis of gestures in spatial relationships, feelings and moods, the logic of movement actions, harmony of gesture, physiology and psychology of dance, the dancing "being," dance as an art, dance as a science and the significance of dance notation, as well as dance as an experience if living.[6]

6. Juana de Laban, "Modus Operandi," *Quest* 2:15, April, 1964.

Laban, therefore, not only set the intellectual parameters of the concept, but also did much to refine the empirical approaches to the study of human movement.

Within professional physical education there does not seem to be a discernible consensus view on how the concept of human movement should be interpreted. This is due, at least in part, to the fact that different writers use different sets of terms to discuss their interpretations of the concept. This is not surprising and happens often with educational concepts that are as young as is the movement movement. It remains to be seen whether the various professional leaders are merely using different sets of terms to describe what will eventually be seen as a unitary concept, or if, indeed, there are basic differences in the interpretations.

Brown and Cassidy have defined human movement in terms that most professionals would find acceptable.

> By definition, therefore, human movement is the change in position of man in time-space as a result of his own energy system interacting within an environment. Human movement is expressive and communicative, and in the interactive process changes both the individual and the environment.[7]

While this definition would find widespread acceptance, it is likely that the agreement would vanish when it came time to translate the definition into a program of physical education. The definition does use terms most commonly applied to human movement; the terms which stem directly from those first used by Laban. Lawrence Locke has described Laban's four aspects of movement. You should note both the categorization and the particular terminology.

1. The Body: What moves? This includes: (a) the activity of the body, locomotion, gesture, manipulative transport, (b) the body parts involved, limbs and trunk, (c) the degree of symmetry in the movement of body parts, and (d) the flow of body movement—the degree to which movement is simultaneous or successive.
2. Effort: how does the body move? This includes the organization of basic effort elements: (a) weight (force), (b) time (speed), (c) space (path), and (d) flow (constraint or freedom).
3. Space and Shape: Where does the body move? This includes: (a) size or extent of movement (large or small), (b) level of transit (high or low), (c) direction (high-right-backward, low-forward-left, etc.), and (d) pattern through the air or over the floor (straight, angular, curved, twisted, etc.).
4. Relationship: With what does the movement occur? This includes: (a) relation of movement in one body part to another body

---

7. Camille Brown and Rosalind Cassidy, *Theory in Physical Education* (Philadelphia: Lea and Febiger, 1963) p. 54.

part, (b) relation of one moving individual to another, and (c) relation of one moving group to another group.[8]

The above set of terms is obviously most useful for *describing* movement, and this is both its strength and its weakness. Many physical educators feel that to interpret human movement adequately, one must move beyond description into the realm of meaning.

Eleanor Metheny and Lois Ellfeldt[9] have focused particularly on interpreting human movement in terms of its meaning within the philosophical context of the theory of symbolic transformation. To do this, they created a whole new set of terms.

A body in motion creates a dynamic, somatic pattern which is visually perceivable. This visually perceivable form of human movement is a "kinestruct." The kinestruct is a symbolic form because it can be meaningfully interpreted by an observer. Thus, the kinestruct becomes a "kinesymbol" or a "kinesymbolic form." The body in motion is also perceptible to the mover through the kinesthetic senses. This kinesthetically perceivable form is a "kinecept." The kinecept is also a symbolic form because it can be meaningfully interpreted by the mover. Thus, the kinecept is another kinesymbol or kinesymbolic form. The individual, therefore, expresses the meaning of the kinecept in kinesymbolic form through the kinestruct. The value of this approach is that it investigates the question of meaning from: 1) the point of view of the mover, 2) the point of view of the observer, and 3) the interaction between the two. The limitations of this approach come from manipulating the completely new set of terms and, indeed, their originators now seem to have abandoned the terms.

THE RELATIONSHIP BETWEEN
PHYSICAL EDUCATION AND HUMAN MOVEMENT

It becomes obvious, therefore, that there is no one set way to approach and interpret the concept of human movement. Likewise, when discussing the idea of physical education as human movement, more than one approach is available; in fact, at least four different approaches can be identified. These approaches are most easily discernible when viewed as prescriptions for school programs of physical education.

---

8. Lawrence Locke, "Movement Education—A Description and Critique," in *New Perspectives of Man in Action,* edited by Roscoe Brown and Bryant Cratty, (New York: Prentice Hall, 1969), p. 208.
9. Eleanor Metheny and Lois Ellfeldt, *Connotations of Movement in Sport and Dance* (Dubuque: Wm. C. Brown, Company Publishers, 1965), pp. 57-62.

1. *The approach which views human movement as the central core of meaning for what has heretofore been called physical education.* This approach calls for the reorganization of the content of physical education with human movement as the central focus. It does not necessarily mean new content, but it does mean some slight shifts in emphasis and a new methodology. It requires the development of new concepts and, most importantly, it requires a new way of looking at sports, dance, and games. Brown and Cassidy have provided the most thorough articulation of this approach. As they have suggested, physical education should be seen as human movement.

> Physical education has the same designation as movement, as human movement. Throughout history, movement has been the central core of the meaning attached to what has been called physical education, physical training, or physical culture.[10]

This approach requires a new definition for physical education, one that has human movement as the generic focus. Again, Brown and Cassidy have provided the best example.

> Physical education is the school program of the study of the art and science of human movement needed in today's world designed for development through movement, and human performance restricted to expressive form and/or restricted through the use of representations of environmental reality.[11]

This approach to physical education is *through* the concept of human movement. Basketball, dance, handball, and creative rhythms all are viewed from the perspective of human movement. The variables which facilitate the viewpoint are a mixture of kinesiological concepts, biomechanical concepts, and movement concepts drawn primarily from Laban. The chart on the following page shows how physical education activities are viewed from the theoretical perspective of human movement.

While it is entirely possible, and even probable, that all of the traditional activities of physical education would be utilized in this type of program, the approach to the activities and the activity experiences themselves would differ from the traditional approach. First, there would be more emphasis on intellectual content. Why and how a student moves, how people in other cultures move, and what constitutes efficient movement are all questions that would require a great deal of cognitive activity along with the actual participation. Second, the increased intellectual emphasis would require that a greater amount of

---

10. Brown and Cassidy, *Theory in Physical Education*, p. 33.
11. Ibid.

Individual Variables Affecting Human Movement	Change this:
Start with this:	
	Environmental Variables Affecting Human Movement
Fundamental Movements:	
Flex-bend	Time-space
Extend-reach	Speed, acceleration
Rotate-twist, wring	Space
Circumduct-swing	Distance
Abduct-push	Direction
Adduct-pull, bring	Force
Glide-glide	Amount
Elevate-raise, lift	Direction
Depress-lower	Air-liquid resistances
Supinate-turn	Matter
Pronate-turn	Sense objects
	Objects of simple location
Fundamental Movement Patterns:	Man as Mass
Maintaining equilibrium: stand, sit, lie, upright, while moving, etc.	Media
	Land
Giving impetus to self: walk, run, jump, crawl, leap, skip, etc.	Water, other liquids
	Air
Giving impetus to object: throw, strike, bat, kick, etc.	Relationships
	Attitudes of valuing
Receiving impetus of self: land, etc.	Cultural conditions necessary for healthy growth and development
Receiving impetus of object: catch, etc.	
	Total situation as perceived by an individual
Combinations of Fundamental Movements and Movement Patterns	Events

Camille Brown and Rosalind Cassidy, *Theory in Physical Education* (Philadelphia: Lea and Febiger, 1963), p. 76. Used by permission of the publisher.

FIGURE 5.   Variables of Human Movement Possibilities

time be allowed for verbal activity in the form of lectures (the lecture-laboratory concept is very popular in the movement movement), or in the form of discussion groups. Third, there would be an increase in emphasis on analysis. This ranges from analyzing the meaning of a movement to a bio-mechanical analysis of the forehand tennis stroke. Fourth, there is an emphasis on understanding rather than on skill development. This is not to say that high levels of skill are not sought.

It merely suggests that understanding movement is at least as important as moving skillfully.

2. *The approach which views physical education as an applied field of the broad discipline of human movement.* The discussion in chapter three will be of interest to you in understanding this approach, which has been best articulated by Ruth Abernathy and Maryann Waltz. Here a distinction is made between a discipline and an educational profession. The discipline is human movement and the educational profession is still called physical education. This is the primary difference between this approach and the first approach discussed in this chapter.

Abernathy and Waltz have explained the distinction between discipline and profession as follows.

> It is important to emphasize the distinction between terms, for physical education and human movement are not synonymous. Physical education is viewed as the school or college program utilizing movement experiences in developing concepts, enriching percepts, and otherwise modifying the organism in keeping with broad educational goals. Physical education is, in this sense, an applied field. . . . Inquiry into the phenomenon encompasses a search for knowledge beyond the scope of immediate or even subsequent application in physical education.[12]

In this approach, human movement is viewed as a discipline and entails the value-free search for knowledge that is characteristic of disciplinary investigation. Physical education is viewed as a process which utilizes movement experiences as a vehicle for achieving the goals of education. This is, of course, very much in the tradition of the education-through-the-physical approach. The only essential difference is that instead of describing the "through" part in terms of sports, games, and dance, it is described in terms of movement experiences.

The primary focus of attention in this approach is on the discipline of human movement. This is important because it takes the primary focus out of the realm of educational programs and into the realm of the value-free discipline. This focus of attention is necessary because physical education is interpreted to be the application of the knowledge gained in the discipline. The goal, then, becomes to achieve a well defined body of knowledge about human movement. The better organized and defined this body of knowledge becomes, the more easily and efficiently it can be applied in school programs of physical education. Abernathy and Waltz have offered a preliminary schematic which ex-

---

12. Ruth Abernathy and Maryann Waltz, "Toward a Discipline: First Steps First," *Quest* 2:1-2, April, 1964.

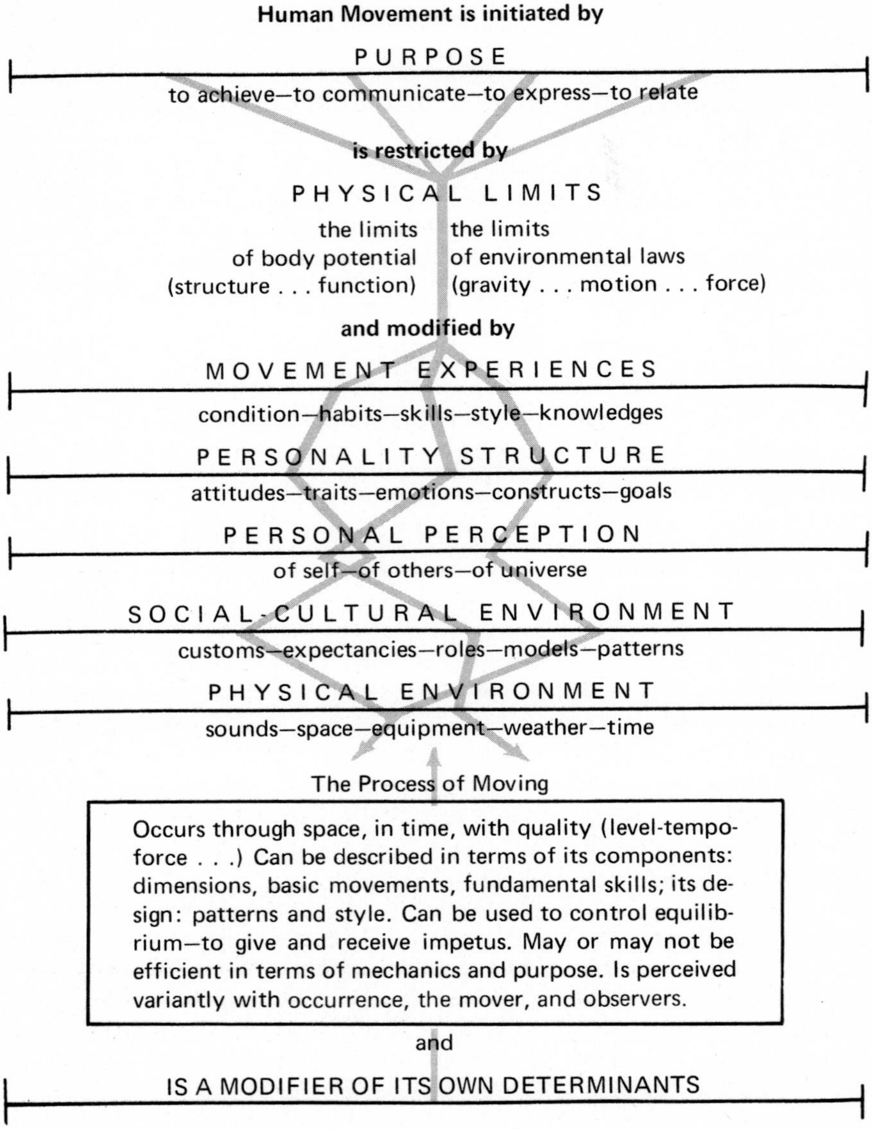

Human Movement is initiated by

P U R P O S E

to achieve—to communicate—to express—to relate

is restricted by

P H Y S I C A L   L I M I T S

the limits | the limits
of body potential | of environmental laws
(structure . . . function) | (gravity . . . motion . . . force)

and modified by

M O V E M E N T   E X P E R I E N C E S

condition—habits—skills—style—knowledges

P E R S O N A L I T Y   S T R U C T U R E

attitudes—traits—emotions—constructs—goals

P E R S O N A L   P E R C E P T I O N

of self—of others—of universe

S O C I A L - C U L T U R A L   E N V I R O N M E N T

customs—expectancies—roles—models—patterns

P H Y S I C A L   E N V I R O N M E N T

sounds—space—equipment—weather—time

The Process of Moving

Occurs through space, in time, with quality (level-tempo-force . . .) Can be described in terms of its components: dimensions, basic movements, fundamental skills; its design: patterns and style. Can be used to control equilibrium—to give and receive impetus. May or may not be efficient in terms of mechanics and purpose. Is perceived variantly with occurrence, the mover, and observers.

and

IS A MODIFIER OF ITS OWN DETERMINANTS

Ruth Abernathy and Maryann Waltz, "Toward A Discipline: First Steps First," *Quest* 2:3, April, 1964, used by permission of the *Quest* Board.

FIGURE 6.   Schematic representation of variables and interactions which define the parameters of the discipline of human movement.

plains the important variables and interactions that make up the discipline of human movement.

This approach allows for the utilization of all the traditional activities of physical education. Like the first example, the primary differences are in how activities are approached. Abernathy and Waltz have emphasized that the discipline of human movement does not automatically mean an applied program of movement education.

> It is evident that this approach, in which subject matter in physical education is seen as an application of knowledge, is not synonymous with that in which the descriptive emphasis is upon a program of movement exploration, exercise, or activities. . . . Attention to the structure of physical education as an application of disciplined knowledge, does not negate the functional role of traditional activities in the conduct of the program. Organized experience in sport, dance, gymnastics . . . is not incompatible with a program based upon movement inquiry. However, in such a program, activities can not be perceived as ends in themselves since they do not define the nature or purpose of the experience.[13]

The last sentence in the above quotation is quite important. It shows clearly that the study of human movement is an end in itself for the discipline of human movement, but not for the profession of physical education. In fact, we might label the applied aspects of this approach as education-through-movement-experiences. Implementation of this approach no doubt would be quite similar to programs developed from the first approach discussed in this chapter. The two approaches, in fact, are not very far removed from one another, and it is easy to see how they might merge in the future.

3. *The approach which views human movement as a part of physical education.* The third approach has much in common with the first two approaches, especially in terminology and methodology. The basic difference among them is that this approach sees the concepts, content, and methods of the movement movement as comprising only one part of a total physical education program. Traditional categorizations such as sport and dance are considered to make up the other parts of the total physical education program. This approach is most often called "movement education," and its practitioners are called movement educators.

The part of the physical education program that is usually considered to be the movement education phase is what has traditionally been called the "self-testing activities" part of the program. Other terms that are commonly used with this approach are "movement

---

13. Ibid., pp. 6-7.

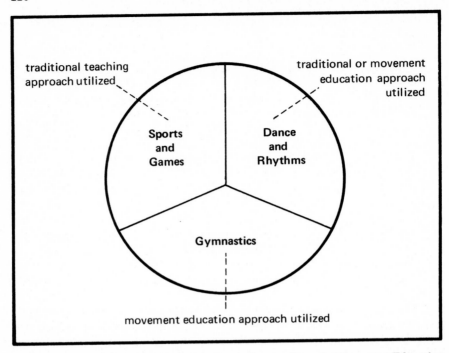

FIGURE 7.   The Physical Education Curriculum as Regards Movement Education

exploration" and "educational gymnastics." With this approach, the physical education curriculum is usually divided into three equal parts.[14]

Dance activities may be taught either by the traditional approach or by using the movement education approach. From this point of view, there is a fundamental difference between methods of approaching movement education and traditional physical education activities such as team sports. Glenn Kirchner, Jean Cunningham, and Eileen Warrell have emphasized this in their explanation of movement education.

> There is a fundamental distinction that must be made between the organizational structure of contemporary Physical Education and Movement Education. In the former, *the activity itself* (volleyball, track and field or folk dance) provides *the structural basis* for developing a curriculum. Skills within each area are arranged from the simple to the complex and presented to children in accordance with their physical maturity and general readiness.

14. Glen Kirchner, et al., *Introduction to Movement Education* (Dubuque: William C. Brown Co., Publishers, 1970), pp. 16-17.

> Within the organizational structure of Movement Education, the con-
> cepts and underlying principles of "body awareness," "space," and
> "qualities" of movement provide a basis for *understanding* all move-
> ment. In Movement Education, *all* activities are selected on the basis
> of how well they can foster and develop the concepts and movement
> principles described under the concepts and movement principles
> described under *body awareness, space,* and *qualities* of movement.
> These concepts or *elements of movement* thus become the *frame-
> work* of a *Movement Education Curriculum.*[15]

Thus, unlike the two previous approaches, this viewpoint accepts a
difference in the organizational structure of the various phases of the
total physical education program. This approach stresses a different
teaching method, a different organizational structure, and a different
explanatory terminology for the movement education phase of the total
program. On the other hand, this approach also suggests that team
sports and individual sports are probably better learned using traditional teaching methods and organizational structures. This, in itself, is
a departure from the first two approaches, each of which suggested that
all activities should be approached from the human movement point
of view.

Another difference, finally, is that movement education is almost
entirely an elementary school approach. Those who view human movement as only a *part* of physical education almost always confine themselves to discussions of physical education at the elementary school
level. There is no attempt to incorporate movement education into
senior high school or college programs of physical education (this should
not be confused with college courses in body mechanics or movement
fundamentals which are conducted in an entirely different manner
than are movement education programs in elementary schools). Because of the emphasis on elementary school physical education, this
approach does not utilize as intellectualized an approach as did the first
two.

4. *The approach which views human movement as the catalyst
for bringing about an entirely new program of physical education.* The
fourth and final approach which I will suggest is, perhaps, the most
radical departure from what we have traditionally called physical education. This approach suggests that the study of human movement
requires new methods, new content, and new programs. This approach
is best exemplified by the work done by the faculty of the Department
of Physical Education for Women at Purdue University.

More than any other of the approaches, this viewpoint was born out
of a discontent with the results of traditional programs of physical

---

15. Ibid., pp. 13-14.

education. Hope Smith has spoken of both the discontent and the fundamental basis of the human movement approach which grew out of this discontent.

> Only in rare instances did we leave twelve years of physical education behind us knowing much more about our motor performance except that we play some games well enough to engage in them occasionally and that we play others poorly or not at all. We may know that regular, vigorous exercise and "fitness" are closely related, but since we seem to get along without the exercise, why should we worry? Consider, then, all the things we have *not* learned about physical activity, for example, very few of us know that certain ways of approaching the learning of a new activity, or the refining of a familiar activity, are far more effective than others; that selecting certain sensory information to attend to is important for improving performance; that the design of the human body is such that it permits an enormous number of movements and movement combinations; that the physical environment in which we live imposes certain restrictions on our movement behaviour (if the laws of the environment and the operational principles derived from these laws are understood and applied, one may move efficiently despite the restrictions); that our socio-cultural environment affects the ways in which we use space-time with our bodies and body segments and that our environment influences the value we assign to various activities and our ability to perform them.[16]

The goal of this approach to physical education is to refine individual movement behaviour. This is accomplished by helping the student to understand principles of efficient movement; to know the best way to learn skills; to understand the role of movement in his own culture and in other cultures; and to explore his own potential for movement through various movement experiences.

The structural organization in this approach is built around the various aspects of studying human movement: principles of motion, biomechanical analysis, principles of learning movement skills, posture, rhythm, and aesthetic expression through movement. The basic method utilized in this approach is the lecture-laboratory method with a high priority placed on students doing individual movement experiments.

Obviously, such an approach emphasizes the intellectual content of physical education. Great priority is placed upon *understanding* the role that each of these variables plays in movement behaviour. The assumption is that if the student gains basic understandings in these areas, they will enable him to develop efficient movement behaviour;

---

16. Hope Smith, ed., *Introduction to Human Movement* (Reading, Mass.: Addison-Wesley, 1968), pp. iv-v.

whether this movement behaviour is necessary for recreation, work production, survival, or for the maintenance of health.[17]

To what degree the actual development of skill is a primary objective is more difficult to judge. Obviously, the ultimate goal is efficient movement behaviour which implies a high level of skill. The means for reaching that goal, however, appears not to be in the direct development of the skill, but rather in the development of understanding what skill is and how it can be achieved.

THE FUTURE OF MOVEMENT EDUCATION

In 1966, Locke[18] suggested that the movement movement might progress in any one of three directions. The first possibility was that it might go nowhere; that is, that it was merely another label to be promoted without any basic change in content or method. The second possibility was that it might become the unifying factor that results in the creation of a new theoretical framework for physical education. Locke saw this as a distinct possibility because of his observation that many individuals with diverse backgrounds were finding it profitable to consult with each other because each shared a common interest in problems related to the study of human movement. The third possibility was that the movement movement would progress in different directions. One direction would be the disciplinary route, while another would be the pedagogical process, and these two would not necessarily be related.

It is difficult, now several years later, to offer predictions that are any more accurate than were Locke's. Many professionals feel that the movement movement should go nowhere (notice I said should rather than will). Among the most articulate of these spokesmen is sports philosopher, Harold Vander Zwaag.

> Since 1964, there has been a wild and scrambling search to identify the disciplinary nature of our field. Human movement has emerged as the favorite concept because it represents another umbrella, even though it is woefully deficient in concreteness. . . . Physical education should not and will not be replaced by the concept of human movement. There has been a tendency to contrast the profession of physical education with the discipline of human movement. The net result is a comparison of one abstract entity with another.[19]

---

17. Ibid., p. v.
18. Lawrence Locke, "The Movement Movement," *JOHPER* 37:26, January, 1966.
19. Harold Vander Zwaag, "Historical Relationships Between the Concepts of Sport and Physical Education" speech delivered at the 73rd Annual Meeting of the National College Physical Education Association for Men, December 29, 1969, Chicago, Illinois, p. 11. For a summary of Vander Zwaag's proposals see Chapter Three, Physical Education as an Academic Discipline.

The interdisciplinary dialogue that Locke observed in 1966 has continued to grow, and it would not be inaccurate at this stage of our professional history to suggest that the concept of human movement is now accepted by most physical educators as the core concept of physical education and the source of a growing theoretical framework. It could be, however, that we are still in a honeymoon period, and that human movement advocates may find in developing the theoretical framework that they do not share as much in common as may now appear.

The third possibility, while theoretically plausible, is most unlikely, simply because the structure of higher education in the United States is unlikely to support a discipline of human movement that is divorced from programs of movement education in the schools.

What might be predicted about the four approaches suggested in this chapter? At least two predictions are possible. First, I suggested earlier that approaches one and two were not far apart in terms of program implementation and could conceivably join together if some differences on the theoretical level could be worked out. This is a distinct possibility; the two together may in the future provide one distinct movement within the profession. It is also possible to foresee a wedding of approaches three and four. The movement education approach was seen to be almost exclusively the interest of elementary school physical educators. On the other hand, approach four was seen to be mostly applicable to high school and college programs of physical education. Such a union would provide a total human movement curriculum that would be radically different from anything we have known in physical education.

If this is the direction in which the various components of the movement education concept progresses, then the result might be two approaches (one and two together and three and four together) that would have some similarities (terminology and some parts of methodology) on the theoretical level, but would be radically dissimilar on the program level. This is one possibility. There are certainly others that may be equally possible, and you can test your predictive powers about the future of the movement movement.

IMPLICATIONS FOR PHYSICAL EDUCATION

Perhaps here it will be helpful to summarize a critique of movement education that was recently prepared by Locke who presented the strengths and weaknesses of movement education, and I believe that his appraisals are equally relevant to all forms of the movement. I will present a summary of his thoughts in hopes that it will whet your appetite and cause you to read this excellent article.

STRENGTHS

1. Movement education has provided the first stimulating break with a long tradition of inadequacy in treatment of teaching method.
2. Movement education has caused an increased interest in the crucial elementary school years in which instruction is most profitable.
3. Movement education has encouraged interest in self-directed learning.
4. Movement education has encouraged interest in observing and analyzing movement.
5. Movement education, by individualizing the rate of learning, allows for adequate introductory experiences.
6. Movement education has brought about a new interest in theory, subject matter organization, and methods of instruction.

WEAKNESSES

1. Movement education, by proposing to teach readiness for future movement demands, may have an ultimate objective that is unobtainable.
2. Movement education, by relying heavily on concepts of general abilities and transfer of training, does not have the support of a research consensus.
3. Movement education, by emphasizing the understanding of movement, runs the risk of losing the source of pleasure in movement.
4. Movement education, by focusing on advances in methodology, has underestimated the central problems in physical education.
5. Movement education, to be successful, requires teachers who have very special abilities.
6. Movement education may not be the best program for all children.
7. Movement education tends to intellectualize too much and to make physical education an accessory to academic learning.
8. Movement education, by emphasizing the kinesthetic elements does not always provide the learner with the best focus.
9. Movement education is very difficult when there is a wide range of abilities and experiences in one class.[20]

Locke is a benevolent critic. On the whole, he feels that this movement has been very beneficial for American physical education, but he also recognizes the dangers in the potential solidifying of the theoretical position to the point where no synthesis with traditional programs of physical education is possible.

---

20. Lawrence Locke, *New Perspectives of Man in Action.*

Movement education is, as it was in the beginning, more relevant to expressive movement (dance, etc.) than it is to sport. Despite the fact that many promoters of the human movement viewpoint have insisted that sport forms can be relevantly examined through the parameters associated with human movement, there still has been no convincing argument presented which explains how sport can retain its unique meaningfulness when studied through the perspective of human movement.

It also seems apparent that beyond the elementary school level some programs that utilize the human movement approach are no longer activity courses. With lectures, discussions, and experiments, there is little time left for the kind of practice that has most often been associated with activity courses.

A third observation is that all approaches to physical education as human movement result in an intellectualization of content. This is necessary because the assumed source of meaning is in the form of human movement which in itself is an abstraction. The focus for meaning is not badminton, but rather, the movements associated with badminton. To know badminton requires very little intellectualization, but to understand the movements of badminton requires more than a little. The obvious implication of this focus of meaning is that the activities, in themselves, are not of primary importance.

It can also be said that while the movement movement promotes a methodology that places the student rather than the subject at the center of attention, it assumes, erroneously I believe, that the student would rather explore his movement potential than learn to play badminton. The young child still asks his mother, "May I go out and play?" rather than, "May I go out and move?"

Another problem is that there is no evidence to support the idea that movement exploration provides a better readiness for sports skills than does the traditional "lead-up games" approach. The entire concept of readiness for sports skills needs to be evaluated, especially when one bears in mind Jerome Bruner's now famous statement that a child is always ready for an activity if it is presented in an understandable form.

Another observation is that the basic assumption of the inherent meaning in human movement is questionable. I do not doubt that there is meaning inherent in sport, games, and dance. The question is, to what is that meaning attributable? What is its source? The movement movement has as a basic assumption that the meaning is attributable to the experience of movement. If this assumption could be refuted, then the entire theoretical structure would lose its relevance.

The movement education approach has enjoyed a honeymoon status in terms of building its theoretical structure. In the near future we might see a movement-backlash which will be primarily critical and, no doubt, quite emotionally prejudicial. This backlash, however, should be good for the advocates of movement education because it will cause them to tighten their theoretical structure and to eliminate some of the concepts which are not easily defended.

As you can tell, I am not exactly a proponent of the concept of human movement. This should not deter you from reaching conclusions about the movement movement that differ from mine. Each of us must reach conclusions as objectively as possible, particularly on this topic which will remain very emotionally charged far into the future.

What Questions Can You Ask About the Following Statements

1. Human movement, as a designation for our field of study, is less abstract than physical education.
2. In sports, the performer's focus of attention is seldom on the movement itself, and because of this it is incorrect to say that the perception of movement produces meaning.
3. Movement education is really a different teaching method rather than a new theory or content.
4. Women physical educators support the human movement concept because it is more intellectual than physical education.
5. Since sports and dance both involve skilled human movement, the ideas and concepts of the movement movement are relevant to both pursuits.
6. The movement movement is merely a restatement of education-through-the-physical, using different terms but no new ideas.
7. Basketball is not human movement, it is a game.
8. Self-analysis of movement is an aid to learning.
9. The public will more readily accept movement education than they have physical education.
10. The emphasis on expression makes human movement more relevant to dance than to sports.

Chapter 7—Some Other Current Approaches to Physical Education

. . . the spirit of innovation is perhaps the most outstanding characteristic of the world of education today.

Max Friedlander, 1965

INTRODUCTION

We live in a period which is best characterized by an unprecedented rapidity of change. That education in general and physical education in particular reflect the prevailing mood of change was evidenced by AAHPER President (1969–70) John Cooper's choice of "Preparation for and Adjustment to Change" as the theme for the 1970 National Convention. Much of the focus of this convention was on innovative programs, equipment, and ideas, and how individuals and a profession can cope with them.

Impetus for change comes from many different sources. One major source is the general field of education, and the questions that are most hotly debated within the circles of professional education have their correlates within the profession of physical education. Increased interest in the process and content of early childhood education has sharpened the interest of physical educators in the contributions that physical education can make in this critical period. As relationships between students and teachers are examined closely, physical educators have begun also to reassess their traditional roles as teachers and coaches. As relevancy becomes a key word in planning educational curricula, physical educators have begun to redefine the scope of activities which can be included within programs of physical education. As core courses and requirements come under close scrutiny at the college level, physical educators have been required to reassess the question of "required physical education"; this time without the basic assumption that requirements are necessarily good for the profession or the student. Questions of classroom management, grading, motivation, and many others have all been raised during this period of change. Sooner or later these questions all get applied to programs of physical education at the various educational levels, and what this does more than anything else is to create a climate in which innovative suggestions are accepted as routine.

This is not to suggest that a great deal of change has taken place in physical education in the past few years. Many observers have rightly suggested that the "educational establishment" is often highly resistant to innovative change. What has taken place during the past decade is not so much actual change, but rather, the development of a new attitude toward change. It is a spirit of innovation rather than innovation itself which has recently come to characterize education. New ideas are no longer met with hostility, and each of us has come to expect that new approaches are just around the corner. What this has done, of course, is to create a climate within which change can be much more easily effected. If we have just lived through a period in which the spirit of innovation was dominant, then, we are very likely approaching a period in which innovation itself will be much more prevalent.

This means that physical education programs will change. The three major theoretical influences on physical education—physical fitness, education-*through*-the-physical, and human movement—have already been examined in previous chapters. There are, however, many other potential influences which could bring about new directions in physical education. To examine some of these is the purpose of this chapter. Whether these forces *will* influence physical education significantly remains to be seen. This is a judgment that only history can provide. Whether these forces *should* affect physical education to any significant degree, is a judgment that can more reasonably be made at the present time.

PATTERNING, NEUROLOGICAL ORGANIZATION, AND PHYSICAL EDUCATION

If, twenty years ago, someone had taken a physical educator into a gymnasium to observe a group of children crawling around the floor in a very precise, stereotyped pattern, and then attempted to convince the physical educator that what he had observed was a class in physical education, it is unlikely that the physical educator would have had a very sympathetic view of the entire affair. If today, however, the same scene were to be replayed, it not only is much more likely that the physical educator would be more ready to accept the idea, it is even possible that the person proposing the idea might be a physical educator himself.

The hypothetical scene depicted above is an outgrowth of theories and programs that have been established at the Institutes for the Achievement of Human Potential located in Philadelphia. The names most often associated with these programs are Robert Doman, a specialist in physical medicine; Carl Delacato, an educator who has specialized in reading problems; Glenn Doman, a physical therapist; and Eugene Spitz, a specialist in pediatric neuro-surgery. The theory and method promoted by this group is most often referred to as "the Doman-Delacato method." The entire project has received a great deal of publicity in popular media over the past few years—"The Boy Who Would Not Die" *(Look)*, "Hope for Brain-Injured Children" *(Reader's Digest)*, "Train Your Baby to be a Genius" *(McCall's)*, and "Unlocking the Secrets of the Brain" *(The Chicago Tribune)*. It also has attracted considerable attention within professional physical education because many of the remedial activities suggested in the program are gross motor activities which could easily be incorporated in programs of physical education, especially at the elementary level.

The basic supposition of the Doman-Delacato theory is that intellectual functioning can be improved by adherence to a progression of activities which purportedly increases the neurological organization of the child. In this way, severely traumatized children (brain injured, supposedly retarded, minimal brain dysfunction) can be helped to achieve normal and supranormal status, and normal children can be helped to achieve even higher states of intellectual ability.

The basic principles of the Doman-Delacato theory can be summarized as follows:

1. The central nervous system develops in a definite pattern from conception to age six to eight.
2. The pattern is such that ontogenetic development of individual nervous systems recapitulates the phylogenetic development of the species.
3. Progress of this development can be measured on a scale of neurological organization in six areas: 1) body movement, 2) speech, 3) manual skills, 4) visual skills, 5) hearing skills, and 6) tactile skills.
4. Although developmental speed varies widely among children, the pattern is nevertheless consistent.

5. Cortical hemispheric dominance is the final stage of development, and this stage is brought about by lateral dominance (right-eyed, right-handed, right-footed, etc.).

6. If development of neurological organization at any one of the stages is impaired, the total pattern will be adversely affected.

7. The development of neurological organization can be slowed down by some methods of rearing children; it can be slowed down very much when a child is deprived of necessary environmental stimulation; and it can be stopped completely by injury to the brain.

8. Learning problems in general and reading difficulties in particular are the result of neurological disorganization due to some retardation of this developmental pattern.

9. The diagnosis of trauma, learning problems, and reading difficulties, therefore, becomes an evaluation of the degree of neurological organization.

10. By stimulating the development of the central nervous system in simple, non-surgical ways, it is possible to push children considerably up the ladder of neurological development.

11. By the same methods, the neurological development of normal children can be stimulated, i.e., their mental abilities can be increased.[1]

When a child is brought to the institute, he is put through a battery of extensive tests, and from the results of these tests a thorough diagnosis is made. On the basis of the diagnosis, the parents of the child are given a precise series of tasks which they must see that the child performs consistently. Each child receives a "program" that is suited to his individual needs, but the method involves similar activities for all children. As a whole, these activities have come to be known as the "Doman-Delacato Method" and they include the following:

1. Cross pattern creeping: left leg and right arm move forward simultaneously as the head and neck turn slightly toward the right or forward hand. At the next step, the left hand and right leg move forward, as the head and neck turn toward the left hand. With traumatized children, five adults are usually needed to manually manipulate the child through the patterning. With normal children, instruction as to correct form is usually sufficient to allow hundreds of children to crawl around a gymnasium floor.

1. Carl Delacato, *Neurological Organization and Reading*, Charles Thomas Company, Springfield, 1968; Joan Beck, "Unlocking the Secrets of the Brain," *Chicago Tribune Magazine,* September 13 and September 27, 1964; Virgil Engles, "Patterned Movements: A New Justification for Physical Education?," *The Physical Educator,* December, 1968, pp. 170-172.

2. Cross pattern walking: rhythmical walking in bare or stockinged feet. As each foot moves forward, the child points to its toes with the opposite hand. While pointing, the head and body turn toward the forward foot and the eyes focus on the forward hand.
3. Sleep position: Each night the child is to sleep on his stomach and left cheek, facing right. The right elbow should be bent so that the right hand rests about twelve inches from the face, palm down. The right leg is flexed with the knee opposite the right hip. The left arm is placed by the side with the palm up, and the left leg is stretched straight down (this is for a left-handed child, the position would be reversed for a right-handed child).
4. Visual pursuit: horizontal and vertical tracking of a pencil held in child's hand from twelve to twenty-four inches in front of his face.
5. Sidedness training: complete cortical hemispheric dominance is developed through arranging the child's environment so he is forced to become laterally dominant, i.e., right-eyed, right-handed, right-footed (or left-eyed, left-handed, left-footed). This is emphasized in writing, reading, eating, throwing, kicking, and all other activities.
6. Removal of music: removed temporarily from the child's environment because tonality is a function of the non-dominant hemisphere of the cortex.
7. Red-green reading: Transparent green paper covers material to be read and transparent red paper covers the non-dominant eye, causing the child, without his being aware of it, to use his dominant eye for reading.
8. Red-red writing: using transparent red paper, and a red pencil for writing, forces use of dominant eye.[2]

It is not too difficult to see that physical education provides a "natural" place to pursue some of the activities used in the Doman-Delacato Method. If elementary school children are going to be required to crawl and walk for fifteen minutes each day, what better place to do it than in the gymnasium during their physical education period? If children are going to receive sidedness training, how better could it be accomplished than by the kicking, throwing, and striking activities used in physical education? When the activity opportunity is considered in conjunction with the long-standing propensity of many physical educators to be supportive of programs which purport to give direct evidence of mind-body unity, then the potential influence of the Doman-Delacato system on physical education becomes readily apparent.

2. See Beck, "Unlocking the Secrets of the Brain" *Chicago Tribune Magazine;* Carl Delacato, *Treatment of Speech and Reading Problems,* (Springfield: Charles Thomas Company, 1963).

The Doman-Delacato system, perhaps more than any contemporary mental-development program, has, however, been continuously surrounded by controversy. Nearly all who visit the Philadelphia based institute come away impressed with some or all of what they have seen. Some of the case studies of youngsters who have undergone the treatment are truly amazing. For parents whose children have benefited from the treatment, the Doman-Delacato system takes on almost religious significance. To many others, however, the system appears to be totally invalid.

The criticisms can be broken down into two groupings. First, there are criticisms which are directed at the theory of neurological organization which purports to explain how and why the improvements take place. Second, there are criticisms directed at the method used to bring about the changes.

CRITICISMS OF THEORY

1. Evidence from comparative neurology fails to support the theory that ontogeny recapitulates phylogeny, and it has long been discarded as an important educational and psychological concept.[3]
2. The implication that early motor development is predictive of later cognitive performance is unwarranted on the basis of research findings.
3. The nervous system does not function in the simple way implied by the theory. Voluntary motor patterns are caused by complex, dynamic interactions of many parts of the brain.[4]
4. Experimental data does not support the assumption that gross motor activity affects the visual or associative centers of the brain.[5]
5. Research regarding the relationship of lateral dominance to cognitive performance is inconclusive.
6. The assumption that children who are not genetically defective may have above average intellectual potential is unwarranted.[6]

CRITICISMS OF METHOD

1. The assertion that their method treats the brain directly while others deal only with peripheral symptoms is not justified.[7]

---

3. Theodore Perkins, "Problems Arising From the Assertions of Assumptions of Delacato," in *Claremont Reading Conference 28th Yearbook,* Claremont Graduate School Curriculum Laboratory, 1964, p. 125.
4. Bryant Cratty, "On the Threshold," *Quest* 8:10, May, 1967.
5. Ibid.
6. Roger Freeman, "Controversy over Patterning as a Treatment for Brain Damage in Children," *Journal of The American Medical Association* 202:385, October, 1967.
7. Ibid.

2. The use of observational case studies does not allow for generalizations, especially generalizations made to a normal population from case studies of impaired children.
3. The hypothesizing of neurological patterning on the basis of clinical observations is totally unwarranted.[8]
4. Making parents play the role of therapists is questionable.[9]
5. The willingness to allow such terms as "miracle" and "maxichild" to be associated with the system is questionable.
6. The few experimental studies that have investigated the effects of the treatment have reported contradictory findings.[10, 11]

Professionals, outside of those directly involved with the Doman-Delacato system, seem to be overwhelmingly skeptical of the theory and the method. The degree of that unanimity was made apparent recently when seven major medical and health organizations[12] issued a joint statement which held that the Doman-Delacato theory and treatment were "without merit." This, however, has not prevented the Doman-Delacato system from gaining adherents across the country and in foreign lands also. A *Saturday Evening Post* article about the system pointed to its rapid growth.

> Satellite institutes based on the same plan have been springing up in a number of U.S. cities, 10 at last count. The system also has spread to Latin America; 9 institutes now are operating in Brazil alone. Dozens of schools in the U.S. have established special classes in which children with learning problems crawl, creep, and practice visual exercises for certain periods of the day. The Roman Catholic Archdiocese of Baltimore is experimenting with neurological organization as part of an extensive remedial-reading program in parochial schools. And near Dallas, Texas, a new university, established to rescue dropouts, has a required course in neurological organization—that is, patterned crawling and creeping.[13]

It is in light of this type of controversy and conflicting opinion that physical educators must make judgments about their stance toward the potential influence on their programs.

---

8. Cratty, "On the Threshold."
9. Freeman, "Controversy over Patterning . . ."
10. John Kershner, "Doman-Delacato's Theory of Neurological Organization Applied with Retarded Children," *Exceptional Children* 34:441, February, 1968.
11. Melvin Robbins, "A Study of the Validity of Delacato's Theory of Neurological Organization," *Exceptional Children* 32:517, April, 1966.
12. "The Doman-Delacato Treatment of Neurologically Handicapped Children" *Archives of Physical Medicine and Rehabilitation,* April, 1968, p. 184.
13. "When Children Can't Learn," *Saturday Evening Post,* 240:27-31, 72-74, July 29, 1967.

IMPLICATION FOR PHYSICAL EDUCATION

There are two ways that the Doman-Delacato phenomenon can be approached, and the two are not necessarily interdependent. First, it can be approached with scholarly open-mindedness in the spirit of investigation; i.e., an attempt to find out if it is true or not. Physical educators at the disciplinary level legitimately could assist in this task, particularly by isolating the specifically motor type activities in the treatment and conducting experimental studies to determine their effects on various measures of cognitive performance. The second approach must be to decide whether any part of the treatment deserves to be incorporated in programs of physical education. Even if some causative relationships between gross motor activity and cognitive development are uncovered, the question still remains as to whether these activities should become parts of programs of physical education.

It would appear that, at this point in time, any defense of the theoretical assumptions of the Doman-Delacato system must be made on the basis of belief rather than on any argument based upon scientific fact. This should not, however, cause anyone to view the treatment with anything but open-mindedness. To suggest that the treatment is without merit is hardly a defensible position, when viewed in the light of numerous case study successes and at least one experimental success. This is not to suggest that one must accept the successful results as having been *caused* by the particular factors which are claimed as causative factors; i.e., the patterning. One very fruitful avenue might be to accept the idea that successes have occurred and then begin to examine more closely the factors that might be potentially responsible for the successes. Many physical educators have suggested that successes may be due to: 1) the increase in the quantity of sensory input and sensory stimulation which the child experiences when patterning occurs, 2) the physical closeness of many adults who obviously care about the child's improvement, 3) the reward factor of having success marked in small observable increases in performance output, 4) the reduction in tension that results when all concerned are involved totally in a prescribed series of activities, and 5) the role of the clinician as friend and protector.

What are your judgments regarding some of these questions? I seriously question whether crawling should become a physical education activity even if it is shown to improve reading performance (and I doubt that it will). I would view it, if indeed it is shown to be effective, as a remedial reading activity rather than a physical education activity. In answering this question for yourself, you must examine closely your views on the potential relationship between physical education and academic learning. Does a belief in mind-body unity necessarily mean that physical education must, if possible, be used as a vehicle for improving the mind? Or can physical education exist merely for its own sake—for the sake of the experiences gained from participating in the activities themselves? When you formulate a viewpoint on a specific phenomenon such as the Doman-Delacato system, you should recognize that your viewpoint will reflect your judgments on these much deeper and ultimately more important questions.

BODY IMAGE AND PERCEPTUAL–MOTOR DEVELOPMENT

For many years now, experts in psychology, psychiatry, child development, and physical education have attributed significance to the role that early motor experiences play in how a child perceives his physical and social world. Arthur Steinhaus has suggested that much of our knowledge of the world comes through our muscle sense; i.e., unless we had held an orange or thrown a ball, we would merely see a circle instead of a sphere when we look at the moon. Jean Piaget, the eminent Swiss scholar, believes that concepts of force have their origins in childhood when heavy objects are manipulated or immovable objects are pushed against. Psychiatrists believe that an individual's ability to trust others is determined, at least in part, by his ability to trust the movements of his own body. Reading specialists suggest that some problem learners need certain types of motor activity in order to develop their perceptual readiness to read. Optometrists now regard certain childhood vision problems as problems in motor coordination, and it is not at all uncommon to have balance beam and jump rope activities prescribed for visual problems.

While not all of this increased interest in early motor experiences is undergirded by a unitary point of view, most of it does rely, either implicitly or explicitly, on a theory of perception which views vision and movement as interdependent modalities. In other words, our spatial orientation to the physical environment and our social orientation to the social environment, depend in part on the quality and quantity of childhood motor experience.

One of the most thorough explanations of the basic importance of early motor experiences, and the one most widely known within professional physical education, has been provided by Newell Kephart. His book, *The Slow Learner in the Classroom,* has become a classic in elementary education. While the basis for Kephart's orientation is the development of readiness skills that allow children to perform academic skills, his terms and concepts have been widely adopted by educators also interested in social skills and emotional development.

The basic concept undergirding all this is that our own bodies are the point of reference from which we organize and interpret sensory information (tactile, kinesthetic, visual, etc.). Since there are no directions in external space, the body becomes the point of origin for all spatial relationships, even those among objects outside of the body. It is an easy task for any elementary school child to look at several classmates sitting to one side of a classroom and to determine that Nancy is sitting to the left of Johnny. It is a bit easier to appreciate the skill involved in moving along a crowded school corridor, and it is even easier for physical educators to recognize the degree of skill necessary to dribble successfully down a basketball floor on a fast break. Each of these tasks, however, is dependent on perceived relationships among stationary and moving objects, and this ability is, in turn, the result of a series of developmental tasks which are largely learned through motor experiences. The sheer quantity of experience needed to progress through these developmental steps is enormous, but most children are provided the opportunity for the necessary random experimentation with their environment which eventually brings about the needed abilities. Some children, however, do not progress as rapidly as others, and some even fall far enough behind their age groups that they exhibit serious behaviour and learning problems when they reach the elementary school.

The basic developmental step from which this all develops is called laterality.[14] Laterality can be defined as an internal awareness of the two sides of the body and their difference. Laterality is learned through experimentation with the movement of the two halves of the body, and the primary form this experimentation takes is balance activities. The spatial direction "right" and the visual recognition of "right" grow out of this internal awareness of the sides of the body. Kephart[15] has pointed out that laterality should not be confused with handedness or lateral dominance; a concept that is important to the Doman-Delacato system. There is no evidence that laterality (Kephart) and lateral dominance (Doman-Delacato) are related in any way.

After a child has developed a fairly solid laterality, he begins to project the directional concepts he has learned into external space, and this is called directionality. Spatial directions and relationships develop first in relation to the child himself (called subjective space or egocentric localization), and only later develop as relationships between objects (called objective space or objective localization). First, the child locates two objects independently, each in relationship to himself (sub-

---

14. Newell Kephart, *The Slow Learner in the Classroom* (Columbus: Charles E. Merrill Books, Inc., 1960), p. 42.
15. Ibid., p. 44.

objective space: the car is considered to be moving to the right throughout the visual field. In this case no shift in spatial direction is made.

subjective space: the car is considered to be moving from the outside toward the midline, and then from the midline to the outside. In this case a shift has been made in spatial direction.

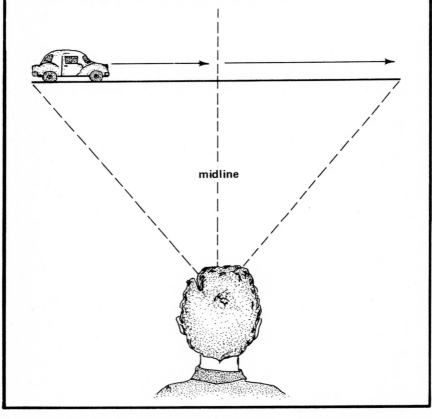

midline

FIGURE 8   Objective space, subjective space, and the midline problem.

jective space), and later he is able to conceive of one object to the right of another without the intervening step of locating each object in relation to himself (objective space).

It is as Kephart has explained, at this level, that the relatedness of the visual and motor modalities is most evident.

> The child learns that when his eyes are pointed in a given direction, this means that the object lies in that same direction. In order to learn this, he must make a complicated series of matches between the position of his eyes and the position of his hand in contacting an object. . . . When the child has learned this control, he matches the movement of his eye to a movement of his hand and thus transfers the directionality information from the kinesthetic pattern in his hand and arm to the kinesthetic pattern in his eye. This is, of course, a very precise and very complex matching procedure and a great deal of skill and learning is required to perfect it. When this matching has been perfected, the child can use his eyes as a projection device to determine directionality in space outside the reach of his hand.[16]

Without the development of this kind of directionality, a *b* and a *d* would not be different, and it is in this sense that you can begin to recognize the implications this all has for academic readiness skills.

The one most serious impediment to the development of directionality is the "midline problem." Since the human body is a nearly perfect example of bilateral symmetry, our first sense of spatial awareness is in our own laterality. In this subject space, however, we move from left to right (or vice-versa) as we cross the midline of the body. Once laterality is projected into external space as directionality, however, the subjective direction must be reversed when the midline is crossed. Following a car from one side of the visual field to the other, for example, requires an in-out change in subject space; but in objective space, the movement is in one direction. This is one of the more difficult of the developmental tasks, and many "midline problems" are evident in young children, even those of school age.

Laterality, directionality, and midline abilities combine to form a basic body image in the sense that they allow a child to know where he exists in terms of his environment and to define his spatial relationship to other objects in his environment. It gives him the confidence, for example, to move in and among other moving bodies. Bryant Cratty has provided a description of the systematic steps necessary to achieve this developmental level.

There are sixteen developmental steps in the formation of the body image and the body's position in space.

---

16. Ibid., p. 47.

1. Identification of body planes
2. Body planes in relation to objects
3. Objects in relation to body planes
4. Body part identification
5. Movements of the body
6. Laterality of the body
7. Laterality in relation to objects
8. Static objects related to laterality
9. Laterality and moving objects
10 Moving body's laterality in relation to objects
11. The left and right of objects
12. Static directionality with other people
13. Laterality of other people in relation to static objects
14. Relation of static objects to laterality of other people
15. Moving objects in relation to other's laterality
16. Laterality of others' movement[17]

Roach and Kephart[18] have developed a survey to measure a child's status along these developmental lines. The *Purdue Perceptual-Motor Survey* is a diagnostic instrument, rather than a test which yields precise data. It measures development of laterality, directionality, midline, perceptual-motor match, form perception, and occular pursuit. Any classroom teacher or physical educator could use this instrument with minimal training.

Kephart's system has been well received by many physical educators, one primary reason being that the activities he recommends have long been common to elementary physical education programs: balance beam activities, balance board, rope jumping, trampoline skills, gymnastic stunts, and rhythm games. Kephart also strongly endorses ball games (soccer, baseball, etc.) as a means for training perceptual-motor match and ocular pursuit.

Kephart, as we have seen, has promoted a theory which aims to develop a group of generalized movement skills which, if mastered, presumedly provide a readiness for the mastery of academic skills. In this sense, body image is seen as a specific developmental goal that requires the mastery of a set of sequential tasks. Others, however, have been interested in body image more for the social and emotional benefits which accrue from an intact or acceptable body image. This is not to suggest that they would not agree with the Kephart approach; it is merely to point out that others are working on body image problems at a different level or from a different point of view.

---

17. Bryant Cratty, *Developmental Sequences of Perceptual-Motor Tasks,* (Freeport: Educational Activities, Inc., 1967). 88 pgs.
18. Eugene Roach and Newell Kephart, *The Purdue Perceptual Motor Survey,* (Columbus: Charles E. Merrill Publishing Co., 1966).

Psychiatrist Joseph Jacob gave evidence of his interest in this problem when he spoke to a 1962 AAHPER special conference convened to study problems related to the development of values through sport.

> A proper appreciation by the individual of his or her own body needs constant reinforcement, not by preachments, but by proper use, proper sense of "what I can do," not too competitively tinged (this brings too much self-consciousness), and proper enjoyment. (I am not opposed to competitive games for those who enjoy them, but the basic health of the masses of young people involves leadership and activities of more routine and fundamental nature.) I believe that much more emphasis is needed in the elementary grades on the fields which give a sense of body mastery and a sense of identity, or oneness with others, so that each child has a reasonable feeling that "I can do this or that," or at least a sense of confidence that "I can learn to do this if need be."[19]

Providing this kind of experience, has been the task of physical educator, Warren Johnson, at the Children's Physical Developmental Clinic associated with the University of Maryland. Johnson[20] believes that a "critical period" exists in childhood when an adequate body image must be developed through physical movement activities; and if a satisfactory body image is not formed, a child may experience emotional, social, or academic difficulties. Johnson further suggests that therapeutic programs of physical movement activities can remedy damaged or retarded body image development. For Johnson, however, neither the nature of the body image development nor the activities used to achieve it are as precise and stereotyped as they are in the Kephart system. The key, according to Johnson, is to approach children on the level of big muscle play activities, which he believes to be the level which most contributes to psycho-social development in childhood.

It should be mentioned at this point that the relationships between movement activities and the development of body image presented in this chapter have been of a cause and effect nature. Each of the above mentioned experts suggests programs which they believe *cause* improvement in body image, which in turn supposedly effect improved academic, social, and emotional functioning. The assumption is that each child should have an intact body image which would allow him or her to function to the limit of his capabilities. It is a long step, and one that cannot be logically taken, from this position to a position which suggests that improvement or excellence in specific sports skills will

---

19. Joseph Jacob, "Psychiatry, The Body Image, and Identity," in *Values in Sport,* AAHPER, 1963, p. 30.
20. Warren Johnson, "Critical Periods, Body Image, and Movement Competency in Childhood," *Symposium on Integrated Development,* Purdue University, 1964, pp. 55-57.

enhance self-esteem; i.e., will improve the view that a boy or girl has of himself or herself.

There is ample evidence that success in athletic skills enhances a boy's self-esteem, especially in adolescence, but this phenomenon is not a correlate of the causative relationship that body-image specialists have suggested. The self-esteem gained by success in athletic skills is the result of increased status in a peer group which values the particular skill in question. The more the skill is valued, the greater the potential for increased status with success. The status, however, is not caused by the physical performance itself. The increased status is due to the fact that the person is quite a bit better than average in skills that are considered to be important by the peer group. If every student reached the particular level of skill, the status would automatically disappear. It is status, not skill development, that causes the increased self-esteem. A basketball player at a small high school might be a big hero in the eyes of his peers, but his level of ability might be such that he could compete only at an intramural level in a larger high school, thus achieving no particular status through his skill. His skill in basketball might enhance his self–esteem in the former case, but not in the latter. To examine objectively the relationship between athletic skill and self–esteem, experimenters will have to control the status factor if the research is going to be meaningful.

IMPLICATIONS FOR PHYSICAL EDUCATION

Again, there are two basic categories of decisions which must be made regarding the theories and programs described in this section. First is the scientific-experimental decision about the validity of the claims made for physical activity. One of the obstacles to gaining a clear picture of the role of motor activity in the development of body image is the lack of precise measuring instruments for gathering data about body image. Like the *Purdue Perceptual–Motor Survey,* almost all tests of body image are more useful as clinical diagnostic instruments rather than as experimental data gathering instruments.

Research data dealing with relationships among the motor, emotional, intellectual, and social behaviour domains are almost all based on correlational analysis, which gives evidence of relation but not of causation. In one of the more extensive studies undertaken, Roscoe Brown[21] conducted a four-year longitudinal investigation, collecting data on fifteen variables. When he omitted the intellectual factors, and attempted to predict academic achievement from the remaining vari-

---

21. Roscoe Brown, "The Contribution of Physical Activity to the Integrated Development of Man," eds. Brown and Cratty, *New Perspectives of Man in Action,* pp. 6-17.

ables, he obtained correlations from .18 to .24, with the physical performance and emotional factors making the largest contributions. The
important point to recognize is that while these correlations were statistically significant, they were of little practical importance—a correlation of .24 accounts for less than six percent of the variance between
the two variables, thus leaving ninety-four percent of the variance
specific to the two measures. The results of experimental studies are no
more conclusive. Some studies report statistically significant gains in
emotional or intellectual performance after participation in a motor
activity program, but others report no significant gains. Bryant Cratty
has summed up the importance of more and better investigation in this
area.

> Perhaps in no other area can researchers competent in carrying out
> studies in perceptual-motor functioning make a more significant con-
> tribution. Proponents of various systems of perceptual-motor training
> continue to postulate various relationships between motor, percep-
> tual, intellectual, and emotional functioning. The data supporting
> these contentions, however, frequently contradicts the supporters of
> these theories.[22]

It would appear, then, that the most that physical educators can do as
regards these programs is to view them with cautious optimism.

The second set of decisions that can be made is in the pedagogical-
program area. If research does uncover evidence which supports the
basic ideas advanced in perceptual-motor development programs, then
physical educators will increasingly have to make decisions about the
role that such activities are to play in the elementary school physical
education program. Such activities could conceivably become the major focus of physical education in the primary grades; or the activities
could be viewed as a peripheral part of the program having only diagnostic and corrective importance. If all of this can be described as
"motor therapy," then the decision will be the extent to which motor
therapy becomes a central or peripheral element in elementary school
physical education programs. In high school and college programs,
physical activity which is primarily therapeutic or corrective in nature
has been traditionally a peripheral aspect of the total physical education
program. It will be interesting to see if this pattern is followed in the
elementary schools as well.

THE CONCEPTUAL APPROACH TO PHYSICAL EDUCATION

A new approach to physical education has recently begun to make
significant impact on college physical education, and it should be ex-

---

22. Bryant Cratty, *Movement Behaviour and Motor Learning,* 2nd edition (Philadelphia:
Lea and Febiger, 1967), p. 67.

pected that it soon will begin to make significant inroads into programs of physical education at the secondary school level. I have used the term "conceptual" to describe this approach, but you should recognize that this is an "umbrella" term that includes many different programs which operate under many different labels. Such programs are often called "foundations of physical education," "values of physical education," "fitness in the modern world," or "concepts of physical education." At some schools, this approach comprises the entire physical education program, while at others it may be only one part of the physical education requirement—usually a one semester course that acts as a first course in a total physical education requirement of two or four semesters duration.

The goals usually stated in the various conceptual approaches to physical education can be divided into two main groups: 1) appraisal goals, and 2) awareness and understanding goals. The differences among the various programs are most often the result of which group of goals receives the primary emphasis. Appraisal goals are implemented through diagnostic testing in areas such as endurance fitness, strength, motor fitness, motor ability, flexibility, and posture. The student is guided through a series of these diagnostic tests in order to develop a complete profile of his status in these abilities. Most approaches then utilize this profile in attempting to develop a program of exercise that is designed to meet the particular needs of the individual student.

Awareness and understanding goals are common to all programs that come under the umbrella of the conceptual approach to physical education. While not all programs stress appraisal goals, they do all stress awareness and understanding goals; i.e., instead of stressing the development of fitness, they stress the understanding of fitness and the awareness of how to keep yourself fit. At Texas A & M University, a "concepts" course has been developed which provides a good example of awareness and understanding goals.

COURSE OBJECTIVES

The primary purpose of this course is to acquaint students with basic knowledges, understandings and values of physical activity as it relates to optimal healthful living.

The specific objectives of the course are:

1. To develop an understanding of the role of physical education within our society.
2. To briefly acquaint the student with the human organism, its structure, function, capabilities and limitations in relation to physical activity.

3. To present information concerning the values of exercise in developing each of the many aspects of physical fitness.
4. To aid the individual in becoming aware of personal fitness needs through a testing program to evaluate physical fitness status.
5. To develop a more adequate understanding of the concepts of physical fitness, skill performance, body mechanics, posture, obesity, stress, and the value of exercise.
6. To expose the student to several programs for aiding him in becoming physically fit and more efficient in daily life.
7. To help the student understand his attitude toward physical activity.
8. To provide counseling and guidance in the selection of activities for immediate and future needs.
9. To help the student learn to perform exercise correctly.
10. To acquaint the individual with modern techniques of resuscitation (artificial respiration and artificial circulation) and the values of such methods.[23]

As you can readily see the emphasis is on "understanding," "acquainting," "becoming aware," and "helping to understand." Evaluation in such courses is almost entirely based upon the student's mastery of knowledge, and any physical performance testing (fitness or skill) is useful for the purpose of developing awareness and insight rather than for other evaluative purposes.

The teaching method used in the conceptual approach to physical education is the lecture-laboratory approach, with problem solving and experimentation being the primary methods used in the laboratory sessions. There is usually extensive use made of visual-aids in the lecture sessions, and a basic textbook is often mandatory. There is seldom any primary emphasis placed upon skill development, although some programs do attempt to advance the student's level of fitness through "homework" exercise programs.

There are several explanations that might be offered as reasons why the conceptual approach to physical education has developed rapidly and found such widespread acceptance.[24] Many educators feel that this approach is more academically respectable. William S. Carlson,[25] President of the University of Toledo, has suggested that this approach emphasizes the "education" in physical education, thus allowing physical education to achieve its proper role in an academic institution.

23. Charles Corbin, et al., *Instructor's Handbook for Concepts in Physical Education* (Dubuque: Wm. C. Brown Company Publishers, 1970), p. 1.
24. Max Cogan in a paper presented at the 73rd Annual Meeting of the National College Physical Education Association for Men, indicated that responses to his survey of trends in college programs showed a strong new emphasis on intellectual content, implemented with a lecture-laboratory approach.
25. From the Foreword of *Physical Education: A Problem-Solving Approach to Health and Fitness,* by Perry Johnson, et al. (New York: Holt, Rinehart, and Winston, 1966), p. v.

Others feel that the development of skill alone is not enough to make a student physically educated, especially at the college level.

Still another possible explanation is to be found in the changes that have occurred within the discipline of physical education. As the scope of physical education broadens to include more fields of inquiry, and as the depth of analysis within each field becomes more sophisticated, the body of knowledge in physical education will expand; and as it does, it is logical that physical educators will more and more want to pass that body of knowledge on to students via the conceptual approach to physical education. It should certainly be further expected that this approach will begin to find its way into programs of physical education at the secondary school level.

Another impetus for this innovative approach is found on a more pragmatic level. Enrollment in colleges and universities is such that it has become quite difficult to service large numbers of students in a traditional skills-oriented program of physical education. Even with thirty to forty students in each class, the strain on facilities and staff is so great that any alternate method of providing a physical education experience becomes very attractive. The lecture-laboratory method used in the conceptual approach usually allows administrators to serve twice as many students as they could with the activity course approach. For many harrassed administrators, the conceptual approach seems like an almost providential innovation.

IMPLICATIONS FOR PHYSICAL EDUCATION

The conceptual approach to physical education is likely to continue to make inroads into college and university programs and, also, to filter down to high school programs. It is also quite likely to become a controversial topic simply because it necessarily raises a question about whether students should "know about" or to "know how to do." To me there is a very substantial and basic difference between "knowing about" something and "knowing" something. To know what fitness means, you have to experience the feelings, psychological and physiological, that accompany the training effect; but to know about fitness, you do not necessarily have to experience the thing itself. The conceptual approach to physical education will provide the catalyst for examining this question closely in the future.

A second observation is that both this approach and all other approaches suggested in this chapter are aimed at improving the mind. For people who deal on a day to day basis with motor activity, physical educators seem to be amazingly receptive to any program that will improve the mind—be it a direct improvement of the mind (Doman-Delacato), an indirect improvement in the form of readiness skills

(Kephart), or the accumulation of knowledge (the conceptual approach). Perhaps this receptivity is based, at least partially, on a deeply imbedded inferiority complex that has plagued physical education for many years, and which has implicit in its manifestations the idea that mental or cognitive experiences are of greater value to the individual than are motor play experiences. Now, this is not intended to raise the old mind-body argument, which is at best an argument that has little to do with the present question.

A third observation is that more evidence is needed to support the assumption that the possession of knowledge about physical education will help students to make choices that will result in participation in beneficial physical activities. Knowing about anything is of value only if it finds outlets in behaviour patterns that enhance the individual's life.

It should also be noted that the conceptual approach to physical education has a very strong "health-orientation." When these programs are examined, it is impossible to say whether they are more health education or physical education. Perhaps what is being implied is that there is no difference between the two. If so, this should provide another interesting development, because the professions of health education and physical education now are in the process of moving toward status as independent disciplines.

Some strong reactions no doubt have been raised in your minds, simply because these are areas of professional thought which are usually accompanied by strong emotional overtones. Would you prefer the conceptual approach to the activity approach? Do you sense a kind of inferiority complex in physical education? Do you feel that there is a difference between "knowing" and "knowing about"?

WHAT QUESTIONS CAN YOU ASK ABOUT THE FOLLOWING STATEMENTS
1. Since man acts as a unified organism, it should be expected that motor experiences will influence his mental development.
2. If physical education is to gain acceptance, it must become more academically oriented.
3. In the primary grades, a large part of the child's education should be physical education.
4. If students know more about physical fitness, they will have a greater tendency to maintain an adequate level of fitness.
5. Lectures, laboratories, and text books are utilized more to enhance the physical education program in the eyes of the academic community than to provide a good physical education for the student.

6. If people cared more about helping children and less about so-called scientific proof, they would see the value in the Doman-Delacato program.

7. An adequate body image is so important to development that it should become the primary goal of elementary physical education.

8. Because of the high incidence of degenerative disease in our society, it is necessary that students learn about diet, weight control, and exercise in their physical education programs.

9. Since most children develop normally, these theories are more relevant to adapted and corrective physical education than they are to general programs.

PART THREE

A New Approach
for Physical Education

Introduction—The Nature of a Theory of Education

What follows in Part III of this text can be described as a theory of physical education. The use of the phrase "theory of education" must be clarified, especially in reference to the terms "philosophy" and "scientific theory."

Philosophy generally suggests inquiry into areas such as metaphysics, epistemology, and axiology. Philosophers are generally concerned with abstractions such as experience, knowledge, truth, nature, mind, and God. The problem with using the term "philosophy of education" is that it suggests utilizations of these categories for the purpose of guiding educational practice, but the truth of the matter is that most often knowledge developed in these categories is somewhat unrelated to the practice of education. Epistemology, for example, may be defined as the branch of philosophy that deals with relationships between the knower and the known; yet epistemological philosophers, with the exception of Jean Piaget, have over the years failed to shed any appreciable light on the conditions which affect learning.

When attempting to deal with problems of education, philosophical premises must be considered, but so must information from a host of other disciplines. Thus, an attempt to provide some systematic direction for educational practice, though the attempt may be philosophical in nature, is more than philosophy, and it is in this sense that educational philosopher Paul Hirst has made the distinction between educational philosophy and educational theory.

> The traditional view that there is a direct connection between philosophy and educational practice either totally ignores, or heavily underestimates, the significance of education theory in this sense. It

151

fails to recognize the important truth that unless philosophical beliefs are to influence it through the medium of education theory where they are considered conjointly with many other elements before any particular principles for educational practice are explicitly formulated.[1]

A major goal of Part III is to consider, philosophically, the source of meaning in physical education, but after this task is accomplished the results are used to suggest a systematic orientation to guide programs of physical education; as such, it is more correct to describe the results as a physical education theory rather than a philosophy of physical education.

A further distinction must be made between scientific and educational theory. Scientific theory attempts to describe *what is* and says nothing about *what ought to be.* The purpose of scientific theory is to describe relationships that exist, and to describe them as precisely as possible so that they can be tested and refined, thus extending the limits of knowledge. Edward Best has described the differences between the two:

> For whatever linguistic subtleties lie hidden in the statement of a scientific theory it is obvious that its purpose can never be to advise or commend a course of action. On the other hand, it would be wholly impossible to give a faithful version of one of the well-known educational theories without implying advise or, in more general terms, a prescription.[2]

Theories of education tend to originate not in questions of metaphysics or epistemology, nor in a desire to define relationships precisely, but rather in dissatisfaction with current educational practices. This was true when the theory of education-through-the-physical developed in the early part of this century, and it was equally true when human movement theory more recently began to gain widespread acceptance. Such theories, and the one suggested in the following pages, attempt to provide a specific framework within which physical education can be changed from *what is* to *what ought to be,* and the essence of each theory is, of course, in the clarification of what ought to be.

---

1. Paul Hirst, "Philosophy and Educational Theory," *Philosophy and Education,* ed. Israel Scheffler (Boston: Allyn and Bacon, Inc., 1966), p. 80.
2. Edward Best, "Common Confusions in Educational Theory," *Philosophical Analysis and Education,* ed., Reginald D. Archambault (London: Routledge and Kegan Paul, 1965), p. 40.

Chapter 8—The Role of Physical Education in the Last Quarter of the Twentieth Century

A friend of mine says that Homo sapiens *have now reached the stage of being* Homo sedentarius. *And there are only two more possible stages of evolution:* Homo sportivus *or* Homo obesus. *Americans are, at the moment, making the wrong choice.*

Jean Mayer, 1970

Physical education does not exist in a vacuum. It is part of a total educational program which involves local school systems, state organizations, regional organizations, and strong national organizations. Education is, in turn, affected by the various cultures and subcultures which together form a national society, and the national society must exist as a member of a world community. The number of factors which can influence the theory and practice of physical education is, therefore, virtually limitless. Any attempt to predict the possible directions in which physical education might move in the last quarter of this century must be made within a framework which takes into consideration at least the strongest of these influencing factors. This framework should include judgments about the interactions among societal, individual, and educational factors.

FOR SOCIETY: A GLOOMY FUTURE

It is difficult to find a forecast for the future that is at all bright. Scientists, politicians, public speakers, newscasters, novelists, and artists all reflect the general feeling of doom and gloom which seems to pervade any attempt to look into the future. A myriad of societal problems is brought into each home every evening, and for many they appear in

153

living color. The proliferation of mass media has created what Marshall McLuhan has called the "global village" in which each of us is made constantly and vividly aware of contemporary threats to human existence. All of this has created a kind of mind-set toward the future which can only be described as fear—fear of disorder, fear of injustice, fear of economic failure, fear of poverty, and fear of disease.

It is too easy, however, merely to catalog the many ills that beset us and to suggest that the enormity of the problems has created the fear. Society has faced enormous problems before; yet has met them with an underlying faith in the future. This faith is not nearly so evident today, and neither the number or depth of the problems is enough to explain its absence.

What is different about today, and the underlying cause for the doomsday predictions, is that for the first time man is beginning to question his rational capacity to deal with societal problems by improving his technology. The development of nuclear weaponry was frightening enough, but not nearly so much as the growing fear that man might be unable to control the use of these weapons. Since the dawn of the industrial revolution, man has depended upon technological progress as a means not only for meeting his problems, but also as a basis for an optimistic view of the future. Today, however, technology not only does not seem to be the saviour it was once thought to be, but its side effects now can be seen as mankind's greatest threats—the doomsday weapons of military technology, the social pollution created by unplanned urbanization and over population. This dent in man's faith in the all-encompassing problem solving ability of technological progress is being filled by a growing doubt and fear of the future.

What this has to do with the theory and practice of physical education is difficult to assess. Physical educators and their students have to live with this future just as others do. The most foolish, dangerous response would be to suggest that it has little to do with physical education.

The response on the professional level is the easiest to gauge. It can be seen now in the AAHPER's Committee on Professional Services to Ethnic Minority Groups, and Project Man's Environment. It can be seen also in the new interest being shown in programs of physical education designed specifically to help remedy problems encountered in ghetto areas and in the growing emphasis on lifetime sports which can supposedly help to buffer the anxiety that is the natural by-product of civilized, contemporary life. These programs, though tremendously important, are, however, largely peripheral in nature. Designed to help meet specific societal needs, they have only minor influence on the evolution of the theory and practice of physical education. To gauge accurately the possible avenues of movement for physical education, it is much more profitable to examine the individual's role within society, and the influence of all this on general educational theory.

FOR THE INDIVIDUAL: ALIENATION, ANOMIE, OR ACCEPTANCE

In one of their popular songs of several years ago, John Lennon and Paul McCartney provided a general description of contemporary man that finds great acceptance among today's social critics: A nowhere man, living in a nowhere land, without any particular point of view, and without any clear idea of where he is headed. In the more scholarly literature, one finds various labels attached to descriptions of particular facets of his behaviour: a "marketer," an "adjusted other-directed," a "role-player," an "organization man," a "middle-class male child." Most social critics would agree that man has been somewhat cut adrift from the traditional guideposts which gave security to his ongoing existence. Things have been changing too rapidly, and contemporary man has been bearing the psychological and emotional burden of that change. Social critic, Kenneth Kenniston, has spoken of the nature of that burden.

> Increasingly, the vocabulary of social commentary is dominated by terms that characterize the sense of growing distance between men and their former objects of affection. Alienation, estrangement, disaffection, anomie, withdrawal, disengagement, separation, noninvolvement, apathy, indifference, and neutralism—all of these terms point to a sense of loss, a growing gap between men and their social world. The drift of our time is away from connection, relation, communion and dialogue, and our intellectual concerns reflect this conviction. Alienation, once seen as imposed *on* men by an unjust economic system, is increasingly chosen *by* men as their basic stance toward society.[1]

Man has always been able to define his relationship to society by referring to the stable traditions associated with family structure, community structure, occupational hierarchy, church, and social mores. With the accelerated rate of change that characterizes life in a technocracy, these points of reference not only are less easily defined, but some seem to be disappearing entirely, while others change so quickly that they provide no basis for defining relationships in any stable way. When his relationships to his social environment become unclear, man comes

---

1. Kenneth Kenniston, *The Uncommitted: Alienated Youth In American Society* (New York: Dell Publishing Co., 1960), p. 4.

under a great deal of stress, and it is this that plagues modern man, contributing to the high incidence of mental illness, emotional disturbance, psychosomatic illness, and general anxiety. Faced with the psychological and emotional stress inherent in his social environment, modern man drifts into or chooses alienation, suffers anomie, or comes to some sort of limited acceptance of his precarious social existence.

Alienation most often characterizes much of man's behaviour in the technocracy. Erich Fromm has defined alienation as follows.

> By alienation is meant a mode of experience in which the person experiences himself as an alien. He has become, one might say, estranged from himself. He does not experience himself as the center of his world, as the creator of his own acts.[2]

Man feels alienated when he no longer believes that he has control over his own destiny; when he feels that he is being pulled along by the course of events and the impersonal forces of society. To overcome his feelings of alienation, man often "drops out" of some portion of society, or in some cases all of his social behaviour is affected.

Anomie refers to the personal disorientation, anxiety, and social isolation that characterizes the behaviour of many who cannot cope adequately with the stress of life. Anomie can also refer to those who seem to be coping with their social environment but are paying such a terrible price that they "break down" suddenly.

The majority of people, of course, come to accept technocratic existence in most phases of their life. While they experience some tension and anxiety, they have found ways to cope with this aspect of modern life; and although they may not see their way of life as the "ideal," they accept it as a reasonable compromise with the social, political, and economic forces which make the technocracy go. Many accept a degree of alienation in their economic lives in order to practice a degree of individuality and freedom in their social lives. Some accept a degree of alienation in their political existence while attempting to achieve a higher degree of freedom in their economic lives.

This seems to be the plight of modern man, at least if one is willing to accept the consensus of critics who attempt to analyze man's relationships with his environment; writers such as Karl Jaspers, Rollo May, George Orwell, David Riesman, and Carl Jung. In response to this predicament, several concepts have been developed, and they tend to appear whenever solutions are sought which might help man to arrive at more acceptable relationships. In their more popular forms, they appear as "autonomy" in the works of David Reisman, as the "fully

---

2. Erich Fromm, *The Sane Society* (Greenwich, Conn.: Fawcett Publications, 1955), p. 111.

functioning person," in the works of Carl Rogers, or as "self-actualization" in the works of Abraham Maslow. The denotation of such terms
always involves self-sufficiency, independence, self-reliance, and individuality. In the lingo of the youth culture, it comes out as "doing your
own thing." It perhaps is best explained by Abraham Maslow's descriptive phrase "not-needing-other-than-itself-in-order-to-be-itself." Wherever contemporary life is examined, these phrases are likely to be
utilized in some way, and nowhere is this more true than in the literature and thought which speaks about questions associated with contemporary education.

FOR EDUCATION: SELF-CRITICISM AND RENEWAL

Almost all of the literature dealing with analyses of contemporary
education is critical. The more severe criticism comes from analysts
such as Paul Goodman whose *Compulsory Mis-Education* is typical of
the blanket indictment of public education and the radical innovative
suggestions for improving its status. What is truly amazing is that the
more mild and constructive criticism is typified by writer-educator
Charles Silberman, in a book he has chosen to entitle, *Crisis in the
Classroom.* Other men who are reasonable, realistic, and conscientious
in their criticism, agree that American public education badly needs
change. John Gardner, former HEW Secretary, has said that it educates
for obsolescence; psychologist Jerome Bruner has said that it does not
develop intelligence; media expert Marshall McLuhan believes that it
is irrelevant; educator John Holt has observed that it is based almost
wholly on fear; cybernetic expert Norbert Wiener believes that it
shields children from reality; psychologist Edgar Friedenberg has
shown that it punishes creativity and independence; and psychoanalyst
Carl Rogers has said that it avoids the promotion of significant learnings.[3]

Has the American system of public education largely failed? You
should recognize that such a question cannot be answered without
making some determination about what the system has been trying to
do. Thus, the question of success or failure can be judged both in terms
of the goals of the system and the degree of success the system has had
in achieving its goals.

In terms of its *stated* goals, there is very little evidence that American public education has accomplished its purpose. Of the 1938 goals
established by the Educational Policies Commission—self-realization,

3. Postman and Weingartner, *Teaching as a Subversive Activity* (New York: Delacorte
Press, 1969), p. xiv.

human relationships, economic efficiency, and civic responsibility—
only the area of economic efficiency rates any measure of successful
achievement; and in terms of the 1961 revision—to develop the rational
powers of students—there is, again, little evidence of large scale success.

We have always assumed that our system of free public education
would act as a leveling influence among the diversity of economic,
regional, and ethnic subcultures which populate this nation. In 1966,
the Coleman Report[4] branded this assumption as almost universally
untrue and clearly indicated the total failure of public education to
overcome and prevent a growing alienation among students in
minority groups. Minority children are at an understandable disadvan-
tage in verbal and non-verbal skills when they enter school, but the
assumption has always been that our system of public education would
minimize these differences, thus creating a climate of equal opportunity. The Coleman Report, however, produced data which showed
that during their twelve years in school these initial differences are not
lessened, but rather are increased. School factors—such as libraries,
facilities, laboratories, teacher training, salaries, etc.—bore relatively
little relationship to the growing differences, but the attitude survey
used in the study uncovered one significant factor.

> For example, a pupil attitude factor, which appears to have a stronger
> relationship to achievement than do all the "school" factors together,
> is the extent to which an individual feels that he has some control over
> his own destiny.[5]

The last clause of the above quotation is almost a duplicate of the
definition of alienation given earlier in this chapter. This report, as
Harvard educator James Kent[6] has said, exploded many myths about
American public education and showed that children who "survive"
this education are not equipped to cope with the technology-oriented,
multiracial world they must enter.

From another point of view, however, the system of public education has worked quite well. There are many critics who suggest that the
"de facto" purpose of American public education is to fill the needs of
the technocracy, in terms of workers, managers, researchers, and executives. Evidence of the efficiency of the system can be seen in the
response of the system to the post-Sputnik need for scientists; a need

---

4. James Coleman et al. *Equality of Educational Opportunity* (Washington: United States
Government Printing Office, 1966), 737 pp.
5. Ibid., p. 23.
6. James Kent, "The Coleman Report: Opening Pandora's Box," *Phi Delta Kappan*
49:242-245, January, 1967.

that has been met so satisfactorily that many top graduate schools have now cut down on their graduate enrollments in the sciences. The system accomplishes these purposes by a process of "weeding-out," primarily through a massive system of testing and grading. The high schools weed-out for the colleges and also supply workers for the lower levels of the technocracy; the colleges further weed-out for the graduate schools and also supply the lower level technicians; and the graduate schools weed-out for the upper levels of government, industry, and the professions. Thus, the entire system seems to operate so as to faithfully produce Conant's "academically talented" fifteen percent, who are necessary to maintain and improve the technocracy.

From this point of view, the critics believe the system to be a failure in terms of its goals and purposes. They see it as an efficient system with invalid goals, mostly because those who have been weeded-out consider their experience to be irrelevant and debilitating, while those who survive the process have become conditioned to competitive and organizational behaviours that take great tolls on their psychological and emotional lives. What is important to a student in this system is his I.Q., G.P.A., and S.A.T., because these indicate and control his success or failure. Educator-psychologist Jerome Bruner, has labeled this type of system a "meritocracy."

> A meritocracy, however, implies a system of competition in which students are moved ahead and given further opportunities on the basis of their achievement, with position in later life increasingly and irreversibly determined by earlier school records. Not only later educational opportunities but subsequent job opportunities become increasingly fixed by earlier school performance. The late bloomer, the early rebel, the child from an educationally indifferent home—all of them in a full-scale meritocracy, become victims of an often senseless irreversibility of decision.[7]

One of the important points to recognize in the midst of all this criticism is that much of it is *self-criticism;* that is, educators themselves are perhaps the most concerned about the state of educational affairs, and this force of self-criticism is providing a solid base for renewal and change. This force for renewal and change accurately reflects the general concern within society for experiences which will help young people to pursue meaningful lives in the technocracy. Thus, the literature of contemporary education is replete with terms such as self-realization, self-actualization, fully-functioning, free expression, liberated mind, authenticity, autonomy, and sensitivity training. Content is more and more being examined in terms of its meaningfulness and relevancy to

---

7. Jerome Bruner, *The Process of Education* (Cambridge: Harvard University Press, 1960), p. 77.

life in the technocracy, and the process of education is more and more being examined in terms of its psychological and emotional effects on students. It seems to be characteristic of Americans that they want "things" to be "better" for their children, and, increasingly, "things" are being defined in terms of quality and authenticity; and "better" is being defined in terms of more meaningful, rather than just more in number.

It is within this general framework that physical education will evolve in the last quarter of the twentieth century. The overriding factor in society and in education is the search for meaning, and it should be expected that this will be a dominant theme in education for some time to come. With this in mind, it should now be possible to make some judgments about how physical education will reflect this theme both in content and in the process of physical education.

FOR PHYSICAL EDUCATION: A TIME FOR CHOOSING

For physical educators, a time of choosing and decision-making lies ahead. Certainly, some things will remain constant, and there are other matters about which enough evidence exists so we can make intelligent predictions. It is difficult to predict the course of theory and practice in school programs of physical education, however, and the only thing that appears certain is that some far-reaching decisions will have to be made.

Part I of this text speaks to some matters about which rather certain predictions can be made. The activities of physical education will continue to have historical, cultural, and personal significance. Indeed, we might expect that these activities will become more culturally important and also of greater personal significance. Sociologist David Riesman[8] has suggested that the sphere of play can increasingly become the sphere for the development of skill and competence in the art of living. He notes that in the technocracy, a person's play or recreational life is one of the few remaining spheres of activity in which autonomy may be achieved. Sport and dance activities could become of enormous importance culturally and personally.

Karl Jaspers, the great German philosopher, has described in beautiful metaphors his belief that sport can be an important avenue for the expression of personal liberty in the face of an alienating technocracy.

> Contemporary man, when engaged in sport, does not indeed become a Hellene, but at the same time he is not a mere fanatic of sport. We

---

8. David Riesman, *The Lonely Crowd* (New Haven: Yale University Press, 1950), pp. 326-347.

see him when he is engaged in sport as a man who, strapped in the strait-waistcoat of life, in continuous peril as if engaged in active warfare, is nevertheless not crushed by his almost intolerable lot, but strikes a blow in his own behalf, stands erect to cast his spear.[9]

We might expect, therefore, that the activities of physical education will assume even greater importance in the lives of men and women; and in so doing, it is not unreasonable to expect that they might take on new cultural roles, possibly being important with reference to psychological and emotional survival.

Another assumption that might be reasonably made is that physical education will enter a period of rapid change in terms of theory, organization, and practice. Chapter Two of this text showed that it has operated for the most part under one unified theory for the past fifty years. There is much to suggest that this theory—education-through-the-physical—has lost its position of preeminence; and although it may be assumed that another will evolve into a position of prominence, that change will not take place without far-reaching effects on the entire profession of physical education. The fact that general educational theory and practice is in a period of rapid change will only heighten the possibility of far-reaching changes in physical education.

A third factor that might be accurately predicted is the emergence of a discipline of physical education, although it may well operate under a different label such as human movement, or sport and exercise science. Within this discipline, scholarly work will progress and specialized fields will continue to develop, even to the point that specializations within the sub-disciplines may emerge. Thus, within the sub-field of sport psychology, investigators will probe further into variables associated with learning, and specialists may develop in sub-sub-fields such as feedback control, reinforcement, and practice and rest distribution. All of this scholarly and research effort should provide a constant flow of information into the profession of physical education; and if ways can be found to translate this information from the precise and technical terms of research into the practical terms of teaching, we might expect that physical educators will rapidly improve their grasp of the theoretical and technical aspects of their teaching and the effects of the activities on their students.

While the aforementioned predictions can be made with a reasonable degree of certainty, they do not give any substantial indication of what physical education programs will be like in the future. It is easy to predict the further evolution of a specialized discipline, but it is quite

---

9. Karl Jaspers, *Man in the Modern Age* (Garden City: Doubleday and Co., Inc., 1951), p. 79.

difficult to predict what kinds of physical education programs will exist at the various levels of formal education. In Part II of this text, an attempt was made to survey critically the major approaches to physical education which now appear to possess the greatest potential for influencing the future course of the profession: 1) physical education for physical fitness or education-of-the-physical, 2) physical education as a means for achieving the goals of general education or education-through-the-physical, and 3) physical education as human movement or movement education. While the other approaches suggested in Chapter Seven will no doubt influence the future course of the profession, they do not appear to have the makings of major theoretical positions. It may develop that physical education theory and practice will pursue an essentially eclectic approach in the future, but it is more likely that one theoretical position will exert the greatest influence just as the education-through-the-physical philosophy has done during the past fifty years.

The fact that we are now in the embryonic stage of investigation and discussion about physical education theory—a stage that will necessarily precede any important decision-making stage—was made evident in a recent article in the *Journal of Health, Physical Education, and Recreation*,[10] where six people, associated at various levels with the profession, offered philosophic interpretations of physical education. Anthony Annorino, a university professor in physical education, suggested a refinement of the traditional education-through-the-physical approach; one that would place greater emphasis on the "unique" objectives or organic, neuromuscular, and interpretive development. Paul Varnes, a departmental chairman of intramurals and recreation, suggested that the profession should concentrate on enhancing the "physical-me" concept of the child and prepare him for his recreational life. Betty Lou Murphy, another university teacher, made a case for the study of sport as the proper focus for the profession of physical education. Edward Kozloff, a junior high school teacher of physical education, viewed physical education as the primary means for developing skills necessary for successful participation in a democratic society. Charles Schmidt, a college senior majoring in physical education, talked about exciting experiences and developing "physical self-awareness." Evelyn Triplett, a college physical educator, indicated that fitness should be the primary emphasis in physical education, but her definition of total fitness placed her more in the education-through-the-physical than in

---

10. "A Personal Philosophy of Physical Education," *Journal of Health, Physical Education, and Recreation* 41:24-30, June, 1970.

the strict physical fitness category. The six contributions illustrate the kind of introspection that is now occuring within professional physical education.

One of the keys that will help you to better understand the potential of theories of physical education is how well they can be adapted to fit the general mood of change that now prevails within society in general and education in particular. It appears that a successful theory of physical education must evidence potential in contributing to self-realization, self-actualization, fully-functioning-personhood, and other such goals. Future theories of physical education will have to focus on providing meaningful experiences for students, experiences that can help them to achieve a fuller, more authentic existence in the technocracy. In several of the personal philosophies cited above, you can recognize a trend in this direction in the use of such terms as "enhancing the physical-me" and "physical self-awareness." How well, then, do the major theories of physical education rate in terms of their "meaning-making potential"?

It seems doubtful to me that, in their present forms, any of the three major theories of physical education have enough meaning-making potential to be successful in a meaning-centered education. The physical fitness viewpoint might suggest that the *feelings* associated with vigorous exercise and a trained state are a source of meaning. The phenomenological evidence for this type of claim is abundant and has been summed up well by existential philosopher Jean-Paul Sartre, whose intellectual pursuits focus on sources of meaning.

> The initial feeling of enterprise, the fulfillment of fitness and the subsequent fatigue belong to one cycle of the full measure of corporal existence or of being-in-the-world. Concomitant ingredients are emotional curiosity, the peak of satisfaction and the plane of quiet exhaustion concluding the cycle.[11]

What is also obvious, however, is that the meaningful feelings associated with "using oneself fully" are entirely dependent upon the type of exercise involved. A two-mile run in a park during the twilight hours might provide great meaning, but it is doubtful that a ten-minute bout on a treadmill would produce much meaningful experience, even though the physiological effects might be the same. A physical fitness approach to physical education does not in itself differentiate between those two experiences. Something would have to be added to the physical fitness approach but this addition might well subordinate the physical fitness factor to a point where the approach could no longer be

---

11. Jean-Paul Sartre, *Philosophical Psychoanalysis* (New York: Philosophical Library, 1953), pp. 117-118.

described as an education-of-the-physical theory. It does not appear that the physical education as physical fitness viewpoint does in itself possess sufficient meaning-making potential to survive as the dominant theory of physical education.

Education-through-the-physical seems to have a better chance to survive as the dominant theory if it can be reinterpreted to emphasize the kinds of goals that are becoming popular in general education. By its very nature—physical education as a means for achieving the goals of general education—this theory should be easily adaptable to new approaches to education. Even in its original forms, education-through-the-physical emphasized meaning-making potential, as is evidenced by Jesse Feiring Williams' consistent insistence that physical education would be judged ultimately by the contribution it made to fine living. Recent interest in physical education theory suggests, however, that this approach has not produced the desired results. Perhaps, as I suggested earlier, the biggest reason for the lack of meaningful results has been the insistence on a multi-goal approach—organic, neuromuscular, interpretive, social, and emotional. In attempting to be all things to all men, education-through-the-physical has not focused on the nature of meaningful experiences enough to be able to promote them in school programs. In attempting to help students become fit, skilled, emotionally stable, knowledgeable, and good citizens, education-through-the-physical has not only neglected meaning-making, but too often has provided programs that tend to prevent the experiencing of meaning in activity. In order to re-focus on its meaning-making potential, education-through-the-physical would necessarily have to undergo some extensive changes both on the theoretical and practical levels.

Several of the major promoters of physical education as human movement, Eleanor Metheny in particular, have placed great emphasis on the importance of meaningful experiences in physical education; and in this sense, the movement movement has somewhat of a theoretical head start over the other two major approaches. This might be one reason why the concept of human movement has met with extensive acceptance and has provided a potential focus for the discipline of physical education. There seem to be two major obstacles—one theoretical and one applied or practical—that the movement movement will have to overcome if it is to become the theory which will contribute to a meaning-centered education.

The theoretical obstacle is that movement itself will have to be defended as the source of meaning in physical education activities. Few would doubt that playing handball provides meaningful experiences for the players, but there might be considerable debate about the source of that meaning. The meaning is difficult to conceptualize and difficult to verbalize. It is at least debatable that the main source of meaning is attributable to movement experiences. Others may argue that the source of meaning lies in play, sport, exercise, or competition. This debate will have to be decided in favor of human movement if it is to assume the central role in physical education theory.

Another obstacle to the meaning-making potential of the movement movement is in applying the theory in programs of physical education. It is easy to see how movement education programs in the elementary schools have meaning-making potential, but it is much less clear how high school and college programs based on human movement alone will provide significant meaning-making experiences. A major obstacle is the tendency to intellectualize physical education at this level, to take it out of the gymnasium, dance studio, and playing field and to put it into the classroom. This is not to suggest that a conceptual approach to physical education cannot be meaningful—that is not the point of contention here. What is being suggested is that the conceptual approach provides a different kind of meaning, one that is far removed from the innate meaning of the handball court or the gymnasium.

Several contesting points of view will probably vie for dominance in the foreseeable future. The need and desire for a meaning-centered physical education is likely to be the primary criterion by which the contesting approaches will be judged. The three theories that have been examined here are certainly not the only ones that will be in contention. Recently, in fact, there has been renewed interest in the concept of sport as the source of meaning, and it should be expected that there will be considerable support for a theory of physical education that focuses on the meaning inherent in sport.

You should recognize that a different analysis of the general factors that characterize society, the individual, and education might result in different judgments about the adequacy of the three major physical education theories. The alarming increase in the incidence of diseases associated with the cardiovascular system, for example, might be considered of greater importance than the need for meaningful experience. Jean Mayer, Director of the Harvard Nutrition Laboratory and one of the foremost experts on the subject of weight control, has said that we are in the midst of a "cardiovascular plague."

> We tend to think of the plagues as forgotten dangers of the Middle Ages. But close to half of our men, and an increasing proportion of our women, are dying of one cause—cardiovascular disease and, more

specifically, coronary catastrophe. We are again in the age of the great pandemics. Our plague is cardiovascular.[12]

You might want to proceed with an analysis similar to the one presented in this chapter, except with the "cardiovascular plague" as the central theme. This would require examination of the major theories of physical education in light of this factor.

SOME PRACTICAL FACTORS

In any discussion of the evolution of educational theory, it is always healthy to mention some of the more important practical factors which might have considerable potential influence on the development of any theory.

One such factor is certainly the amount of time and money that the public will be willing to devote to programs of physical education. No theory can hope to develop programs which will produce results, if the programs consist of two thirty-minute classes a week, little equipment, and forty students in each class. The amount of meaningful experience that can be gained in such a situation is negligible. It is quite difficult to forecast the mood of the public regarding its willingness to provide for any certain kind of education, but it is certainly hoped that an increasing public interest in meaning-centered education will result in a substantial increase in the funding and time allotment for physical education. If physical education programs do not provide meaningful experiences, then no longer will public support continue.

Another factor which has in the past had significant influence on programs of physical education is the results of physical fitness tests. When draft rejections in time of war have gone up, physical education programs have emphasized physical fitness training. During the 1950's, a similar "fitness boom" started because of widespread dissemination of the results of the Kraus-Weber tests. Though promoted as tests of "minimum muscular fitness," it would be more accurate to describe them as strength and flexibility tests for the lower back. Because European children were shown to be more proficient on these exercises, a "fitness boom" started and grew rapidly with the creation of the Council on Youth Fitness and the President's Citizens Advisory Committee on the Fitness of American Youth. The AAHPER jumped on the bandwagon in 1959 with its "Operation Fitness" programs. It should be noted that

---

12. Jean Mayer, "Affluence: The Fifth Horseman of the Apocalypse," *Psychology Today* 3:47, January, 1970.

this later "fitness boom" was the first such movement that the physical education profession has dealt with and supported without drastically refocusing its other aims.

A third factor, closely related to fitness because both result from public pressure, is potential sports failures, particularly in international competition. While the impact of the Kraus-Weber research data was obviously significant, a strong case can be made which suggests that an equally significant factor in the overwhelming public acceptance of the "fitness boom" was the weak showing of the 1960 United States Olympic Team. Russia had first entered Olympic competition in 1952 and had surprised the sports world with its excellent team. By 1956, the Russians were clearly challenging the United States for Olympic supremacy. An important turning point occurred in the 1960 Olympics at Rome when the Russians had progressed to a point where they excelled not only in their traditional events but also began to win medals in events that had for sixty years been dominated by American athletes. The high jump presented a miniature picture of the entire drama. John Thomas, a twenty-year-old black high-jumper from Boston University, (note the essential elements of the American dream present in this drama) went to Rome as the world record-holder and with the reputation of the greatest jumper in the history of the sport. He was beaten! He was beaten not only by one but by two Russians (one of them being the great Valery Brumel). This single defeat may have had as much to do with public acceptance of the "fitness boom" as all the publicized data.

A fourth factor that should not be neglected is the inevitable emergence of new professional physical educators who will be the leaders in a time when the profession may have to move in new directions. The wide acceptance and persistent longevity of the education-through-the-physical philosophy must to some degree be attributed to the influence of Jesse Feiring Williams and Jay B. Nash. These men were dedicated, articulate, and particularly charismatic, and it may well be that their personalities were as much responsible for the acceptance of their philosophy as was the philosophy itself. New leaders, with new ideas, will develop, and they might command a similar following; in fact, you might be able to see some leaders today who may exert that kind of leadership.

SOME THOUGHTS ON THE FUTURE OF PHYSICAL EDUCATION THEORY

It should be expected that the near future will bring a flurry of activity about the "aims" of education, and the terms that will most likely find great acceptance are currently used in "humanistic psychology"—such as self-realization, self-actualization, peak experiences, fully function personhood, autonomy, and authenticity. These or similar terms are already beginning to be used in physical education. Adherents of the education-through-the-physical and human movement viewpoints probably will be most likely to utilize such concepts.

This author has absolutely nothing against the concepts of humanistic and existential psychology; rather he has great respect for the work of Gordon Allport, Rollo May, Abraham Maslow, and Carl Rogers. This, however, does not prevent expression of caution with reference to an aim of education (or physical education) such as self-realization. I would look with reservation, for example, on the following: "The aim of physical education is to produce a fully functioning person through the medium of physical activity." The problems as educational philosopher R. S. Peters[13] has pointed out, is that such aims presuppose standards of value which determine the kind of "self" that is to be realized or the kind of "personhood" that is "fully functioning." While self-realization sounds impressive in a statement of educational theory, it is very difficult for the teacher in the classroom to decide what sort of "self" John in the first row or Jane in the second row is supposed to be realizing, and there is always danger that some preconceived notion of "self" will inhibit or retard development of the very quality that is embodied in the aim.

No matter how inviting concepts such as "self-realization" seem, they do encourage an instrumental way of looking at education. A sometimes nebulous end is invented which the activities of education are supposed to lead toward; this being required because it has been assumed that education must be justified by reference to an aim which is extrinsic to it. This, it seems to me, has been one of the weaknesses of the education-through-the-physical viewpoint which attempts to justify physical education by reference to fitness and social development and, in doing so, promotes a utilitarian approach to the activities of physical education. The danger of this is that it risks losing the inherent meaning and significance in the activity. If badminton, for example, is promoted because it leads to approved democratic behaviour and emotional stability, there is danger that the meaning-making potential of badminton itself might be jeopardized.

Can physical education be justified by reference to the activities of physical education itself? Is *it* self-justifying? This, indeed, may be the pivotal question that must be answered. It should be obvious by now

---

13. R. S. Peters, "Must an Education Have an Aim? " *Philosophy of Education* by William Frankena (New York: The Macmillan Co., 1965), pp. 44-51.

that the author is convinced that the activities of physical education are self-justifying; that learning to play badminton or handball skillfully is worthwhile and sufficient cause for their inclusion in a school curriculum.

There is a quality of life which is self-justifying. When education is seen in this perspective, the primary aim becomes that of providing experiences which will allow students to come to know that quality of life. As Peters has suggested, it is a matter of helping those on the "outside" to get on the "inside" of the activities.

> Now anyone who has managed to get on the inside of what is passed on in schools and universities, such as science, music, art, carpentry, literature, history, and athletics, will regard it as somehow ridiculous to be asked what the point of his activity is. The mastery of the "language" carries with it its own delights, or "intrinsic motivation," to use the jargon. But for a person on the outside it may be difficult to see what point there is in the activity in question. Hence the incredulity of the uninitiated when confronted with the rhapsodies of the mountain-climber, musician, or golfer. Children are to a large extent in the position of such outsiders. The problem is to introduce them to a civilized outlook and activities in such a way that they can get on the inside of those activities for which they have aptitude.[14]

The role of the teacher becomes that of initiator as he tries to help others know and appreciate the qualities and meanings that he considers to be worthwhile.[15] The remainder of this text presents a theory based on the belief that the activities of physical education are intrinsically worthwhile and sufficient to justify their existence in our schools. I hope to show that this perspective can best maximize the meaning-making potential of physical education during this last quarter of the twentieth century.

WHAT QUESTIONS CAN YOU ASK ABOUT THE FOLLOWING STATEMENTS

1. The "cardiovascular plague" is something immediate and important and physical education should gear itself toward combatting this problem.
2. The reason that men like to play golf every weekend is that it is the only time during the week when they feel like they are their own bosses.
3. If we bring politics and social problems into physical education, we are just going to spoil what we have.

---

14. R. S. Peters, "Reason and Habit: The Paradox of Moral Education" *Philosophy of Education*, p. 109.
15. R. S. Peters, "Education as Initiation," *Philosophical Analysis and Education,* Reginald Archambault, ed. (London: Routledge and Kegan Paul, 1965), pp. 87-111.

4. The problem with contemporary society is that we have too much leisure.
5. The aim of physical education should be to achieve autonomy in self-actualizing leisure.
6. Physical education should not be swayed by whatever educational theory happens to be popular.
7. The American way of life has always been best reflected in sport, and we should cling to that as our guide for the future of physical education.
8. The greatest failure of physical education has been that many students come to dislike sport and dance because of their participation in physical education.

Chapter 9—The Derivation of a Conceptual Definition of Physical Education

For, to speak out once for all, man only plays when in the full meaning of the word he is a man, and he is only completely a man when he plays.
Friedrich Schiller, 1902

AN ANALYSIS OF TWO DEFINITIONAL EFFORTS

The concept of physical education is an abstraction and tends to defy conceptual or logical analysis and definition.[1] We could merely point to a certain activity in-process and say "that is physical education," or point to another and say "that is not physical education." It is a very difficult task, however, to compose a logical definition for such ostensive judgments.

Jesse Feiring Williams conceptualized physical education as follows:

> Physical Education is the sum of man's physical activities, selected as to kind, and conducted as to outcomes.[2]

This definition does not adequately express the meaning of the concept of physical education. The class (man's physical activity) does not in itself imply any particular meaning; its choice places physical education along side such activities as digging ditches, typing, chewing, and breathing, for they are all forms of physical activity. These activities do not connote feelings which are similar to those associated with golf, tennis, or baseball. Neither does this definition offer any real basis for

---

1. A conceptual or logical definition places the subject (species) in a class (genus) and then differentiates it from other members of the same class. See page 7.
2. Jesse Feiring Williams, *The Principles of Physical Education, 6th ed.,* (Philadelphia: W. B. Saunders Co., 1954), p. 9.

differentiation among the activities. It suggests that there are certain "kinds" of physical activity that comprise the field of physical education, and that these activities are to be conducted in terms of certain "outcomes," but neither the kinds of activity nor the outcomes are stipulated, therefore, the definition provides no real basis for understanding the meaning of the concept. An adequate definition requires, at least, delineation of the restrictions which would clearly delimit the "kinds" of physical activity which are logically subsumed under physical education.

The definition developed by Camille Brown and Rosalind Cassidy is one of the most thorough attempts to define physical education.

> Physical education is the school program of the study of the art and science of human movement needed in today's world designed for development through movement, and human performance restricted to expressive form and/or restricted through the use of representations of environmental reality.[3]

Here, physical education is placed in the class of human movement, which is defined as "the change in position of the individual in time-space resulting from force developed from the individual's expenditure of energy interacting with the environment."[4] The differentiae in this definition are: 1) the school program, 2) today's world, 3) development, 4) human performance, 5) expressive form, and 6) representations of environmental reality.

It is my opinion that "school program" signifies a restricted application of the concept of physical education rather than a restriction on the concept itself. If an attempt is being made to generalize and explain what is meant by "a physical education experience," then it is doubtful that it can be restricted in this way, thus ruling out the possibility that such experiences might occur in a YMCA program or a summer recreation program.

The "needed in today's world" restriction refers to judgments that physical educators must make about the relative values of activities; and in a certain sense, this restriction is implied in the word education. The "development" restriction excludes all human movement which has some objective other than individual development, and it can be defined in the narrow sense of therapeutic exercise or in the broader sense of the general development of the whole man.

The fourth restriction deals with "human performance" which Brown and Cassidy defined as "moving and not specifically for his own

---

3. Brown and Cassidy, *Theory in Physical Education* (Philadelphia: Lea and Febiger, 1963), p. 36.
4. Ibid., p. 33.

development but for some other purpose, but moving."[5] This restriction is not totally satisfactory because of its open-ended nature (some other purpose), which does in fact make necessary the limitations imposed by the fifth and sixth restrictions. There also seems to be some contradiction between the third and fourth restrictions (development and human performance); the former excludes all human movement that does not have development as the primary objective and the latter gives approval to human movements which have purposes other than development.

The "expressive form" and "representations of environmental reality" restrictions clarify the "other purpose" suggested in the fourth restriction. While the expressive form restriction is abundantly clear, the meaning and purpose of the sixth restriction is rather vague. It can be seen easily that the swimming pool represents the "reality" of the lake or ocean, but it is less clear what "reality" the golf course or the handball court represents; and if this restriction implies, as it seems to, that these activities be carried on so that students can learn to cope with the "realities," then it becomes even more confusing, especially when an activity such as fencing is considered.

It can be seen from this analysis of these two illustrative efforts that a logical definition requires first and foremost a judgment about classification of the subject, and then the development of a set of restrictions which clearly differentiate the subject from other members of the chosen class. While I do not agree with the Brown and Cassidy statement, it provides a good example of how to derive a logical definition.

DETERMINING THE CLASSIFICATION

There are several classes under which physical education can be subsumed as a species, without damaging the "logical" adequacy of its definition: physical activity, health, human movement, and sport. Since the "meaning" of the concept would emerge differently when derived from each of these classes, it becomes useful to distinguish between "logical meaning" and "psychological meaning." The former is satisfied more by the development of adequate restrictions, while the latter is primarily determined by the choice of class.

If the meanings in physical education are to be appreciated to the fullest, then it will be necessary to define the concept with reference to the source of meaning inherent in the activities of physical education. An analysis of societal problems which concludes that the presence of a "cardiovascular plague" is the most serious consideration for the fu-

---

5. Ibid., p. 35.

ture of physical education naturally considers "health" to be a logically and psychologically satisfactory classification for the concept of physical education. What must be found is a classification which immediately conveys the totality of meaning so easily observed in a class of second graders seriously creating movement ideas with musical accompaniment; that which is so evident in the behaviour of sixth graders learning gymnastic skills; that obtained in a heated volleyball contest between high school seniors; and that derived from intramural competition, interscholastic competition, and leisure-time recreation. To what can we attribute the meaning? What is its source? The answer should provide the necessary classification of the concept of physical education. Let us examine the classifications of physical activity, human movement, and sport.

Physical activity, as a logical class, is essentially meaningless. While badminton can be meaningful, it is not specifically so because it is physical activity, and other forms of physical activity can be pure drudgery. Mastication and respiration are also forms of physical activity, but they bear little meaningful relationships to badminton, and, therefore, it is doubtful that they are species of the same class.

Advocates of the human movement viewpoint have suggested that that classification explains the meaning available in the activities of physical education. Eleanor Metheny,[6] in a sensitive and inspiring call for a meaning-centered philosophy of physical education, has discussed the "inherent meaningfulness of kinesthetic perception" as if the Pacinian Corpuscles could actually discriminate between two similar movement patterns and attach meaning to one but not the other. Running, for example, can be meaningful or it can be drudgery; nevertheless, the same movement pattern is involved. Do the kinesthetic receptors attach meaning to one running experience and not to the other? Obviously not, and neither Metheny nor any other advocate of the human movement position would suggest that the perception of meaning is so peripheral in nature. Metheny's "kinecept" concept is evidence of her recognition of the central nature of the perception of meaning. Kinesthetic perception, no matter how important it might be in movement experience, does not explain the experience of meaningful participation, simply because to move one's body through time-space does not inherently imply meaning. Thus, as with physical activity, when other members of the human movement class are examined, no feelings are evoked which would provide essential links with the worlds of the dance studio or the handball court. Certain forms of

---

6. Eleanor Metheny, *Connotations of Movement in Sport and Dance,* (Dubuque: Wm. C. Brown Co., Publishers, 1965), p. 105.

physical activity and human movement are meaningful to human be-
ings, but neither the concept of physical activity nor the concept of
human movement provide any real clues about the source of that meaning.

Thomas Sheehan[7] in a recent *Quest* article rejected physical
fitness, human movement, and social values from physical education
activities as potential classes for the concept of physical education, and
he concluded that "sport" was the proper focus (generic focus) or classification. While I have a considerable amount of sympathy for this
viewpoint, I do not feel that it goes far enough in attempting to place
physical education in proper perspective in terms of its meaning-
making potential. To utilize sport as the basic classification is too limiting because it explains physical education in terms of other members
of that class; in other words, in terms of other forms of sport. Thus,
physical education would be a species of sport as would professional
sport and leisure-time sport. While this might be a very useful classification in a certain sense, it does not sufficiently indicate the meaning-
making potential of physical education.

PHYSICAL EDUCATION AS A SPECIES OF PLAY

It is this author's contention that the source of meaning in physical
education is best explained by the concept of play, and that play is the
classification that is necessary in order to fully indicate its meaning-
making potential.

When a person is at play, he is *by definition* engaged in experience
which is inherently meaningful. It is interesting that the basic importance and meaningfulness of play is given recognition in ordinary language. The call is always "let's play" and almost never "let's move," or
"let's have activity," or even "let's have sport." Both the child and the
adult desire to play; and if they find meaning in their movement, it is
only to the degree that they are at play, and as the play element is
diminished, the movement loses its meaningfulness.

Johan Huizinga defined play as follows:

> Summing up the formal characteristics of play we might call it a free
> activity standing quite consciously outside "ordinary" life as being
> "not serious," but at the same time absorbing the player intensely and
> utterly. It is an activity connected with no material interest, and no
> profit can be gained by it. It proceeds within its own proper bounda-
> ries of time and space according to fixed rules and in an orderly
> manner.[8]

---

7. Thomas Sheehan, "Sport: The Focal Point of Physical Education," *Quest* 10:59-67, May,
1968.
8. Johan Huizinga, *Homo Ludens: A Study of the Play Element in Culture* (Boston:
Beacon Press, 1962), p. 13.

This definition was an important attempt to understand the significance of play. It was refined and expanded by sociologist Roger Caillois, who developed the following characteristics of play.

1. Free: it is voluntarily entered into
2. Separate: the temporal and spatial limits are defined and fixed in advance
3. Uncertain: the results and course of action are not predetermined
4. Economically unproductive: neither good nor wealth is produced
5. Regulated: underconventions that suspend ordinary laws and for the moment establish new laws which alone count, or
6. Fictive: accompanied by a make-believe, a free unreality[9]

Play is activity that is free, separate, uncertain, unproductive, and regulated or fictive. You will notice that both definitional efforts are of the conjunctive, bi-verbal type, which means that all the characteristics named must be present before the term is applicable; to the extent that any one of the characteristics is impinged upon, the degree of play which is present in the situation is lessened. You will notice that as in all bi-verbal definitions, no attempt is made to reach the meaning of the concept; instead its characteristics are cited so that we might know when the concept applies and when it does not. Thus, the less voluntary or the less uncertain any activity is, the less the play element is present.

No attempt is made here to explain why play is inherently meaningful, because it is assumed that play is an irreducible form of behaviour present in all animal life, finding its fullest expression in human behaviour. As Celeste Ulrich has said: "Play is a basic mode of behaviour, an integrating thread in the design of life."[10] The view that play represents a fundamental category of human behaviour is widely accepted and has been so for many years, even in professional physical education, as was evident in Edward Hartwell's keynote address to the Boston Conference of 1889.

> The plays of the kindergarten, the athletic sports to which British and American youth are so devoted, and the systematic gymnastics of the Swedes and Germans have all developed from one germ, from healthful play, that is; the vital energy of this germ is found in the *universal and ineradicable* impulse of all healthy children to play.[11] (Italics added)

---

9. Roger Caillois, *Man, Play, and Games* (New York: The Free Press of Glencoe, Inc., 1961), pp. 9-10.
10. Celeste Ulrich, *The Social Matrix of Physical Education* (New York: Prentice-Hall, Inc., 1969), p. 99.
11. Edward Hartwell, "A Nineteenth Century View of Physical Education," Arthur Weston, *The Making of American Physical Education* (New York: Meredith Publishing Co., 1962), p. 127.

Play, then is an essential source of human behaviour and has great importance culturally, being present in law, literature, philosophy, and even war, as well as in the more obvious cultural institutions of sport, dance, and theatre. Play is, as Johan Huizinga[12] made absolutely clear in his monumental *Homo Ludens,* (Man the Player) a "significant form" which should be taken as the player himself takes it, in its primary significance.

When one accepts the premise that play is a basic form of behavior, as do virtually all behavioural scientists, then theories concerning the origin of play, like definitions of play, do little to shed any further light on the meaning inherent in play. It matters little whether play is explained by reference to a "surplus-energy theory," a "self-expression theory," a "recapitulation theory," a "sublimation theory," or a "preparation for life theory." Each of these approaches has some obvious validity, but none begins to be sufficient to explain the endless variety and meaningfulness of play in human behaviour. The fact that no one theory has ever achieved any lasting support among a majority of scholars has not prevented the development of a scholarly body of knowledge which gives evidence to the importance of play in human life.

The literature which speaks to the various aspects of the concept of play—psychological, sociological, anthropological, mathematical—is vast, but the major steps in the modern development of the concept can be cited.

1. Freidrich Froebel linked the importance of play in the life of an individual to educational theory by recognizing the importance of play in childhood, recognizing it as a basic aspect of human nature which reveals fully the present and future life of the child.

2. The poet-philosopher Friedrich Schiller stressed the basic importance of play in the development of culture and initiated attempts to deduce the character of different cultures by analyzing their games and forms of play.

3. Karl Groos in *The Play of Animals* and *The Play of Man* began to study seriously the nature of play in an attempt to define its characteristics.

4. The genetic epistemologist, Jean Piaget, noted the dichotomy between imaginary play and regulated games, recognizing both as important play forms.

5. Johan Huizinga in *Homo Ludens* developed the first compre-

---

12. Huizinga, *Homo Ludens:* . . .

hensive definition and theory of play, and examined the concept as a basic animating principle in all of human culture.

6. Erik Erikson in *Childhood and Society* refined the Freudian view of play and the psychological importance of play in human behaviour.

7. Virginia Axline combined the basic elements of the Freudian view of play with the non-directive approach of Carol Rogers and formed the basis for non-directive play therapy.

8. Roger Caillois in *Man, Play, and Games* refined and expanded the examination of play originated by Huizinga, and developed a typology of games categorized by irreducible play impulses.

9. David Miller in *Gods and Games: Toward a Theology of Play* synthesized the contemporary utilizations of the concept of play and developed a theology of play that breaks down the dichotomy between play and the serious.

It is within the context of this body of thought that play can be recognized as the proper classification for physical education. It places physical education (sport and dance) along side of music, art, and drama as the primary institutionalized forms of play (in the terms of a logical definition they are *species* of the same *class*). Within this classification it becomes quite easy to recognize the various cultural counterparts that are present in the other members of the play class. Figure 9 illustrates these relationships.

The listings in Figure 9 are obviously not exhaustive, and it would be good for you to decide what the various counterparts might be in dance or drama and to examine other cultural forms of play than those mentioned in the left-hand column. The important point to recognize is that the weekend golfer is motivated by the same impulse that activates the weekend painter, the member of the community theatre, or the amateur musician: each is at play, and it is only the species of play that distinguishes one from the other.[13] By placing physical education within this class, the meaning inherent in the activities of physical education becomes immediately apparent; and by alluding directly to this source of meaning, it is possible to define the concept of physical education in a way that takes cognizance of its meaning-making poten-

---

13. This obviously suggests that the student learning physical education skills has as his counterpart the student learning art, drama, or music skills, thus placing physical education clearly within the humanities, where it rightfully belongs. It is interesting, however, that in most schools physical education is included with the biological sciences or the social sciences, but almost never with the humanities.

Cultural Form	Species of Play		
	Sport	*Music*	*Art*
childplay	kick the can	playing a toy horn	drawing a picture
basic education	physical education class	music class	art class
education for special skilled interests	varsity sports with interschool competition	band/ orchestra with regional & state competition	art clubs with group & individual shows
private individualized instruction	tennis lessons	piano lessons	lessons in watercolor
community oriented leisure	softball league	community band concerts	summer art fair
professionalized*	pro athlete	professional musician	professional artist

FIGURE 9.   Counterparts in play

tial. Play, then, is the classification for physical education that is most logically and psychologically satisfactory.

THE DIFFERENTIAE WHICH DEFINE THE CONCEPT OF PHYSICAL EDUCATION

If play is the proper classification for the concept of physical education, then the differentiae must be determined; that is, those character-

---

* It would seriously underestimate the complexity of human behaviour to suggest, as many do, that the professional does not play because he is paid, therefore making it work. As with all the characteristic of play, the importance of the "getting paid" would impinge upon the play factor, but would not necessarily eliminate it completely. Often times, when he is financially secure, the professional athlete is very much at play. The uncertain characteristics of play is just as important as an illustration of the fact that the play factor is on a continuum. The more uneven a contest, the less the play factor, and it is because of this that spectator and participant alike do not realize much meaning from a one-sided contest.

istics that differentiate it from other play-forms such as art, music, and drama. It is assumed, of course, that physical education is an educational process, and this is why it is incorrect merely to suggest that physical education is play. It would be more nearly correct to suggest that it is a form of play education.

Education is a process in which the action of the environment produces valuable changes in the modifiable aspects of human behaviour.[14] This definition obviously implies a value judgment. It tells us what education *is,* but it does not tell us what education *should be,* and it is in the determination of the *should be* that the value judgments must be made. I prefer to accept John Dewey's concept of growth as the criterion by which any educational experience should be judged. The growth criterion simply means that for it to be a true educational experience: 1) the activity must be considered to be valuable, and 2) the process must contribute to the growth of further experience. If the activity process arrests or distorts the growth of further experience, this would have to be called, in Dewey's words, a mis-educative experience (this also explains the title of Paul Goodman's book, *Compulsory Mis-Education*). In our case, if participation in a junior high school physical education program results in experiences which cause a student to avoid future physical education experiences, then physical mis-education has occurred. When the term "process" is used as a restriction in defining the concept of physical education, it should be understood as an educational process which contributes to the growth of further valued experiences.

Determination of the activities that are logically subsumed under physical education can only be made by reference to some method of categorization of play forms; and while several are available, the typology of play developed by Roger Caillois in *Man, Play, and Games* is perhaps the most refined attempt to date. Caillois has divided play forms into four categories: *agon, alea, mimicry,* and *ilinx.* The definitive character of each category corresponds to an essential and irreducible impulse in human behaviour: competition (*agon*), chance (*alea*), simulation (*mimicry*), and vertigo (*ilinx*). It will be helpful to explain the substance of each category in Caillois' words.

Agon: It is therefore always a question of a rivalry which hinges on a single quality (speed, endurance, strength, memory, skill, ingenuity, etc.) exercised within defined limits and without assistance, in such a way that the winner appears to be better than the loser in a certain category of exploits.

---

14. Charles Hardie, *Truth and Fallacy in Education Theory* (New York: Bureau of Publications, Teachers College, Columbia University, 1962), p. 73.

Alea: This is the Latin name for the game of dice. I have borrowed it to designate, in contrast to *agon,* all games that are based on a decision independent of the player, an outcome over which he has no control, and in which winning is the result of fate rather than triumphing over an adversary.

Mimicry: One is thus confronted with a diverse series of manifestations, the common element of which is that the subject makes believe or makes others believe that he is someone other than himself. He forgets, disguises, or temporarily sheds his personality (sometimes his conventional self) in order to feign another (sometimes his true self).

Ilinx: The last kind of game includes those which are based on the pursuit of vertigo and which consist of an attempt to momentarily destroy the stability of perception and inflict a kind of voluptuous panic upon an otherwise lucid mind. In all cases, it is a question of surrendering to a kind of spasm, seizure, or shock which destroys reality with sovereign brusqueness.[15]

It becomes immediately obvious that physical education includes the play principle characterized in the category of *agon* and, indeed, the vast majority of activities used in physical education fall within the boundaries of this category. From the first competitive attempts in childhood games to the sophisticated and highly skilled areas of varsity competition, much of physical education thrives and grows around the principle of competition, and much of what we value is intrinsic to the spirit of this category of play.

> The point of the game is for each player to have his superiority in a given area recognized. That is why the practice of *agon* presupposes sustained attention, appropriate training, assiduous application and the desire to win. It implies discipline and perseverance. It leaves the champion to his own devices, to evoke the best possible game of which he is capable, and it obliges him to play within the fixed limits, and according to the rules applied equally to all, so that in return the victor's superiority will be beyond dispute.[16]

Virtually all of the world of sport is found in this category of play. It includes competition with an opponent, as part of a group against another group, a standard, an ideal form, some aspect of the environment, or a previous performance. Regardless of the form of competition, the animating principle remains the same.

Forms of play in the *alea* category, however, have no place in physical education, simply because they are based upon the principle of chance which requires the player to be passive. The deployment of the player's resources does not affect the outcome of the play, and,

---

15. Caillois, *Man, Play, and Games,* Chapter Two.
16. Ibid., p. 15.

because of this, *alea* tends to negate practice, training, experience, and qualifications. For these reasons it is not possible for *alea* to have any place in an educational program. This does not mean that "chance" occupies no role in the other forms of play. It must be remembered that one of the defining characteristics of play is its uncertainty. In sports competition, it is obvious that chance plays an often significant role; the bounce of the ball and the toss of the coin. This kind of uncertainty should not be confused with the implications of the *alea* category.

Physical education does include the play principle characterized in the category of *mimicry*. It is found often in children's games; it is an essential spirit underlying creative movement activities; and it assumes a very important role in the field of dance. The idea of *mimicry*, however, cannot be viewed too narrowly or part of the essential spirit of the category will be lost. In modern dance, for example, much of the motivation comes from the free expression of the individual ideas of the dancer, which in essence is a shedding of the conventional self in order to reveal the expression of the real self. It should be thought of, therefore, not only as literal simulation but also as the expression of ideas.

Physical education does not directly include activities from the category if *ilinx*. There is, indeed, considerable doubt as to whether the pursuit of vertigo comprises a fundamental category of play. British sport sociologist, Peter McIntosh[17] has suggested that the activities presented in this category can be shifted into the categories of *agon* or *alea;* the determination being based on the role of the performer. The child tumbling down a hill is resigned to the tumble and to the accompanying sensation of vertigo, and, therefore, this activity would be logically placed in the *alea* category. The tumbler and diver, however, are not passive or resigned. They put forth their skill and resources in an attempt to complete an imposed task; and even though they may experience vertigo, the goal is always to overcome it, control it, and complete the task despite its presence, rather than to passively accept it. This places their activity in the realm of *agon.* Thus, Caillois' category of *ilinx* seems to be subdividable within his classifications of *agon* and *alea* depending on whether the player may be best characterized by resourcefulness or resignation. It appears, then, that physical education is concerned with competitive *(agon)* and simulative *(mimicry)* activities, but not with activities of chance *(alea).*

McIntosh has further criticized Caillois' classification of play by suggesting that the category of *agon* is too narrow to subsume the entire world of sport. He is particularly concerned with the inclusion of what

---

17. Peter McIntosh, *Sport in Society* (London: C. A. Watts, 1963), pp. 126-128.

he calls non-competitive sports; and in an attempt to remedy the dilemma, he offers a classification of sport which includes competitive sports, combative sports, conquest sports, and expressive activities. The differences between McIntosh and Caillois obviously hinge on different interpretations of the term "competition." I would argue that McIntosh's interpretation is too restrictive and misleading because it fails to make clear that the impulse motivating the mountain climber is the same as that motivating the football player; and that shooting baskets in the backyard (what he calls a non-competitive sport) is either a relaxed expression of the competitive impulse or, as it often is with young players, a combination of *agon* and *mimicry* in which the player is as likely to be playing the role of John Havlicek as he is practicing for a future competition.

In this sense, the McIntosh classification can be reduced to the two categories of sport and expressive activities, which is virtually identical to the Caillois classifications of competitive and simulative activities. At this point, it becomes a matter of which terminology you prefer, recognizing that the essential meaning is the same in both sets of terms. I prefer to be a bit eclectic and to use the terms "competitive" and "expressive" as restrictions on the concept of physical education, because these terms best express to me the fundamental play impulses which motivate the activities of physical education.

One more restriction should complete the analysis of the concept of physical education. From the analysis thus far completed, it is easy to recognize that riding in a roller coaster is not a physical education activity because it involves passive resignation to the vertigo, and thus belongs in the *alea* category, which is antithetical to an educational enterprise. It is not yet clear, however, why chess, which is obviously competitive, is not a physical education activity. Nor can it be yet determined why acting, indeed the whole realm of drama, which is clearly expressive, is just as clearly not physical education. What differentiates chess from gymnastics? What differentiates drama from modern dance? Each is an expression of the same vital play impulse. The differences obviously hinge upon the point of emphasis. In gymnastics, the competition focuses on gross motor performance even though the planning and execution of the skill reflects many cognitive judgments. In chess, the competition focuses on mental performance even though a motor act is required to move the figures on the chess board. The same analysis is applicable to the differences between theatre and modern dance. This is not to suggest that successful actors do not express themselves through their movement, nor is it to say that dancers do not reflect a considerable amount of mental expression.[18] Obviously, there is a motor element in the primarily-cognitive activities, and there is a cognitive element in the primarily-motor activities.

The use of the term "motor activities," hereafter, should be taken to mean activities in which gross motor performance is the focal point of the competition or the expression, and it is in this sense that the term can be useful as a restriction on the concept of physical education. When this restriction is coupled with the restrictions of "competitive" and "expressive," they form together a restrictive phrase—competitive and expressive motor activities—which delineate the play activities which are logically subsumed under physical education.

The physical educator has come to adopt competitive and expressive motor activities as his distinct area of concern. There is a considerable amount of historical and anthropological evidence to support the idea that these activities have provided men with meaningful experiences throughout time. Why these play activities seem to be particularly meaningful is beyond our present scope. Some might suggest that its source of meaning is something akin to that which the Freudians have described in infantile motor play as "muscle eroticism," but whether this helps us to understand the special play-meaning that man seems to experience in sport or dance is open to question. It would be presumptuous to suggest that the meaning available in the primarily-motor activities is superior to the meaning available in the primarily-cognitive activities.

It is now possible to arrive at a logical definition that reveals the meaning of the concept of physical education. *Physical Education means any process that increases human abilities to play competitive and expressive motor activities.* In this definition, physical education is classified as a species of play, and differentiated by: 1) an educational criterion—any process that increases human abilities, 2) competitive activities, 3) expressive activities, and 4) a dominant motor emphasis.

This definition may have several advantages. First, it places sport and dance in their proper class, so that they take their rightful place alongside art, music, and drama. Second, it requires that experiences must lead on to further valued experiences. Third, it logically categorizes the activities of physical education in terms of the motivational

---

18. Before I am accused of being a dualist, I should suggest that these illustrations have nothing to do with the mind-body controversy. Acceptance of the "whole-man doctrine" does not preclude recognition that activities can be either primarily mental or primarily motor.

impulses responsible for their development as meaningful institutional forms. Fourth, it allows physical education experiences to occur in many places—such YMCA programs, summer camps, etc.—thus defining the concept in terms of behavioural experience rather than institutional processes such as schools. Fifth, and perhaps most importantly, it defines the concept by referring to its irreducible source of meaning, thus taking advantage to the fullest of the meaning-making potential of the definition.

This definition could not have been derived from any of the basic viewpoints associated with the three major theories of physical education discussed in Part II of this text. It, therefore, requires the fuller explanation which is presented in the next two chapters.

WHAT QUESTIONS CAN YOU ASK ABOUT THE FOLLOWING STATEMENTS

1. Students must work hard to become well educated, and it therefore follows that play is inconsistent with educational efforts.
2. Because there is too much emphasis on winning in education and life, we should emphasize the play element in physical education.
3. Since the very nature of games is winning or losing, it is not possible to stress winning too much.
4. Too much stress on winning or gaining skill takes all the fun out of physical education.
5. If play becomes the generic focus for physical education, it will cease to develop as a scientific discipline.
6. Instead of playing so much, we should concentrate on teaching discipline, perseverance, and hard work because these are the qualities that make for success in life.
7. Adults should not waste their time playing games.
8. Physical education is not like art, music, and drama because the people who are interested in those things are not at all like people who are interested in sports.

Chapter 10—The Aims and Objectives of the New Approach

I also wish to point out the fact that the most constructive and beneficial play is something that has to be learned and is not likely to be an accidental ability or an inherited trait.

William Menninger, 1948

THE VALIDITY OF PLAY AS AN EDUCATIONAL CONCERN

The idea that physical education should be perceived as a form of play education will meet with a certain amount of opposition, particularly from within the profession of physical education. Because, in attempting to justify their programs, physical educators have traditionally had their theoretical backs against the wall, they have developed a conditioned apprehensiveness toward any of the terms that are generally associated with play. The physical educator cringes at the idea that his programs might be considered to be frivolous, non-academic, and childish. Play is too often misunderstood because it is thought of only in terms of the spontaneous and carefree play of the young child. Every now and then, someone suggests that an attempt should be made to recapture "the play spirit," and images of carefree and exuberant children are immediately conjured up. These apprehensions and misunderstandings must be eliminated so that public and professional alike can recognize that the controlled intensity of the skilled gymnast is as much a manifestation of the play impulse as is the exuberance of the child tumbling around the backyard.

Two things need to be understood so that play can gain the recognition it deserves. First, it must be made clear that a person's play life is as important as any other part of his life. To describe play as non-serious is misleading and incorrect, because it presumes a value judgment about those parts of life that are other-than-play, and also because it completely disregards the obvious seriousness of the player. More value judgments are implied when the term "frivolous" is used, implying that play is the opposite of work, economically unproductive, and carried on in a special world that is different from the real world. The connotations of these judgments are particularly damaging in our culture, with its Puritan suspiciousness of anything that is not work; a culture in which we tend to label anything that is economically unproductive as frivolous. To describe play in such terms tends to place it on the margin of life, as a diversion, when it would be far more accurate to recognize that play is at the center of life, an important aspect of human existence. Seen in this light, the immense productivity of play becomes immediately apparent (why is it that we tend to equate economic unproductivity with total unproductivity?) for we recognize the enriching and meaningful experiences gained from the play world.

The second factor that must be understood is that *play* is not synonymous with *child's play*. The connotations of play as a meaningful form of behaviour are too often different when used in the contexts of child and adult subjects. When a young boy "plays ball," the connotations suggest the meaningfulness of the activity; but when the young man "plays ball," the full meaning of the term is too often lost, and what is left is considered either a fringe activity or becomes synonymous with the term "perform." This attitude has developed because play has been assumed to mean activity that is unstructured, non-serious, and frivolous. While it is true that spontaneous and exuberant activity is play, what must be recognized is that this is *only one way of playing,* and that other ways exist and are equally playful. The primary contribution of Roger Caillois[1] has been his explanation and clarification of this aspect of the concept of play. He has suggested that ways of playing can be placed on a continuum according to the degree of spontaneity, orderliness, and regulation present in the play.

Caillois uses the term *paidia* to represent the end of the continuum that is characterized by spontaneity, turbulence, diversion, and carefree gaiety; in other words, the kinds of behaviours that are generally associated with child's play (the root of the term *paidia* is the word for child). The other end of the continuum is characterized by contrivance,

---

1. Roger Caillois, *Man, Play, and Games* (New York· The Free Press of Glencoe, Inc., 1961), pp. 13, 27-35.

calculation, and subordination to rules, and is represented by the term *ludus*.[2]

What must be understood is that the primary power of improvisation and joy—which is *paidia*—is in no way to be considered as having more value (or being more playful) than the taste for imposed difficulty —which is *ludus*. They are both play; they are both ways of playing; and, indeed, if there is to be a judgment, it must be that *ludus* contributes increasing meaning to play.

> What I call *ludus* stands for the specific element in play the impact and cultural creativity of which seems most impressive. It does not connote a psychological attitude as precise as that of *agon, alea, mimicry,* or *ilinx,* but in disciplining the *paidia, its general contribution is to give the fundamental categories of play their purity and excellence.*[3]

In this light, it can be understood that the ever increasing regulations and imposed difficulties attached to play activity as it moves from child-play to adult-play do not represent a repression of the play spirit but, rather, a naturally increasing sophistication of fundamental play interests, and to wish longingly for a return to the play spirit—defined as the *paidia*—is akin to wishing that one had not grown up.

Recognition of the *paidia-ludus* continuum is necessary if the concept of play is to be fully understood, and it is the crucial insight lacking in all views of play that do not move beyond the realm of child-play. As play changes from *paidia* to *ludus,* an ever increasing amount of skill, effort, patience, and ingenuity is required in order to be a successful player. The fencer must master the rules, etiquette, skills, and strategies that are imposed upon him in a fencing match, and it is in the mastery of these *ludus* factors that the fencer finds meaning. His play may also be seen, however, as a natural refinement and enrichment of the play impulse that is so easily seen in the *paidia* of "playing swords" in the backyard. Those who recognize only the *paidia* way of playing find it difficult to justify a significant expenditure of time and money in an educational effort which focuses on play, but for those who recognize the *ludus* way of playing, such an expenditure seems to be quite worthwhile.

An understanding of *ludus,* then, is indispensable to an understanding of play education. *Ludus* enriches play and provides increased

---

2. Caillois unfortunately confuses the issue by insisting that certain forms of play are pure *ludus.* These activities should instead be assigned to one of his four categories, which would clear up the contradiction that necessarily exists when he lists activities under *ludus* which he defines as "not a category of play, but a way of playing."
3. Roger Caillois, *Man, Play, and Games,* p. 33.

meaning for the player; it provides an occasion for training; it leads to the acquisition of special skills; it demands mastery; in other words, it requires education; and with such a requirement, play becomes a valid educational concern.

THE NECESSITY FOR INTRINSIC AIMS AND OBJECTIVES

There is always implicit in aims and objectives that are extrinsic to the activities of physical education the feeling that the activities themselves are of doubtful significance. When the central function of play in human existence is not fully understood, it is, in fact, quite easy to doubt the significance of physical education activities. How, after all, can the game of golf be explained? The golfer goes out to a golf course, hits the ball down the fairway (hopefully), walks after it and hits it again until he finally taps it into a small hole, and with the central purpose of hitting it as few times as possible. Such an activity is illogical, contrived, and unreal, and because of this, it is a play environment. It is equally difficult to explain dance, baseball, handball or the trampoline because they are equally illogical, contrived, and unreal. These things can be properly understood only as play environments; and if this understanding is lacking, then it becomes necessary to justify the inclusion of such activities in educational programs by reference to ends which are extrinsic to the activities. Thus it becomes necessary to suggest that the aim of physical education is the development of physically, mentally, emotionally, and socially fit citizens *through* the medium of physical activities. Eleanor Metheny has suggested, rightly I think, that such aims have prevented physical education from focusing on its uniquely educational values.

> I know that physical fitness can be improved through exercise. I believe that the learnings achieved through physical activity are valuable learnings. I recognize that human relationships can be improved through participation in play and games. But, in my opinion the use of the word *through* is the clue to our lack of ability to establish ourselves as anything more than "fringers" in the educational group. I believe that many of the objectives of education can be achieved *through* the medium of physical activity; but in my opinion the word *through* also underlines our own basic uncertainty about the *uniquely educational values* that are inherent in our own kind of subject-matter.[4]

The activities of physical education are intrinsically valuable because they represent institutionalized forms of play and are, therefore, funda-

---

4. Eleanor Metheny, *Connotations of Movement in Sport and Dance* (Dubuque: Wm. C. Brown Company Publishers, 1965) p. 101.

mentally important sources of meaning. This, it seems to me, is the uniquely educational value inherent in our subject-matter.

It is necessary, therefore, to develop an aim and objectives that are intrinsic to the activities of physical education, because the activities, as institutionalized forms of play, are inherently meaningful. If any concomitant values—physical, social, mental, or emotional—accrue from playing handball, basketball, or any other activity, they accrue mostly because the participant has *played.* To suggest aims and objectives which are extrinsic to the activities of physical education focuses the attention of the educator—and too often the student—on the "real world" of social, emotional, mental, and physical development. The problem with this focus is that it tends to impinge upon the play world; and by doing so, it runs the risk of alienating the player from the meaning that is inherent in the play activities.

It is the task of the educator to protect and enhance the play world precisely because it is there that the valued experiences are obtained. Statements from physical educator Howard Slusher, educator George Kneller, and psychoanalyst Erik Erikson help us to understand why the play world must be protected.

> To comprehend the "inner world" of the performer and to understand the reason why each man, as an individual, chooses to partake in sport activity, is to pursue inquiry into personalized forms of *meaningful and significant existence.*[5]
>
> The function of play is one of personal liberation—personal release; in sport man abandons himself to his own freedom, personally choosing the values and rules of his own physical activity, and the desire to play corresponds with the desire to *be* a certain type of person.[6]
>
> The list of playful situations in a variety of human endeavors indicates the narrow area within which our ego can feel superior to the confinement of space and time and to the definitiveness of social reality—free from the compulsions of conscience and from impulsions of irrationality. Only within these limitations, then, can man feel at one with his ego; no wonder he feels "only human when he plays."[7]

To suggest to the student learning to play handball that he pursue this activity in order to become a physically, mentally, emotionally, and socially fit citizen is incongruous. *The idea should be to initiate the student into the ludus that defines the play-world of the handball court, so that he can learn to be fully at play and fully in that play environment.*

---

5. Howard Slusher, *Man, Sport, and Existence* (Philadelphia: Lea and Febiger, 1967), p. 220.
6. George Kneller, *Existentialism and Education* (New York: John Wiley and Sons, Inc., 1958), p. 138.
7. Erik Erikson, *Childhood and Society,* 2nd. ed. (New York: W. W. Norton and Co., Inc., 1963), p. 214.

The meaning obtainable from play experiences is directly proportional to the degree that the player is *at* play and *in* the play environment. It is extremely difficult to explain this meaning verbally, even though recent physical education literature is replete with phenomenological descriptions similar to the following one made by a skilled gymnast.

> There's a feeling of wholeness in doing a routine on the parallels. When I start a routine, I'm not thinking about any part of myself . . . or what . . . or why. I know what I'm going to do; and there are no questions, no indecisions, no holding back, no rationalizing, no self-deceptions. From start to finish, all of me is involved in that action, and nothing is left out, nothing left over . . . It's beautiful . . . it's beautiful to experience your own wholeness . . .[8]

Such a description is quite similar to what psychologist Abraham Maslow has observed as the "peak-experience" of a self-actualizing person; it is very close to what Carl Rogers has described as the fully-functioning person; it is exactly what Erik Erikson means when he suggested that only in play can a person "feel at one with his ego"; it is what Howard Slusher has described as attaining "the being available in sport"; it is what philosopher Simon Wenkart has characterized as "the full experience of one's being in existence"; and it is an experience which Eleanor Metheny has suggested allows the player "some element of self-identification as a significant being in an impersonal universe." It is the opportunity to gain this kind of meaning that must be protected and enhanced, and it is doubtful whether aims and objectives that are extrinsic to the activities of physical education can accomplish that goal. The utilitarian approach attempts to reach extrinsic aims and objectives *through* the use of the activities, thus jeopardizing the meaning that is *in* the activities. The stress of the conceptualization here is neither *of* nor *through,* but, rather, *in.* Physical education should be education *in* competitive and expressive motor activities.

THE AIM

It should now be possible to develop an aim for physical education that is consistent with the framework developed in this and previous chapters. The following points should be remembered. First, physical education must seek ways to maximize its meaning-making potential. Second, there is meaning inherent in the activities of physical education. Third, the source of that meaning is best understood in reference

---

8. Eleanor Metheny, "The Excellence of Patroclus," *Anthology of Contemporary Readings,* 2nd edition (Dubuque: Wm. C. Brown Company, Publishers, 1966), p. 65.

to play—rather than physical activity, fitness, or human movement. Fourth, a definition of physical education should recognize the source of meaning—thus, physical education means any process that increases human abilities to play competitive and expressive motor activities. Fifth, the mastery of *ludus* enriches the play experience and requires instruction, skill, and training; thus establishing play as a valid educational concern. Sixth, and finally, the meaning inherent in playing the activities of physical education can be best protected and enhanced by aims and objectives that are intrinsic to the activities.

As with all educational discourses that achieve a measure of consistency, the aim must develop from the definition: A fitness definition will produce a fitness aim; a movement definition will produce a movement aim; and an education-through-the-physical definition will produce an education-through-the-physical aim. Therefore, *the aim of physical education is to increase human abilities to play competitive and expressive motor activities.* It has previously been suggested that "to play" denotes participation that is free, separate, uncertain, economically unproductive, and regulated or fictive. This full denotation and the connotative meaning associated with it should not be forgotten because it has important implications for the conduct of physical education programs. To substitute "to perform" for "to play" would, for example, alter radically the meaning of the aim and the implications that result from the aim.

The crux of the aim is, obviously, in the phrase "to increase human abilities," because it is in the clarification of this phrase that the objectives should be made clear. The question becomes one of determining *how* abilities to play these activities can best be increased; how, according to Dewey's growth criterion, the process can be conducted so that it leads on to further valued experiences; and how, in the terms of R. S. Peters, physical educators can initiate students into the meaningful inner-worlds of tennis, volleyball, diving, modern dance, and soccer. Objectives, as more precise strategic statements, should suggest how the aim is to be sought.

THE OBJECTIVES

Objectives are quite important because they give structure to the programs which are developed in reference to them. It is entirely possible, for example, to better understand many contemporary programs of physical education by viewing them in light of the objectives generally associated with the education-through-the-physical philosophy. If an activity is not too vigorous—and few of our activities are—

then we feel we must devote a certain amount of time to calisthenics *because* the program has a physical development objective. We test on rules and strategies *because* the program has a mental development objective. We grade partly on citizenship or sportsmanship *because* the program has a social development objective. We practice activities *because* the program has a skill development objective. Obviously, the conceptualization of objectives is a crucial step in the development of a program theory, and the sheer number of objectives tends to give structure to the resulting programs.[9]

With the importance of objectives in mind, and in an attempt to maintain a consistent emphasis on the meaning inherent in playing the activities of physical education, three direct or primary objectives for physical education are proposed here.

1. A development objective: the goal of which is to bring about a state of readiness for playing the activities of physical education.
2. A counseling objective: the goal of which is to provide opportunities for players to match their interests and abilities to various activities with the help of the physical educator.
3. A skill objective: the goal of which is develop competencies in the players' chosen activities.

It is my contention that adherence to these objectives will maximize the probabilities that students will find meaning through their participation, resulting in a substantial degree of aim fulfillment; thus allowing physical education to realize its full potential. In order to clarify this contention, the essential features of the three objectives are now described.

1. *The Developmental Objective.* The ultimate goal of this objective is to make the player *ready* to utilize his full powers and abilities in his play activities, because it is assumed that his participation will be meaningful to the extent that he is able to be completely at play. The objective refers, first of all, to the removal of specific impediments that might hinder the individual's capacity to play. It is not possible for a third grader to discover and enjoy the meaning associated with executing a handspring if he is unable to momentarily support his weight on his hands. It is not possible for a college sophomore to *play* soccer if his cardiovascular system is so inefficient that he cannot sustain a continuous effort for more than several minutes. The meaning available in all

---

9. While it does not necessarily follow that a large group of objectives means that each objective has to be attended to during each class period, such is often the case, and always there remains a pressure to provide some kind of experience that will help to reach each of the objectives. This kind of proliferation of activity has, in my opinion, prevented many programs of physical education from achieving significant results in any of the objectives.

types of ball games cannot be experienced if eye-hand coordination is inadequate. To correct any of these deficiencies would require a remedial effort, and all such remedial or corrective efforts form a substantial part of this objective. Impediments to play may range from somatic handicaps to physiological inefficiency to psychological problems, and they might be present in the child, the adolescent, or in the adult; but if they act as a barrier to realizing the meaning available in play, they become the direct concern of the physical educator.

Development can also be seen in the broader context of the physical educator in the school situation dealing with students who are in various stages of maturational development; childhood, puberty, and adolescence. Each of these maturational stages has associated with it developmental tasks which may directly or indirectly affect a student's abilities to play competitive and expressive motor activities. The development of perceptual-motor abilities, the crucial factor of body images, the coordination problems caused by the development of secondary sex characteristics, and the psychological difficulties encountered in adolescence need to be considered as important factors that potentially can affect the developing player, and as such they are the concern of the physical educator.

The application of this objective can be general in nature, as it is likely to be with younger children in terms of their perceptual-motor development; or it can be specific in nature, as it is more likely to be with older students who need to overcome specific impediments to play that are associated with maturational stages.

It should be remembered that the goal of this objective is to make the player *ready;* and when he is ready to play fully, then the goal is considered to be achieved, and whatever remedial activity that has been utilized to reach the goal can be discontinued. Balance beam activities, therefore, are not advocated for the purpose of helping children to further their perceptual-motor development so they can achieve better in the classroom. Balance beam activities are advocated because being skilled on the balance beam is meaningful in its own right, and because such skill might help a young player to be more ready to play other activities. Cross-pattern creeping is not advocated so that children can learn to read better—not because we are against children reading better or being better achievers in the classroom—it is not advocated simply and only because it is not physical education. Crawling in order to read better may be reading therapy, but it is most certainly not physical education.

The developmental objective is potentially present at all levels of physical education. It is primarily remedial in nature, and it may refer to impediments specific to the history of the player, or to those generally associated with the various maturational stages. Whenever it is applied, the goal is always the same; to remove the impediment as quickly as possible so the player may be more fully at play and more fully in the play environment.

2. *The Counseling Objective.* This objective refers to attempts to guide students into activities in which they may find the most meaningful participation. To attain this objective, the physical educator will have to assume a role similar to that which David Reisman has called an "avocational counselor." There is a close relationship between the counseling objective and the developmental and skill objectives because to attain the latter two, the physical educator will have had to function in his role as avocational counselor.

There are three important aspects of this objective; each of which has important implications for the process of physical education. The first aspect can be best described as "student-evaluation," and it encompasses inventories of student abilities, present interests, anticipated future interests, and vocational aspirations. Objective measurement obviously plays a large and important role in meeting this objective, but the concept of counselor also demands that physical educators develop counseling relationships with students. To know about something—in this case to know about students through objective measurement—is different than to know something—in this case knowing students via the counseling relationship.

A second aspect of this objective can be described as "activity-evaluation." This means quite simply that physical educators must make judgments about the relative values of all the possible activities that might be included in a program of physical education. For various reasons, some activities will be considered of greater value than others. Physical educators should take a more active role in examining activities in this light and must make judgments about the potential of each activity in terms of various important criteria. One such criterion, for example, might be the present and future possibility of playing the activity in urban, suburban, and rural environments. The pursuit of this aspect of the counseling objective will help the physical educator to move "out front" in terms of shaping the activity patterns of society, instead of merely reacting to activity patterns that are imposed from outside the profession. This would be a refreshing change in the traditional state of affairs in physical education.

The third aspect of this objective is the "student-activity-match" in which judgments about students and judgments about activities are brought together in an attempt to help students maximize the meaning

that they obtain from participation in the activities of physical education. It is in this aspect that the real test of the physical education
counselor will be made; as the results of the "match" will tend to give
structure to the activity patterns of the student throughout his school
experience.

The counseling objective is of major importance to the long-term
success or failure of physical education. If physical education is to occupy any major role in developing a "society at play," then it must take
more seriously what physical educator-anthropologist Robert Malina
has pointed out—the importance of establishing beneficial activity patterns during the formative years.

> The notion that regular participation in physical activities during
> childhood tends to persist into the activity patterns of adults is reason-
> ably well established. Although adults can develop new activity hab-
> its, the overwhelming tendency is a reversion to familiar activities,
> most of which are team sports cast in interscholastic settings. Conse-
> quently, it is essential to be concerned with the determinants of
> physical activity during the growing years, for it is at this level that
> the roots of many of the adult problems lie.[10]

3. *The Skill Objective.* This objective refers to the development
of competency in competitive and/or expressive motor activities, and
it is the primary focus of physical education throughout the school experience. It provides the best possibility for meaning, which increases
with the degree of competency developed in the activity.[11] In handball,
the player with little skill is at the mercy of the carom as the ball comes
off the walls of the court. He does not know where the ball will bound
to, and even if he does understand this, he is unable to do much about
it. He flails out, almost in self-defense, hoping first to hit the ball and
secondly, to hit it to the front wall before it hits the floor. As his ability
increases, he begins to gain a greater degree of control over the play
environment of the handball court. First, he begins to anticipate the
carom, and to make sure that he hits the ball to the front wall before it
hits the floor, and later he gains enough control to use the carom, con-
trolling the return of the ball so that it works to his advantage. As the
ball then becomes an extension of his hand, his arm, and his will, the
game takes on greater meaning because he is more able to accomplish
his task, to overcome the obstacles, to defeat an opponent. He is fully
at play, and he is fully in the play environment.

---

10. Robert Malina, "An Anthropological Perspective of Man in Action" eds. Brown and
Cratty, *New Perspectives of Man in Action*, pp. 151-152.
11. The relationship is obviously not linear. It is probably best shown by a negatively
accelerating curve; i.e., there is a point of diminishing returns in the relationship between
competence and meaning.

The object is to develop the competent player, and this entails mastery of the *ludus* of specific sport and dance activities. To do this might require the development of fundamental locomotor skills early in the school experience, and it might also entail early sports skills training of a non-specific type. Primarily, however, it refers to competencies developed in specific activities. The mastery of the *ludus* of any activity obviously entails more than the acquisition of certain motor skills. It is not possible to be a skilled or competent handball player without also mastering the rules, strategies, and courtesies which define the world of the handball court.

By removing impediments and developing capabilities, by guiding students into meaningful activities for which they are suited, and by increasing their skill in these activities, the aim of physical education will be directly achieved. The student who emerges from a program of physical education that utilizes such objectives will have increased significantly his ability to play certain physical education activities, and he will have found the meaning inherent in the activities. If his experiences in physical education also help him in other areas of his life, so much the better, but this is not necessary in order to justify the physical education program. What is necessary is the development of competent dancers, tennis players, and volleyball players; and if programs develop such competencies, then they are totally justified.

A COMPARISON WITH THE MORE COMMONLY HELD OBJECTIVES OF PHYSICAL EDUCATION

The objectives presented above differ considerably from those commonly set forth in physical education. As previously noted (Chapter Five) it has been generally agreed for fifty years that the objectives of physical education are organic development, neuromuscular development, interpretive development, and personal-social development. Recently, the concept of human movement has begun to gain favor (Chapter Six), but its objectives[12] seem quite similar to the traditional ones, the differences being more in terminology than in conception. Instead of organic development, there is development through movement; instead of neuromuscular development, there is development of movement skill and movement expression; instead of interpretive development, there is understanding of development and communication through movement; and instead of person-social development, there is

---

12. Brown and Cassidy, *Theory in Physical Education* (Philadelphia: Lea and Febiger, 1963), pp. 107-108.

movement development enabling a person to learn democratic behaviours through movement.

Because of the historical importance and widespread current acceptance of these fourfold objectives, it will be useful to examine the similarities and differences between them and the objectives suggested here.

Organic Development. It was suggested earlier (Chapter Four) that physical fitness is not a unitary concept, and that it is helpful to recognize at least two basic kinds of fitness; health-fitness and motor-performance-fitness. Traditional objectives of organic development or physical fitness usually include both types. Yet there seems to be no direct reference to physical fitness in the three objectives suggested here, especially when it is recognized that the developmental objectives refer to the readiness of the player rather than to any standards of physical fitness. The question is not whether fitness is good or bad, but rather, what relationship there should be between physical fitness training and physical education. There is no direct reference to physical fitness in the objectives suggested here because this author does not believe that fitness training bears a primary relationship to physical education. Since this is the point where many physical educators will discard these formulations as totally irrelevant, the reasons for this decision should be explained a bit further.

Health-fitness is not a primary objective of physical education because health concepts are rooted in the biological sciences, while the concept of play is rooted in the humanities, being tied most closely to music, art, and drama. Health-fitness most logically and most often should be tied to problems of diet and nutrition, both of which are health concepts that, along with health-fitness, contribute to the maintenance of healthy states of being. This is not to suggest that the physical and biological sciences have nothing to offer play in general and physical education in particular—musical acoustics and sports biomechanics have each proven otherwise. The important point is that health-fitness should be pursued in health education.

When health-fitness is seen as a primary objective of physical education, the resulting focus of attention is extrinsic to the activities and to the meaning of the activities. Health-fitness may well accrue as a concomitant outcome of playing the rhythmical activities—jogging, swimming, etc.—of physical education, but if so, it will be a concomitant outcome, the primary emphasis remaining on a meaningful participation. The recent upsurge of interest in running is only partially attributable to the fact that this is a fine method of increasing and maintaining health-fitness. There has also been a rediscovery of meaning in this age old activity. Part of the meaning is, of course, attributable to the feelings associated with health-fitness, the wholeness which results from a total effort of the human organism. There is also some *ludus* in such play. It may range from running against a clock, to running a certain number of miles each month, to checking the pulse rate each morning. This diffused element of competition reveals the play factor present in such activity. When swimming and running are pursued because the activity has potential meaning, then it is completely consistent with the objectives set forth here because health-fitness would accrue as the player (jogger, swimmer) became more competent. When health-fitness is seen as the objective, however, running or swimming per se, as philosopher Simon Wenkart has pointed out, may hold little meaning to some participants.

> Imposed forcibly on individuals, exercise, and drill can have devastating effects. The humiliation of having one's body used as a mechanical instrument is aggravated by the abuse of one's free will . . .[13]

Under the objectives suggested here, some students will improve their health-fitness because they find meaning in activities which contribute to their cardiovascular efficiency, but it should also be recognized that other students will not improve their health-fitness significantly because the activities in which they find meaning (baseball, golf, etc.) may contribute little to cardiovascular efficiency. If a certain level of health-fitness is thought to be valuable for every student, then the problem belongs to health education rather than physical education, and the forced exercise necessary to achieve such a goal would be most accurately described as health education activity rather than physical education activity.

Motor-performance-fitness is obviously an important part of physical education as I conceive it, but not the primary objective. Motor-performance-fitness is almost always specific to an activity, and the purpose is to improve performance in that activity. The golfer tries to improve his wrist and arm strength (improving his motor-performance-fitness) in order to lower his golf score. The dancer attempts to increase her flexibility and agility so as to better express herself in a dance composition. Each of these situations is entirely subsumed under the skill development objective because the goal is to make the player more competent in order to increase the meaning-making-potential of his or her activity. Seen in this light, it becomes obvious that there is no need

---

13. Simon Wenkart, "The Meaning of Sports for Contemporary Man," *Journal of Existential Psychiatry* 3:400, 1963–64.

for either a health-fitness objective or a motor-performance-fitness objective.

Neuromuscular Development. This objective can be generally taken to mean the development of skill, but the implications are never as broad as those implied in the skill development objective advocated here. Motor-performance-fitness, for example, is not usually considered part of the neuromuscular development objective because it is seen as something that stands alone, requiring status as an objective equal to that of skill development. It has already been pointed out that I view motor-performance-fitness as a part of the skill development objective, thus broadening the concept of skill to include all factors which contribute to increased competence in specific activities.

The skill objective advocated here is also conceptually more important than the neuromuscular development objective because it represents the major focus of physical education programs. In traditional programs, the organic and neuromuscular development objectives have been considered to be of nearly equal importance; and since both objectives had to be worked toward, class time had to be devoted to each. The skill objective suggested here has no such competition. The developmental objective is largely remedial in nature, and many children may never be affected by it; while the counseling objective as a curricular consideration is mostly specific to the junior high school or middle school level, and after that it is most important in terms of counseling activities that occur outside of class time.

The primacy of the skill development objective is based on the assumption that the greater the degree of competency in an activity, the greater is the meaning obtained from participation. It is the highly skilled player who "attains being," has "peak experiences," and becomes "fully functioning" or "self-actualized." This is perhaps due to fulfilling what Gordon Allport has described as the "need for competence."

> It would be wrong to say that a "need for competence" is the simple and sovereign motive of life. It does however, come as close as any need (closer than sexual) to summing up the whole biological story of development. We survive through competence, we grow through competence, we become "self-actualizing" through competence.[14]

For these several reasons, the skill development objective advocated here assumes a far more central role than does the neuromuscular development objective.

---

14. Gordon Allport, *Pattern and Growth in Personality* (New York: Holt, Rinehart, and Winston, Inc., 1937), p. 214. (See footnote 11, p. 198.)

Interpretive Development. As reported in Chapters Five and Seven, to suggest that an interpretive development objective means promoting cognitive or academic growth through physical activity is not a very defensible position; and even if it were, it would still have no place in a program of physical education, the aim of which is to develop competent players. Like health-fitness, interpretive development is an extrinsic objective and, therefore, runs the risk of impinging upon the play environment.

The meaning that is more often attached to this objective is that of developing knowledge about physical education. This can mean knowledge about fitness or health, for example, but it is more often seen as knowledge about the activities of physical education: the history of the game, the equipment used, the dimensions of the playing environment, the rules of the game, the strategies involved in successful participation, and the behaviours which comprise the etiquette of the game. There can be no doubt that knowledge such as this enhances the play experience, because the entire idea of *ludus* is recognition of and devotion to the imposed regulations and courtesies that define the play situation. It is not possible to become a competent and skilled player without mastering the entire *ludus* of the activity.

It is doubtful, however, that this objective should be stated as a major objective, because as a major objective, it implicitly stands on its own and has to be sought along with the other objectives. It is more likely that this objective should be subsumed under the counseling and skill objectives, there to appear as a secondary objective in the natural course of guiding students toward meaningful participation and increased competence. In this way, knowledge will be acquired naturally as skill increases. The more skilled the player becomes, the more he will insist on total knowledge of the rules and strategies that enhance the meaning of the game. He will want to know about the equipment because he will see that it might improve his play, and he will naturally accept the courtesies and etiquette of the game because he will respect the integrity of the play environment. Seen in this manner, the acquisition of knowledge about the activities is put into proper perspective. *The purpose of gaining the knowledge is to enhance the play experience, to make it more meaningful to the player.*

When perceived as a primary objective of physical education, however, the results are all too familiar. Students are too often required to learn meaningless facts and dates that they memorize the night before the "final"—probably forgetting them by the next week—and they are most often tested after the educational situation is completed; so that the acquisition of the knowledge does not benefit their learning experience. Seen as a primary objective, the knowledge stands as an entity in itself, and it gives physical educators a chance to be "objective" in the assigning of grades.

The end result, of course, is that the student tends to be slightly alienated from the physical education experience (physical mis-education?), because he sees that the last minute reading of material and the knowledge testing are irrelevant to his play experience. He also realizes that this type of testing and grading is too often done solely to enhance the status of the physical education program in the eyes of the academic community, rather than to help the student become a more competent player. As a secondary objective to counseling and skill development, the acquisition of knowledge is placed in its proper role as a contributor to the growth of meaningful play experience, and it thus becomes educational.

Personal-Social Development. This objective refers to habits, attitudes, and values that are developed through participation in the activities of physical education. I have already suggested in Chapter Five that little evidence exists which would support the rather pervasive claims that physical educators have traditionally assumed in regards to this objective, and it is high–time that physical educators either alter these claims or provide evidence to defend their positions. Even if the claims were substantiated, this objective would be extrinsic in nature.

It might be suggested that a "play theory" of physical education would favor an emotional development objective, but even here there is doubt that definitive statements can be made. The hypothesis is that emotional control in stress situations can be learned well in competitive games and then transferred to life situations. In this sense, physical education might come close to being a play-therapy environment. There is ample clinical evidence from Anna Freud, Erik Erikson, and Virginia Axline, that play can be therapeutic. The basic premise of play therapy is that the player re-shapes the real world into a play environment in which he can exercise a great degree of control. Here conflicts, frustrations, and aggressions built up in the real world can be worked out to satisfactory solutions—what Martin Capell has called the mastery of helplessness. Norman Reider[15] has questioned the idea that normal play is therapeutic, and his criticism seems to be valid and logical. He suggests that while play might relieve aggressions momentarily, it does nothing to get to the source of emotional problems, unless it is con-

---

15. Norman Reider, "Preanalytic and Psychoanalytic Theories of Play and Games," *Motivation in Play, Games, and Sports* eds. Ralph Slovenko and James Knight, (Springfield: Charles C. Thomas, Publisher, 1967), pp. 13-38.

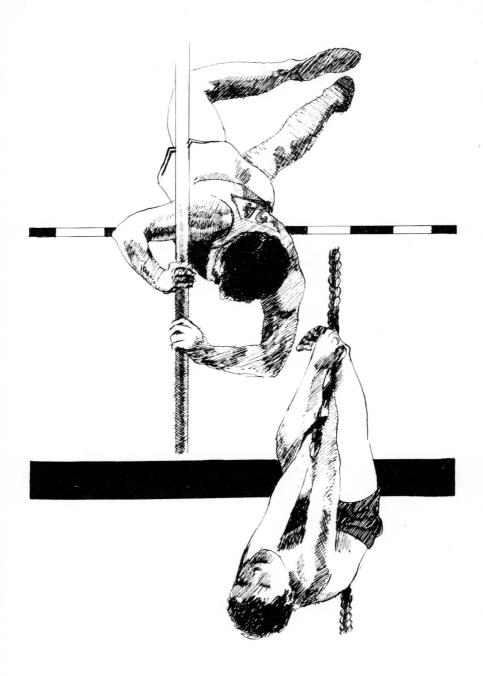

ducted in a clinical setting with a competent therapist. The obvious difference between the therapy environment and the normal play environment is that in the latter the player cannot exercise a significant degree of control because he must respect arbitrarily imposed rules and he must react to other players.

All of this tends to suggest that while play may serve a limited purpose in resolving central conflicts, it is unlikely that it develops emotional stability, unless the play occurs in a structured play therapy environment. Psychologist Karl Menninger believes play is necessary in the well-rounded life not because of its developmental powers, but for its preventive powers, and this may prove to be a more fruitful avenue of inquiry.

How is all this related to a personal-social development objective? The important conclusion is that while the role that play may have in personal-social development is very uncertain, either in a therapeutic or preventive function, it seems to be well accepted that an active play life is very beneficial to the ongoing well being of the individual. William Menninger has underscored this important aspect of play.

> Too many people do not know how to play. Others limit their recreation to being merely passive observers of the activity of others. There is considerable scientific evidence that the healthy personality is one who not only plays, but who takes his play seriously.[16]

It is important to recognize that whatever benefits might accrue, they occur because the participant has *played,* and because of this it seems that the wisest course to follow is to aim at increasing abilities to play, and to state objectives that rigorously adhere to the intrinsic nature of play activities.

The suggestion being made here is that it is time for physical education to take play seriously; to examine the depth and breadth of the implications of play; to recognize it as the source of the meaning that we all have found in the activities of physical education; and to develop theories and programs which are consistent with the overriding human importance of an active play life. If other desirable changes occur as a result of participation in physical education, then so much the better, but we must first recognize if abilities to play are not increased, but instead are held still, stunted, or thwarted, then it is unlikely that desirable changes will occur; and that most importantly, students will be left on their own to discover this important source of meaning. If this occurs, then what has caused it can only be called physical mis-education.

---

16. William Menninger, "Recreation and Mental Health," *Recreation* 42:343, November, 1948.

The best and most direct course to follow to insure that a high degree of aim fulfillment will occur is to: 1) remove impediments that might hinder play, 2) help students find meaningful forms of play and 3) increase their competence as players. These three objectives consequently have been suggested for physical education programs.

WHAT QUESTIONS CAN YOU ASK ABOUT THE FOLLOWING STATEMENTS

1. Development really means the same thing as physical fitness.
2. Physical educators have always been counselors.
3. If a student had to practice one activity for a whole year, he would get terribly bored.
4. Students get bored because teachers don't know enough about the activities to make them interesting.
5. The idea should be to use the activities to make students physically fit.
6. If you believe in the "normal curve" then you know that it is impossible for all students to be skilled.
7. If you expect that knowledge about sport will develop naturally as the student learns the skill, then you are mistaken.
8. Just because the research results do not show that character is developed through sports, this doesn't mean that it isn't happening.

Chapter 11 Some Implications of the Play Approach

Thus we are being forced to re-examine our educational institutions and their curricula to take account of the growing importance of play in the whole economy of life.

Philip Phenix, 1965

HOW NEW IS THE PLAY APPROACH

It would be unfortunate if you were left with the impression that the concept of play has never before been promoted in physical education theory, because this is certainly not the case. During the first quarter of this century, educators showed considerable interest in the concept of play in general and motor play in particular. The concept played a significant role in the ideas of several physical educators. Clark Hetherington used play as the basic means of education in his Play School at the University of California. In 1915, Joseph Lee, who was prominent in the playground movement in this country, published an important book entitled *Play in Education.* In 1920, Luther Gulick, one of America's most important physical educators, published his *Philosophy of Play,* in which he described play as the fundamental means for developing the human being. In 1923, Wilbur Bowen and Elmer Mitchell brought together expertise from the social sciences and physical education to produce *The Theory of Organized Play,* which was revised in 1934, by Mitchell and sociologist Bernard Mason as *The Theory of Play.* Each of these works was significant and each promoted play as a means by which developmental and educational goals could be reached. They can be accurately classified together as attempts to promote education-through-play.

It is also important for you to recognize that each of these important contributions was "pre-Huizinga"; in other words, before the publication of *Homo Ludens* so greatly enriched and expanded the concept of play. The present author would be pleased to have his view of play education considered as a natural development of their thought. The important difference, however, is that here play has been defended as a self-justifying enterprise, not as education *through* play. The early view of play was essentially the same as the education-through-the-physical philosophy, merely substituting *play* for *activity.* Thus, in Mitchell and Mason's book, there are chapters on the physical benefits of play, the mental benefits of play, and the citizenship and character forming benefits of play.

It is also important to note that many physical educators have long considered the activities of physical education to be self-justifying. It is particularly interesting that Jesse Feiring Williams was a strong advocate of this viewpoint, as was demonstrated in the preface to the fourth edition of his classic *Principles of Physical Education,* where he suggested that "unless overly organized for other than its (physical education) own ends, it never is complex. . . ." Williams was always fond of comparing the experience of punting a football to those of other art forms, and he talked often of the contribution that physical education could make to "fine living." What developed out of the Wood-Hetherington-Williams-Nash viewpoint was, unfortunately, a program that was almost wholly designed for "ends" other than its own, and so the program was called education-through-the-physical. More recently, Eleanor Metheny has consistently pointed out that physical education has too often neglected the inherent meaningfulness of its own activities, the source of which she attributes to human movement rather than to play.

The approach to physical education suggested in these pages is "new" in the sense that increasing abilities to play competitive and/or expressive motor activities is considered to be self-justifying because these activities are important forms of inherently meaningful human experience; such a conceptualization of physical education as play education is quite far removed from efforts to describe physical education as education-through-play, education-through-the-physical, or human movement education.

Certain general implications can be drawn from the ideas suggested here and it will be useful to explain some of these. Theoretical formulations are useless if they provide no direct guidance for programs. Ideas about how to move from "what is" to what, in the author's opinion, "should be" are presented here.

IMPLICATIONS FOR RELATIONSHIPS WITH ALLIED FIELDS

In centers of higher education, it has over the years become commonplace to find physical education allied with health, recreation, and safety education. Schools or departments of physical education often have under their administrative guidance programs in these fields, and it is in this sense that they are described as "allied fields."

From the play education viewpoint, no close theoretical relationship between health education and physical education seems apparent. The view taken here is that physical education is most closely related to art, music, and drama, which are rooted in the humanities, while health is rooted in the biological sciences. Both fields might attempt to investigate why an active play life is important to health, and physical education may indirectly contribute to health-fitness when students regularly participate in certain physical education activities. The relationship between physical education and safety education is even less direct.

The same is not true, however, for recreation education, which should bear a very primary and direct relationship to physical education. While the field of recreation is considerably broader than physical education, taking into account many species of play, in our culture the activities of physical education form an important part of any recreational program. The concept of play is, of course, at the heart of any theory of recreation, and because of this its fundamental relationship to physical education is established.

IMPLICATIONS FOR INTRAMURALS AND ATHLETICS

Every view taken here, if carried to its logical conclusion, implies that a broadly conceived, well developed, well financed, and professionally conducted program of intramurals is essential for a program of physical education that aims to increase human abilities to play competitive and/or expressive motor activities. Programs of intramurals and club sports are extremely important because they create environments within which the skills developed in physical education may be tested, practiced, and further extended. Sports clubs in particular seem to offer a great deal in terms of meaning-making potential because they emphasize the social factor of play which as philosopher Eugen Fink has suggested, enriches its meaning.

> Play is a fundamental possibility of social life. To play is to play together, to play with others; it is a deep manifestation of human community. Play is not, as far as its structure is concerned, an individual and isolated action; it is open to our neighbor as partner.

> There is no point in underlining the fact that we often find solitary players playing alone at personal games, because the very meaning in play includes the possibility of other players. The solitary player is often playing with imaginary partners.[1]

Intramurals and sports clubs provide the opportunity for increasing play competencies in an environment that protects the essential characteristics of play.

The implications for programs of interscholastic athletics are not so easily drawn. Athletics are usually conceptualized as the top portion of a triangle that has instructional physical education as its base and the intramural program occupying the center portion. While this is a convenient graphic method for portraying the total field of physical education, it grossly misrepresents the role of athletics in the life of the school, community, state, nation, and world. While it is tempting to suggest that athletics is related to physical education just as debate is to speech and as the school choir is to the instructional music program, this would not give full recognition to the significant cultural position of athletics. The plain fact is that athletics occupy cultural roles that are unparalled by other pursuits that are theoretically similar.

Unfortunately, many aspects of the culture impinge upon the play factor in athletics—the community pressure, the firing of coaches, the overriding importance of eligibility, and the potential for real status all diminish the play element. It would be easy to suggest that what physical education must do is to vigorously guard the play element in athletics, thus maintaining as close a relationship to physical education as possible, but this could be done only if the cultural importance of athletics were ignored. While physical educators, coaches, and athletic directors deplore some of the practices that tend to make interscholastic athletics too much a part of the real world, they recognize the importance of athletics in cultures of school, community, and nation. It would be foolish to suggest that all the play element is completely lost. For many of the participants the play factor is still very important.

Physical educators are more likely to be promoters of sports clubs and intramurals than they are of interscholastic athletics. The more "real" the athletic program becomes, the more apparent and likely the separation between physical education and athletics will probably become. In most major universities, where alumni funds, finances, and scholarships tend to impinge upon the play factor, the separation has become administratively recognized and different departments exist.

---

1. Eugen Fink, "The Ontology of Play," *Philosophy Today* 4:102, Spring, 1960.

CURRICULAR IMPLICATIONS

While the placement of activities in curricula and the relative emphasis given to certain activities might be altered somewhat to be consistent with the ideas presented here, it is doubtful that the activities themselves would change much, simply because broad categories such as dance, ball games, racquet sports, and gymnastics have been institutionalized forms of play for most of recorded history. The persistence with which they are pursued is evidence of their inherent meaningfulness. Certainly, new forms will emerge and be incorporated into programs of physical education, but the basic nature of the activities will not change.

There are, however, some important implications for the placement of activities within curricula, the relative emphasis given to various kinds of activities, and the primary emphasis of curricula at the various school levels. These implications can best be examined by referring to the three objectives.

The Developmental Objective. While this objective does not have any great influence on the development of curricula, two implications are worthy of note. The first is that a certain amount of time should be set aside for diagnostic testing. While a significant amount of time is not required beyond the primary grades, it should be allowed for. The diagnostic testing is, of course, for those students who may exhibit impediments which prevent them from playing fully. The second implication is a closely related one. There must be some flexibility in physical education curricula to allow for remedial work designed to remove the impediments to play, but this remedial work should not interfere with the normal course of affairs in the regular physical education program.

The clear implication of the ideas presented here is that corrective physical education should be pursued only to the point when the student can return to his regular physical education program more *ready* to utilize his full powers in his play education activities. Adaptive physical education, as opposed to corrective, would naturally be a part of any physical education program based on concepts advocated here. If impediments to play cannot be significantly improved through remedial work, then the play environment should be adapted to the abilities of the handicapped student so that he, too, may experience meaningful participation.

The Counseling Objective. The counseling objective has several curricular implications, the major one being that programs of physical education must be as broadly based as possible. Robert Porter[2] has suggested that the great variety of activities germane to the field of physical education offer endless opportunity for a student to find challenges that are emotionally meaningful to him, and Arthur Jersild[3] has suggested that the potential contribution of a physical education program depends entirely upon how broadly the program is conceived. This does not mean, as will be made clear later, that each student must experience a variety of activities. It means instead that students must have many activities available to them so they can find the ones for which they are best suited, and in which they find the most meaning.

Another implication of this objective is that the student must be exposed to a wide variety of activities in hopes that he can learn enough about each activity to be able to make decisions later about specialization. The question is, what is the proper school level for the multi-activity program; which, it should be emphasized, is a curricular-counseling tool and not a primary method of skill development. Most often, it is suggested that the junior high school is the place for the multi-activity program, but in reality it is utilized throughout most high school programs.

The decision on where to place the multi-activity program should be made on the basis of two factors: first, it should come before the student begins to "elect" his activities, and, second, it should come when the student has a broad range of interests and can, therefore, benefit most from this approach. A strong case can be made for offering this program in the fifth and sixth grades, or approximately from ages ten to twelve. According to child development specialist John Anderson[4], students have the broadest range of interests at about the age of eight or nine; thereafter the variety of interests decreases continuously until at the adult level it has been replaced by a narrow range of highly specialized interests. This information coupled with the assumption that the twelve or thirteen-year-old student is beginning to be ready to elect his activities, suggests that the fifth and sixth grade level is most appropriate for this program. It would seem that a two-year program, the primary aim of which is exploration and counseling, would be sufficient to realize this goal.

---

2. Robert Porter, "Sports and Adolescence," in *Motivation in Play, Games and Sports,* Ralph Slovenko and James Knight, eds. (Springfield: Charles C. Thomas, Publisher, 1967), pp. 73-90.
3. Arthur Jersild, *In Search of Self* (New York: Teachers College, Columbia University, 1952), p. 79.
4. John Anderson, "Growth and Development Today: Implications for Physical Education," paper presented at National Conference on Social Changes and Implications for Physical Education and Sports Recreation, Estes Park, Colorado, June, 1958, 14 pp., mimeo.

A final implication is that during the seventh and eighth grade level, the student should begin to assume the responsibility for electing his own activities, and that beyond this level the program should be entirely elective. It may well be that during the first few years of electing activities, the student may have to choose from within categories that tend to develop a range of skills—one racquet sport, one team sport, etc.—but the responsibility for choosing activities should be progressively shifted from the physical educator to the student.

Those who believe that ten and eleven-year-old students are not capable of benefiting from a multi-activity program, and that twelve and thirteen-year-old students are not ready to begin to elect activities, underestimate students. An examination of non-school programs— rocket football, little league, etc.—tends to support the contentions made here. When the full implications of the counseling objective are recognized (the students are not, after all, left on their own, the very purpose of the counseling objective being that of helping them to make the early decisions) it becomes clear that such a view does not "expect too much" from students or "push them too early."

The Skill Development Objective.   It should be obvious by now that the major thrust of the ideas suggested here is in the direction of a high level of competence in a skill or skills for which a student has interests and capabilities. It is not possible to define in quantitative terms just what that level of competence should be, but it should approach what is now described as a "varsity" level ability. As Robert Porter has suggested, it has something to do with a student's ability to compete.

> "Competent" and "compete" both derive from the Latin competere.
> So even etymologically, being well qualified (competent) is clearly
> associated with one's ability to contend with others (compete).[5]

To have reached a competent level of skill means that one is able to compete adequately with others who are considered to be well skilled. Some students will have low skill abilities in virtually every activity, but these are a very small minority; and the more broadly based the program of activities is, the smaller that group will become. Most students have abilities that should enable them to achieve a high level of skill in *some* activity, and the contention here is that physical education should not aim at anything less than this level of skill development.

When specific skill development should begin is a moot point. Physical educators have suggested that non-specific, general motor skills should makeup the bulk of the skill development program at the primary level. If readiness is viewed as it should be—the student is

---

5. Porter, "Sports and Adolescence," *Motivation in Play, Games, and Sports,* p. 81.

developmentally capable of performing the activity in some rudimentary form—then it might be that more specific types of skill development may be started earlier than is normally considered wise. How
"ready" the young student is may be learned by observing his out-of-
school activities. By nine or ten years of age, many children have
learned to swim, had ballet training, and are participating in programs
such as "rocket" football. Many physical education programs for this
age level still are composed mostly of "games of low organization."

Regardless of the specificity or generality of early skill development, the primary implication of this objective is competence through
specialization. Once the multi-activity program has been used to
achieve its counseling function, the student should begin to specialize,
and by specialize I do not mean eight-week units instead of four-week
units. By the end of his high school experience, a student should have
become well skilled in two or three activities. Development of this kind
of competence requires an enormous investment of time, and two or
three six-week units spread over a period of years will not begin to be
enough to reach this goal.

It would be entirely within the scope of the ideas suggested here
for a student to pursue only one activity during an entire school year
if he so chooses, and four activities during a school year probably should
be the maximum allowable. Obviously, beginning, intermediate, and
advanced classes must be offered in many activities. Many students may
pursue certain activities for at least three of the eight semesters of their
high school experience. At higher levels of skill—during the senior year
perhaps—it is entirely possible that an occasional "lesson" or "tutorial
session" might replace regular class attendance. If, however, at the
same level a student already competent in several activities chooses to
begin to learn an entirely new activity, that, too, should be perfectly
acceptable.

While the implications have been presented for an "ideal" program, the same logic should apply to a very limited program. If a certain
high school program had physical education for only two years, and only
twice a week during that time, then it would be consistent with this
approach to have students elect two activities each of which would be
studied for two of the four semesters. If the time restriction is even
more serious, then only one activity should be elected, the point being
that whatever time is available should be used to develop some real
skill.

IMPLICATIONS FOR ADMINISTRATION

The administrator must define his primary role as the protector of the play education environment. While budgeting, scheduling facilities, public relations, and office management are all important, they are only important as factors which contribute to the maintenance of an optimal play education environment. The administrator should see himself more as an applied-social-scientist than as an office manager. All of his decisions, from something as obviously important as the hiring of personnel to something as *seemingly* unimportant as costume requirements, should be made in light of the aim—to increase human abilities to play competitive and/or expressive motor activities.

A great deal of flexible scheduling will be required if skill development at the highest level is sought. Many activities need to be offered, different skill levels of each activity should be available, and individualized instruction (group or individual lessons) is a possibility. Especially in junior high school and high school, where students should elect all their activities, some imaginative administration of time and facilities will be required. A freshman should be able to elect advanced gymnastics if he is interested and capable, and a senior should be able to elect beginning gymnastics if he is interested and has already developed several other competencies.

IMPLICATIONS FOR MEASUREMENT AND EVALUATION

The ideas presented here all suggest that measurement and evaluation are important factors in achieving the aim of physical education. The developmental objective requires diagnostic testing in certain instances, and rather constant evaluation. This might require the use of a diagnostic perceptual-motor inventory at the elementary school level, the use of a vocational inventory during the counseling phase of the program, or the use of a personality inventory with certain students who are experiencing difficulty during adolescence. Adequate evaluation will no doubt require the use of many measures, from the objectivity of a strength test to the subjectivity of a counseling interview, each of which must be judged in the context of the student's total personality and, more specifically, his ability to play.

A major implication of the ideas presented here is that measurement and evaluation must rely heavily on the idiographic approach rather than the nomothetic approach which is used in most cases now. The nomothetic approach abstracts traits from one individual and compares them with similar traits abstracted from other individuals; that is, John's ability to do a handspring compared with all of the other students' abilities to do handsprings, or his ability to do a push-up compared with the rest of the class, school, or national norms. The idiographic approach allows the physical educator to know John better by focusing on how his ability to do a handspring relates to his ability to do push-ups, and also his dominance, intelligence, and other factors which together constitute what Gordon Allport[6] has termed his "patterned individuality." In this way, measurement and evaluation directly contribute to the realization of the aim of physical education, because in diagnosing, counseling, and developing skill, the purpose of measuring and evaluating is to help the student to increase his abilities to play.

It should be equally obvious that grading, which relies heavily on the nomothetic approach, is completely inconsistent with the approach taken here. In the first place, to grade a student on his ability to play is incongruous. There is also the risk that a bad grade might retard or prevent the growth of future play experiences and would, therefore, be directly mis-educative. Students need evaluation, but grades are nothing more than labels that are usually not useful to students and are designed for use by administrators, school officials, and businessmen. In terms of diagnosis and counseling, especially with an idiographic approach, they are not only worthless, but potentially harmful. The view taken here concurs completely with that suggested by physical educators Marjorie Latchaw and Camille Brown.

> If grades or marks were done away with, students, teachers and parents would be forced to face the fact that education should be focused on learning, and that learning takes place in relation to student purposes. Evaluation tools would be used to help students define purposes and appropriate experiences for fulfilling the purposes would be provided.[7]

If grades were abolished, the tools of testing and measuring could be used to contribute directly to an evaluation process that would be intrinsic to the activities of physical education, and therefore would make a significant contribution to the realization of its aims and objectives.

IMPLICATIONS FOR MOTIVATION

It is important to note that the ideas presented here suggest a framework within which motivation in physical education may be understood. The overriding implication is, of course, that motivation increases with competence, which is consistent with Gordon Allport's

---

6. Gordon Allport, *Pattern and Growth in Personality* (New York: Holt, Rinehart and Winston, Inc., 1937), p. 10.
7. Marjorie Latchaw and Camille Brown, *The Evaluation Process in Health Education, Physical Education, and Recreation* (Englewood Cliffs: Prentice-Hall, Inc., 1962), p. 171.

view on the "need for competence" as a primary motive in life.[8] It can also be suggested that the consistently high correlations between interests and abilities demonstrate clearly that people like to do what they do well. The entire focus of the ideas presented here is in the development of competence in activities for which students have abilities. It carries with it, in other words, a built-in reinforcement system.

Another source of motivation that is implied by this approach is in the concept of play itself. Play is an inherently meaningful form of human behaviour, and is, therefore, by definition, a source of motivation. It is impossible to find scholarly articles that speak to the question of how to motivate young children to play games, the obvious reason being that all healthy children are so motivated. Motivation in physical education becomes a problem in puberty and adolescence when too many students seem to be apathetic toward physical education. The problem is how to preserve and develop the motivation found in child's play (how to help students move from *paidia* to *ludus*).

It matters little how the origins of play-motivation are viewed, and it is probably wisest to accept the position that there are many reasons why children play: social incentives, play instinct, surplus energy, expression, ego protection, recreation. The goal should be to bring students to the point where they are motivated to play tennis because they like playing tennis; in other words, so that participation is self-reinforcing. Gordon Allport[9] has suggested that motivation can become "functionally autonomous" of its original source, and it is this type of motivation that is consistent with the views presented here. Early motivations enable children to discover abilities; the abilities then turn into interests, which in turn motivates toward a further increase in abilities. Finally, these "acquired interests" (such as tennis, dance, etc.) become incorporated into the student's life-style, and he begins to define himself partially in terms of these interests. Thus, we would hope to have high school students who define themselves partially as "one who can play tennis well" or "one who can dance well."

It is my contention that such motivation is completely consistent with the counseling and skill objectives presented here. By assessing interest and abilities, the physical educator guides the student toward those activities for which he has the best chance of achieving competence. By increasing his skill in these activities, the physical educator sets the stage for the development of functionally autonomous motivations to play, and his playing of the activities will become part of his

8. see page 202.
9. Allport, *Pattern and Growth in Personality,* pp. 230-237.

life-style. The important point to recognize is that the development of this type of motivation is completely dependent upon a continuing acquisition of skill, which is the basis of the views advocated here.[10]

IMPLICATIONS FOR TEACHER TRAINING

The ideas suggested here would require some rather extensive changes in teacher training programs. In the first place, the growing recognition of the discipline of physical education means that many undergraduate students will have to begin to prepare for graduate study within the discipline, and this specialized study might be quite different than that necessary for entering the teaching profession.

The developmental objective implies that teachers be trained in diagnostic instruments of various kinds, and that they be able to develop specific programs that will remove the impediments. Bryant Cratty has referred to this type of diagnostic and remedial effort.

> It is suggested that the educator ask himself if with what kind of perceptual-motor activities does the child have difficulty? After this has been established, the educator should then attempt to rectify the deficiencies the child evidences through the application of perceptual-motor sequences carefully graded in difficulty and appropriate to the ability levels the child exhibits.[11]

Such diagnosis and therapy might be necessary for assessing and improving perceptual-motor abilities, strength, endurance, body-image, and other such developmental factors.

The counseling objective implies that teachers, particularly those working at the middle school or junior high school levels, be trained in counseling techniques. They must also be familiar with a wide range of activities, and have some rational basis on which to defend their assessments of the relative merits of the various activities. The physical educator must, in the words of David Reisman, "challenge" the young student to explore many activities.

> On the other hand, the other-directed man may in a way not expect enough of himself, may not take his failures in play seriously enough, settling too easily for an adjustment that gets by with the peer-group. The avocational counselor might stimulate, even provoke, such a

---

10. I do not mean to pass this off as an entirely new concept. Jesse Feiring Williams suggested long ago that the criterion for his skill development objective was "enough skill to insure continuation of the activity" (*Principles of Physical Education,* 4th edition, p. 275). My point is that the multi-activity program which developed from Williams' theoretical work was not consistent with his objectives, and if anything that has been suggested here is new, it is that the physical education program must be realistically consistent with its objectives.
11. Bryant Cratty, *Developmental Sequences of Perceptual Motor Tasks,* (Freeport, New York: Educational Activities, Inc., 1967), p. iv.

person to more imaginative play by helping him realize how very important for his own development toward autonomy play is.[12]

The counseling objective is important to the success of physical education, and evidence of its importance is indicated by ranking it as a primary objective. It is not enough for physical educators to plan a multi-activity program that students can experience and then "do their own thing," since such a plan presupposes that they have a "thing" to do. The job of the physical educator is to use his expert judgment to help students find the activities for which they are really suited and, as John Dewey has suggested, such help must be seen as an aid to a student's freedom rather than a restriction on it.

> Since freedom resides in the operations of intelligent observation and judgment by which a purpose is developed, guidance given by the teacher to the exercise of the pupils' intelligence is an aid to freedom, not a restriction on it. . . . That children are individuals whose freedom should be respected while the more mature person should have no freedom as an individual is an idea too absurd to require refutation.[13]

In this sense, the physical educator "initiates" the student into play environments that the physical educator has judged to be particularly meaningful and relevant to a student's interest and abilities.

The skill development objective also implies several important things. Physical educators must receive some differential training on the basis of their projected level of teaching, since teaching elementary skills to young children requires different training than does teaching high level skills to older children. The different problems encountered at the various developmental levels also implies differential training, so that coupled with the need for a different focus on skill development, it seems that elementary physical educators should receive training that is considerably different than that received by secondary physical educators. This means more than just taking different methods courses.

Another clear implication is that those who wish to teach at the secondary level should develop a very high level of skill in certain activities. While it is true that unskilled people can become good teachers and coaches, the exception does not prove the rule, and to expect a high level of skill development in students without preparing teachers to take them there directly is a foolish idea. Undergraduate majors should become specialists in at least one area (racquet sports, aquatics, team sports, etc.) and should have a reasonable level of skill in many

---

12. David Reisman, *The Lonely Crowd,* (New Haven: Yale University Press, 1950), pp. 363-367.
13. John Dewey, *Experience and Education,* (New York: Collier Books, 1963), pp. 71, 58.

activities. Very few teacher training programs today provide opportunities for this kind of skill development.

In teacher training programs, experiences should be provided for the perception and understanding of personal meanings in human behaviour. Indeed, many education departments are now incorporating such techniques as role playing, case-studies, and sensitivity training to meet this very goal. Course work in child and adolescent psychology would be beneficial in this area also.

Another important implication for teacher training can be found in the full recognition that prospective teachers are being prepared for play education programs, and that "play" implies that students be treated in certain ways. A coercive play environment is, for example, incongruous. The physical education process must, as Musska Mosston[14] has suggested, progressively "free" the student (not so much because the goal is a free independent student, but because the true player freely experiences a freedom in his play). The necessity to avoid coercion as much as possible has all sorts of implications for teaching methodology and classroom administration.[15]

SUMMARY

It should be obvious by now that great emphasis has been placed here on skill development. The readiness of students, the counseling function, the administration of the curriculum and facilities, and the training of teachers should all be directed toward the main goal of developing truly competent players. It is believed that such a focus will most benefit students, and that it therefore will be most beneficial to the profession of physical education.

Many students get bored in physical education simply because instructors do not have the knowledge and ability to take them beyond the most rudimentary skills in activities. This must be changed. Physical education will become vitally important when they begin to see that in physical education they can develop important skills. Physical education will become an integral part of the total program when teachers and administrators see the majority of students developing high levels of skill. Parents will begin to actively support physical education when their sons and daughters have the opportunity to choose from a wide

---

14. Musska Mosston, *Teaching Physical Education,* (Columbus: Charles E. Merrill Books, Inc., 1966), 238 pp.
15. If you have read John Holt's, *How Children Fail,* you are already aware of how much student behaviour is best classified as avoidance behaviour and is brought about by the aversive nature of most education environments.

variety of activities and then develop recognizable skill in their chosen field.

I would like to anticipate the reaction that the ideas which have been presented here are too much "ivory tower" or "pie in the sky." When sixty junior high school students are under the direction of one physical education teacher, many of these ideas may seem beyond reach. If a goal is not considered obtainable it is not usually sought after. If it is not, then the situation described above would be more accurately described as a "recreation period" rather than a physical education class. There are many physical educators who believe that we cannot afford not to develop skill for time is running out for those physical education programs which make pervasive claims in several directions, yet produce no measurable results in any of them.

WHAT QUESTIONS CAN YOU ASK ABOUT THE FOLLOWING STATEMENTS

1. It would not be possible to have a schedule flexible enough to meet the demands of the skill objective.
2. If you don't grade students, then they won't be motivated.
3. Students aren't mature enough at the junior high school level to choose their own activities.
4. Since the physical education teacher often has to teach health courses, the two fields must be closely allied.
5. Fifth graders aren't ready for multi-activity sports programs.
6. If physical educators are supposed to be highly skilled, this means that we will end up with teachers who are good athletes but not too smart.
7. Physical education teacher training programs need to be improved academically rather than in skill training.
8. The coach has always been one of the busiest counselors in the school.
9. Students are more interested in having fun than in becoming highly skilled.

Epilogue—The Future Physical Educator

UNDERGRADUATE TRAINING

It is to be hoped that undergraduate preparation in physical education will proceed along two lines. First, the emergence of the discipline of physical education should substantially improve the academic training of the undergraduate major. The emerging fields of sport psychology, sport sociology coupled with the further development of exercise physiology and kinesiology should provide a more sophisticated and meaningful content. Advances in research should not only provide a firmer base of knowledge but should also bring about, at the undergraduate level, a new emphasis on understanding research methodology and statistics.

It should also be hoped that undergraduates will be provided considerably more skill development experiences than in the recent past. In many current undergraduate programs, physical education majors devote twenty per cent or less of their course work to actual skill development. Probably, the major reason for this is that many educators (physical educators too!) still have doubts about offering college academic credit for motor skill training. Someday soon we must face up to the fact that physical educators should be highly skilled in a variety of activities.

GRADUATE TRAINING

Graduate training in physical education will be influenced greatly by trends in higher education. More types of graduate degrees will possibly develop, but it should also be hoped that some standardization will occur. The master's degree program probably will become a dual track program, with the two emphases on teaching and further graduate study. The influence of the discipline of physical education will be most quickly and directly felt in the increasing sophistication of graduate programs.

It is likely that a specialist degree, at an intermediate point between the master's and the doctor's, will become a popular degree for teachers. If standardization of degrees occurs in higher education, then it is likely that the Ph.D. (Doctor of Philosophy) will become a research oriented degree, with the Ed.D. (Doctor of Education) and the P.E.D. (Doctor of Physical Education) degrees oriented toward administration and teacher training.

The graduate student of the future will not only have a broader range of fields and courses from which to choose but he will quite likely have to choose a field of specialization, even at the master's degree level. For teachers this choice will likely be made among programs designed to focus on elementary, middle school, secondary teaching, or athletic coaching; and for students who desire to do further graduate work, the choices will be among the various sub-fields of the discipline of physical education, such as exercise physiology, biomechanics, or sport psychology. Different universities will develop specialties and students will begin to choose among schools on the basis of program strength in a particular area of specialization.

TEACHING

It should be expected that physical education will continue to become a more integral part of school programs, especially if educational theory moves toward a meaning-centered program. At the elementary level this means that more school systems will hire specialists in physical education who will work within one school only, rather than the more currently popular consultant plan in which the physical educator moves around to many different schools, helping classroom teachers to set up programs of physical education.

As programs broaden, time allotments increase, and financial commitment makes possible a reasonable student-teacher ratio, the physical educator-specialist is likely to be more in demand in the junior and senior high school levels. Specialists in aquatics, dance, and gymnastics will be in great demand. It is unlikely that schools will continue to hire the physical educator who "does everything," since this type of person is less likely to be qualified to do particular things well.

Physical educators working within schools should expect to have administrative and supervisory responsibilities in intramural and sports club programs, because parents will be likely to want more emphasis placed on these programs than they have in the past.

Athletic coaching will continue to be a part of the physical educator's responsibility, although many school systems will prefer to have classroom teachers do most of the coaching (for the implicit reason that the physical educator-coach is too much coach and not enough physical educator). We should expect that women physical educators will find a greatly expanded opportunity in athletic coaching in the future, not only of a club variety, but also for interscholastic competition.

Physical educators specializing in adapted and corrective physical education should find many new outlets for their work as more states pass laws requiring adapted programs in the schools. These specialists might also find an outlet in the emerging field of "learning therapy" at the elementary school level, as motor therapy for perceptual, learning, and general behaviour disorders is becoming a very important possibility.

Physical educators should be able to look forward to increased teaching opportunities as specialists in modern dance. There has been some effort to move modern dance outside the realm of physical education, but this would be a most unfortunate occurrence since the possibility that dance training would be as widely experienced by students is unlikely. Certain states are now moving toward certification of dance teachers; this should greatly widen the possibilities for undergraduate training of physical education majors who wish to specialize in dance.

The availability of teaching positions at the college level will depend upon two factors; first, the development of physical education programs in the schools will determine the number of teachers needed, thus, in turn, affecting the number of teachers needed to train prospective teachers. Second, the potential development of the discipline of physical education will determine how many scholar-researchers will be able to find gainful employment in these areas. For the first time in the history of American education, the job market for teachers is reaching the point where the supply is larger than the demand. This creates a "buyer's market" which is good in the sense that the quality of teaching in physical education can be upgraded because school administrators will be able to hire more selectively, but it will be difficult because in such a market some trained physical educators are not going to be able to find teaching positions.

JOB OPPORTUNITIES OUTSIDE THE SCHOOLS

Job opportunities outside the schools should be available in direct proportion to the amount of "extra" money that the average consumer has to spend. If our economic history is to be trusted, then it is likely that such job opportunities will become increasingly available. The dance instructor and the sports teacher have always been able to find summer employment in camps and day schools, but only in private dance studios and in private athletic clubs has there been opportunity for year round employment. The number of such full-time jobs is likely to increase and present another career outlet for the trained physical educator.

The physical educator will also find increased opportunities in the area of physical therapy and exercise clinics. The physical educator can normally fulfill the requirements for the R.P.T. (Registered Physical Therapist) in one or two academic years, and when he does the opportunity for his employment in private practice or in hospitals and clinics is quite good. As the American public gains sophistication in its knowledge of the effects of exercise, it is likely that the "exercise salons and gyms" that promote quick results from a series of machines will lose popularity (an estimated $35,000,000 was spent on exercise machines in 1966); and when they do, it is quite likely that they might be replaced by professionally administered and competently staffed exercise clinics which will combine the efforts of medical doctors, physical therapists, and physical educators.

A very lucrative job market should begin to appear in industrial recreation, which for years has been an accepted part of European industrial life. It will no doubt begin by greatly expanded recreation programs, in which the physical educator can act much like the intramural director in a school. Once the programs are well developed, it is to be hoped that they will be expanded to include regular recreation periods during the work day, such as expanding the noon hour break to one and one-half hours in order to include a recreational period. Once this occurs, physical educators will be in demand.

Physical educators have always been able to contribute to programs connected with religious organizations. The Young Men's Christian Association (Y.M.C.A.), the Young Women's Christian Association (Y.W.C.A.), the Young Men's Hebrew Association (Y.M.H.A.), the Young Women's Hebrew Association (Y.W.H.A.), and the Catholic Youth Organization (C.Y.O.) have widely developed programs, and a large part of the program is in sports and dance training. The Boys' Club of America provides the same kind of opportunity on a nonsectarian basis. The physical educator is usually well qualified to fill the job of program director in these organizations, and as they expand in the future, the number of teaching and administrative positions in such organizations will naturally increase.

Community recreation programs (municipal and state) will continue to grow, although they have primarily operated in the past as seasonal programs, mostly in the summers. With increased urbanization, it should be expected that year-round programs will be developed and this will provide still another opportunity for the employment of the physical educator.

FACTORS INFLUENCING THE FUTURE

While it is tempting to play the role of the forecaster, it is more realistic to recognize the major factors which will actually shape the future of physical education. The first, and perhaps the most important, is the educational philosophy of the society. Education-*through*-the-physical could not, for example, have developed as rapidly as it did without the framework of the Dewey-Thorndike educational progressivism which it reflected. If educational philosophy moves to a meaning-centered approach, then it is likely that many of the opportunities forecasted here will come true. If, however, we return to a more rigid, scholastic philosophy of education, then physical education would no doubt return to a physical training concept.

Another major factor influencing the course of physical education will be the future role of athletics in the schools. Certain universities are at the present time considering the abolishment of all intercollegiate athletics, except those with high spectator appeal such as football, basketball, and hockey, and their replacement with broader sports clubs and intramural programs. At the high school level on the other hand, one is more likely to find a desire to broaden the interscholastic program to include more activities, and more students in each of the activities. It is difficult to predict which course will be taken, and even more difficult to assess the implications for programs of physical education. It has yet to be demonstrated sufficiently that the abolishment of athletic programs necessarily will mean the broadening of intramural programs and sports clubs. Without such broadened programs, however, it will become quite unlikely that students and taxpayers will continue to support the high cost of athletic programs when they recognize the inadequacy of programs which reach the larger student population. What should be most expected is that students will occupy an increasingly larger role in making decisions about such programs; the evidence of the past few years at the university level indicates that they will want their money to go to programs which benefit them directly as participants.

A third factor, and the one that we can do most about, is the quality of physical education programs. If high quality programs of physical education produce measurable and recognizable results in students, then many of these other factors will be less important in shaping the course of the future. The stronger the profession is in terms of the results of its programs, the less likely it is to be buffeted by the winds of educational philosophy or economic change. If, however, physical education programs do not produce such results, then the future will too much resemble the past, and physical education will be considered a "frill," the first program to be curtailed in periods of financial uncertainty.

APPENDIX

A Chronology of Events Important to the Development of American Physical Education 1635–1969

1635   First elementary school is formed in Boston . . . Boston Latin Grammar School formed

1636   Harvard College established

1647   Colonies of Massachusetts Bay and Connecticut enact laws establishing elementary schools for towns with fifty families and latin grammar schools for towns with one hundred families

1743   Benjamin Franklin published *Proposals Relating to the Education of the Youth of Pennsylvania* in which he promotes physical activity

1791   Philadelphia Public Academy becomes University of Pennsylvania . . . First private swimming pool built in Philadelphia

1820   Harvard College constructs first college gymnasium

1825   Charles Beck, an advocate of the Jahn System, is named instructor in Latin and German gymnastics at the Round Hill School in Northampton, Massachusetts, first recognition of teacher of physical education in U.S.

1826   Charles Follen, an advocate of the Jahn System, starts gymnastics program at Harvard

1827   Francis Leiber, a Jahn disciple, opens the first public swimming pool in U.S. in Boston . . . First interclass football game at Harvard

1831   John Warren, Professor of Anatomy and Physiology at Harvard, publishes book on *The Importance of Physical Education* marking first theoretical treatise on subject . . . Catherine Beecher publishes *A Course of Calisthenics For Young Ladies*

1834   First rules of baseball published in Carver's *Book of Sports*

1837   Catherine Beecher founds the Western Female Institute (the Beecher System is built around twenty-six lessons in physiology and two courses in calisthenics; exercises were accompanied by music and designed to produce grace of motion, good carriage, and sound health) Horace Mann reorganizes the Massachusetts system of public education and sets model for years to come . . . Mt. Holyoke Female Seminary offers course in physical education.

1839   First American Normal School for the training of teachers is founded in Lexington, Massachusetts

1848   Girard College opened in Philadelphia with four indoor swimming pools and one outdoor pool; planned by Leiber; marks first swimming pool in U.S. that is connected with school . . . First Turnverein is formed in Cincinnati

1851   First YMCA is formed in Boston

1853   Superintendent of Boston Schools rules that each student should have daily physical or gymnastic exercises

1857   Catherine Beecher publishes *Physiology and Calisthenics*

1859   First intercollegiate baseball game pits Williams versus Amherst

1860   The Dio Lewis program is accepted in West Newton, Massachusetts School System (the Lewis System advocated the use of music to mark rhythm of exercises which were designed to be vigorous enough to increase heart beat and respiration; used beanbags, gymnastic crown, wands, dumbbells, clubs, and handrings)

1861   Dio Lewis founds Boston Normal Institute for Physical Education . . . *The Gymnastic Monthly* and *The Journal of Physical Culture* are first published . . . Edward Hitchcock is named Director of the Department of Hygiene and Physical Culture at Amherst College, marking the first college director in U.S. and the first department of physical education . . .

1866   California passes first state legislation requiring physical education

1869   Princeton and Rutgers play first intercollegiate football game

1874   Lawn tennis introduced into U.S. by Miss Mary Outerbridge

1875   National Bowling Congress is formed

1878   Badminton is first played in the U.S.

1879   Dudley Sargent is appointed Assistant Professor of Physical

Training and Director of the Hemenway Gymnasium at Harvard . . . National Association of Amateur Athletics of America is formed . . . National Archery Association is founded

1881   Sargent organizes the Sanatory Gymnasium in Cambridge, which is later to become the Sargent School of Physical Education and still later The Sargent College of Boston University . . . American Lawn Tennis Association is formed

1883   International Training School of the YMCA is founded in Springfield, Massachusetts . . . Hartwig Nissen introduces Swedish Gymnastics in Washington, D.C.

1885   William G. Anderson invites physical education leaders to a meeting at Adelphi Academy. Sixty leaders attend the meeting and found the Association for the Advancement of Physical Education which is later to become AAHPER. Hitchcock is named first President of the Association . . . Edward Hartwell completes survey on physical education in America for U.S. Bureau of Education

1887   Springfield College begins to offer professional courses in physical education . . . Softball is invented in Chicago

1888   NAAAA (1879) becomes the Amateur Athletic Union . . . Handball is first played in the U.S.

1889   Boston Physical Training Conference is held, the first scholarly convention of physical education leaders . . . The Boston Normal School of Gymnastics is founded

1890   Hartwell is named Supervisor of Physical Education for the Boston Public Schools . . . Posse Normal School is founded in Boston by Baron Nils Posse, an advocate of Swedish gymnastics

1891   Basketball is invented at Springfield College by James Naismith

1893   National Education Association forms a Department of Physical Education for the International Congress of Education

1894   *Mind and Body* first published by North American Gymnastic Union . . . Melvin Ballou Gilbert first teaches esthetic dancing at Harvard Summer School of Physical Education

1895   Through the efforts of J. Anna Novis and the Women's Christian Temperance Union, the NEA makes the Department of Physical Education a permanent unit . . . First public golf courses built . . . Beginning of the National Badminton Association of America

1896   First modern Olympics are held in Athens . . . The *American Physical Education Review* is first published by the American Association for the Advancement of Physical Education . . .

Volleyball invented by William Morgan at YMCA in Holyoke, Massachusetts

1897   Society of College Gymnasium Directors formed, later to become The College Physical Education Association

1899   Anne Barr publishes *Swedish Folk Dances,* first publication in U.S. of folk dances from other lands . . . Basketball first played by women at Smith College . . . Interpretive dancing popularized by Isadora Duncan

1900   (approx) First colleges offer professional physical education: University of Nebraska, Oberlin, University of California, University of Missouri, Normal College at Ypsilanti, Michigan

1901   Graduate instruction in Physical Education is started at Columbia University with a Master's Degree Program . . . Field hockey demonstrated at Harvard Summer School and immediately played by women at Smith, Wellesley, Mt. Holyoke, Vassar, Radcliffe, and Bryn Mawr

1902   Dudley Sargent develops the Universal Test for Strength, Speed, and Endurance

1903   Luther Gulick is appointed Director of Physical Education for The New York City Public School System . . . New Jersey passes legislation making the health examination compulsory for school children . . . The American Physical Education Association replaces the AAAPE (1885)

1904   Gulick develops the first athletic achievement tests . . . R. Tait McKenzie is appointed Director of the Department of Physical Education at the University of Pennsylvania

1905   National Collegiate Athletic Association is formed . . . Springfield College receives authority to grant Bachelor's and Master's Degrees in Physical Education . . . The University of Illinois forms the first Department of Teacher Education in Physical Education . . . *Physical Training* is first published by the YMCA . . . Louis Chalif gave a teacher's course in dance at New York University . . . The National Women's Basketball Committee was established (which evolved eventually into the National Section on Women's Athletics, the National Section on Girls' and Women's Sports and currently the Division for Girls' and Women's Sports, the rules- and standards-making body for all girls' and women's activities)

1906   Playground Association of America is founded

1907   *The Normal Course in Play* by Clark Hetherington was published

1908   The first high school swimming pool is built in Detroit

1909   The Boston Normal School becomes The Department of Hygiene and Physical Education at Wellesley College . . . National Association of Physical Education for College Women (now NAPECW) initiated by Amy Morris Homans

1910   James McCurdy sets up standards for measuring blood pressure and heart rate . . . Thomas Wood begins to advocate natural gymnastics

1913   The University of Michigan and Ohio State University appoint intramural directors . . . Phi Epsilon Kappa, (a physical education fraternity for men), founded at The Normal College of the North American Gymnastic Union in Indianapolis

1915   Wilbur P. Bowen published *Applied Anatomy and Kinesiology*

1916   The American Folk Dance Society is organized . . . Phi Delta Pi, (a national professional fraternity for women), is organized . . . first state supervisor, Thomas Storey, appointed in New York

1918   The National Education Association lists "health" and "worthy use of leisure time" as two of the seven cardinal principles of education . . . U.S. Commissioner of Education calls a meeting to make arrangements for A National Program of Physical Education

1920   Charles H. McCloy develops classification index

1921   Sargent Jump Test is developed

1924   The Department of Physical Education of the NEA merges with The Department of Child Study to form The Department of School Health and Physical Education . . . Columbia University and New York University begin Doctor's Degree programs in Physical Education . . . The National Association of Directors of Physical Education for College Women is formed in Kansas City (now The National Association of Physical Education for College Women)

1925   Organized intramural participation begins in high schools . . . Mary Wigman brings modern dance to the U.S.

1926   Margaret H'Doubler establishes first dance major at the University of Wisconsin . . . American Academy of Physical Education is organized by William Burdick, Jay B. Nash, R. Tait McKenzie, Thomas A. Storey, and Clark Hetherington

1927   Brace Motor Ability Test is developed

1929   Cozens' Tests for General Athletic Ability are developed

1930   American Physical Education Association begins to publish the *Research Quarterly* . . . National Recreation Association is formed ... *Journal of Health and Physical Education* is first published

1932   APEA (1903) adds dance section

1934   The Athletic Institute is founded ... First rope ski tow in U.S. installed

1935   College Physical Education Association is formed

1937   American Physical Education Association and Department of School Health and Physical Education of NEA merge to form American Association for Health, Physical Education and Recreation

1943   Phi Epsilon Kappa begins to publish *The Physical Educator*

1946   Pan American Institute formed to promote research in physical education with McCloy as first president

1948   The Athletic Institute sponsors a National Conference on Undergraduate Professional Preparation in Health, Physical Education and Recreation

1950   The Athletic Institute sponsors a National Conference on Graduate Study in Health, Physical Education and Recreation ... The National Intramural Association is formed

1951   National Athletic Trainers Association is started

1953   Kraus-Hirschland report on minimal physical fitness appears in *JOHPER*

1954   The American College of Sports Medicine is formed

1955   Outdoor Education Project started by AAHPER

1956   Youth Fitness Conference is called by President Eisenhower ... The President's Advisory Commission is created ... The Council on Youth Fitness is created

1957   Governor's Conference on Youth Fitness is held

1959   Operation Fitness is started by AAHPER ... International Congress for Health, Physical Education, and Recreation (ICHPER) is formed as part of the World Confederation of Organizations of the Teaching Profession

1960   President Kennedy's "Soft American" article appears in *Sports Illustrated* ... International Council on Sports and Physical Education organized at Rome

1961   President's Council on Youth Fitness publishes "Bluebook" ... National Conference on Physical Fitness of Youth is called by President Kennedy ... *Journal of Sports Medicine and Physical Fitness* is first published

1962   AAHPER begins projects on Sports Skills Tests, Kindergarten-Fourth Grade Skills Progression, and Sports Knowledge Tests . . . *Gymnasion,* official magazine of ICHPER is first published

1963   *Quest* first published as joint project of National Association for Physical Education of College Women (NAPECW) and National College Physical Education Association for Men (NCPEAM)

1965   Dance is made a division of the AAHPER . . . First International Congress of Sports Psychology is held in Rome

1967   North American Society for the Psychology of Sport and Physical Activity (NASPSPA) is formed

1968   Journal of Biomechanics is published . . . Second International Congress of Sports Psychology is held in Washington

1969   Journal of Motor Behavior is first published

ORGANIZATIONS

1.   The American Association for Health, Physical Education, and Recreation (AAHPER)

The largest professional organization is a department of the National Education Association (NEA). It operates through six (Central, Eastern, Midwest, Southern, Southwest, and Northwest) district organizations. Main divisions are health education, physical education, recreation, men's athletics, girls and women's sports, safety and driver education, and the general division. Main publications are *Journal of Health, Physical Education and Recreation (JOHPER),* and *Research Quarterly.* Membership is open to students.

2.   The American Academy of Physical Education

Primary goal is to foster scholarly work in the various fields of physical education. Main publication is *Academy Papers.* Membership by invitation.

3.   The National College Physical Education Association for Men (NCPEAM)

Focuses on problems related to college physical education. Holds yearly meetings and publishes *Proceedings.*

4.   The National Association of Physical Education for College Women (NAPECW)

Similar to NCPEAM in organization and purpose, and with them publishes *Quest,* a collection of scientific and philosophical papers.

5. *National Recreation Association*

A service organization that provides professional consultation and leadership to individuals or groups on a fee basis.

6. *National Intramural Association*

The purpose of this organization is to provide a forum for the exchange of ideas·about intramurals and generally to promote their development. Publishes *Proceedings.*

7. *American School Health Association*

Designed to promote the dissemination of information about health, and to improve the quality of health services and the teaching of health in schools. Publishes the *Journal of School Health.*

8. *American College of Sports Medicine*

Scholarly organization designed to promote research and to disseminate research findings. Publishes *The Journal of Sports Medicine and Physical Fitness.* Membership is open to students.

9. *The North American Society for the Psychology of Sport and Physical Activity (NASPSPA)*

Scholarly organization designed to promote research in the area of sport psychology. Membership is open to students.

10. *American Physical Therapy Association*

Professional and scholarly organization that is of interest to physical educators in adapted and corrective work. Publishes the *Journal of the American Physical Therapy Association.*

11. *Delta Psi Kappa*

National professional sorority for women. Designed to promote the development of physical education through effective leadership. Publishes the *Progressive Physical Educator.*

12. *Phi Epsilon Kappa*

National professional fraternity for men. Designed to promote physical education, health, and recreation, and to provide a fraternal organization for workers in these fields. Publishes *The Physical Educator.*

13. *Athletic organizations*

The National Collegiate Athletic Association
The National Association of Intercollegiate Athletics
The Amateur Athletic Union
The Athletic Institute
American Association of College Baseball Coaches
National Athletic Trainers Association

National Soccer Coaches Association
United States Volleyball Association
American Football Coaches Association
National Association of College Basketball Coaches

INDEX